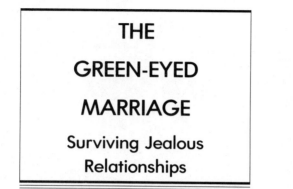

THE

GREEN-EYED

MARRIAGE

Surviving Jealous
Relationships

THE

GREEN-EYED

MARRIAGE

Surviving Jealous Relationships

Robert L. Barker

THE FREE PRESS
A Division of Macmillan, Inc.
NEW YORK

Collier Macmillan Publishers
LONDON

The Free Press
A Division of Macmillan, Inc.
866 Third Avenue, New York, N.Y. 10022

Collier Macmillan Canada, Inc.

Printed in the United States of America

printing number
1 2 3 4 5 6 7 8 9 10

Library of Congress Cataloging-in-Publication Data

Barker, Robert L.
   The green-eyed marriage.

   Bibliography: p.
   Includes index.
   1. Jealousy. 2. Interpersonal relations. I. Title.
BF575.J4B37   1987   152.4   87-19860
ISBN 0-02-901791-2

To My Sister, Bonnie Jean

Her eyes are green but her heart is golden.

Contents

Preface

Those who maintain relationships with jealous people face special difficulties. Anyone who lives with, is married to, or is otherwise involved with a jealous person has to overcome serious and sometimes life-threatening obstacles. It is important to know how to overcome such obstacles in order to cope successfully in life with jealous partners. The basic objective here is to show what the companions of jealous people can do to survive jealous relationships and make the best of life in jealous households. In other words, the primary concern is for the victim (the one who is accused) rather than the perpetrator (the one who makes the accusation).

Exploring jealousy from the viewpoint of the accused is, unfortunately, long overdue. The literature—both popular and scientific—has recently had much to say about jealous people. From reading this material or from watching television, a jealous person can gain a considerable amount of information, understanding, and sympathy. The media have increasingly been explaining how to keep jealousy problems under sufficient control so that they don't become self-destructive. But, so far, little has been said in the media about the plight of the victim of the jealous relationship. No one has been telling the spouses or partners of jealous people how to deal with the situation.

As serious and painful as jealousy can be for those it afflicts, it is usually even more painful for those who have relationships with them. They are the victims, the ones who are suspected of infidelity, disloyalty, or other wrongdoing. Jealous people have a way of bringing down those with whom they share their lives, draining them of their feelings of adequacy and self-worth, contributing to their guilt feelings, and creating an anxiety-filled, stressful environment. Those who live with jealous people develop more than their share of ulcers, colitis, phobias, suicidal thoughts and acts, guilt, feelings of inadequacy, and—most of all—depression. And fewer resources for getting help are available to them than to their jealous partners.

Most of those who are involved with very jealous people face conflict. They are ambivalent about how best to cope with their circumstances. On the one hand, they naturally want to get away from the source of pain. Having tried various stategies without much success, they sense that their only hope is to be away from their jealous partners. On the other hand, they still want the relationship to succeed. They don't want separations. They love their partners, seeing them as good in virtually every way but the jealousy. With so much at stake, often the children, friends, the house, financial security—everything they really care about—they can't leave. They keep hoping that their partners will change and permanently overcome the problem. They don't want to abandon someone who may be sick. They often believe that if they themselves could be a little more understanding, a little less guilty, a little stronger, then things would improve.

Life with a jealous person is like continually walking through a mine field, fearful of taking the wrong step. It means being careful to avoid the wrong company, developing handy alibis, and never getting caught in contradictions or outright lies. Thus, in order to keep the peace, the partners of very jealous people usually find it best to avoid outsiders. When they do seek the advice of friends in making decisions, they are often made to feel even worse. "Why do you put up with that kind of treatment?" is the recurring question they are asked. There is little recognition that the problem is more complicated. There is little credit for sticking it out or wanting to help the one who has the illness. The "me generation" says, "Life is too short to waste it like that. Get out while you can, while your health is still good. Think of yourself. Go and don't look back." Anyone who ignores these admonitions is likely to be labeled a masochist or a martyr, someone who gets pleasure out of suffering.

People in this position even find it difficult to get adequate professional help. Many professionals also wonder why the patient doesn't separate. They, too, often consider those who don't to be masochistic, to enjoy the pain and suffering, and to create situations that permit it. Some therapists feel powerless to help unless the jealous person is involved in treatment. After all, *that* is the person with the illness, the one who should be treated. But jealous people worry about what others might think and perceive being in therapy as having a weakness. Not only are they themselves reluctant to be involved with professional helpers, they try to keep their partners away as well.

For these reasons, the major aim here is to provide an information resource for partners of jealous people. The goal is to answer the questions most likely to be asked by those in this position: What can I do to help my jealous companion? What do I do that causes my loved one to behave that way? How do I know if the problem is really very serious or if I'm just exaggerating? If it really is a serious problem, what are the likely consequences? How can I protect myself from my loved one's jealousy? How can I protect the children? Where can I go for help? What can I do to instill motivation to work on the problem in my jealous partner? If I can't improve the relationship, how can I get out of it without having even more problems?

To answer these questions, the partner of a jealous person first needs to understand the nature and characteristics of jealousy itself. The more one knows about it, its causes, patterns of expression, course, and duration, the more effective one can be in solving the problems it provokes. How much jealousy can be considered a good thing, or at least tolerable, and how much of it is pathological? How does it get started, and what keeps it going? Why does it seem to get worse in some people and go away in others? What's the difference between the normal kind of jealousy that everyone feels and the violently intense kind that causes so much pain?

My own interest and work in this subject began about fifteen years ago when I treated the young couple described in the Prologue. This case inspired me to learn more about the problem of jealousy. I read everything I could find, interviewed my professional colleagues, and began specializing in marital therapy dealing with problems of this type. When information on a specific aspect of jealousy seemed lacking, I conducted my own research. I developed surveys and experimented with different techniques to minimize jealousy confrontations. I developed a test that could be used to determine how serious a jealousy problem was and administered it to hundreds of people. Other professionals, hearing of my special interest in this subject, began sending people with jealousy problems to me for treatment. I conducted seminars for therapists who wanted to share their experiences in working with jealous couples.

This book is a product of these activities. The test, research findings, and a review of the available literature on jealousy are included here, as are numerous examples of couples who have coped successfully with this problem. The cases used to illustrate various aspects of jealousy are taken from my own work with jealous people or have been contributed by several of my professional colleagues. Those who are described have given permission to use their stories as long as I changed names and some identifying details, which I have. Most of the people discussed in the case examples have read my descriptions of their situations and made helpful suggestions, additions, or corrections.

Many people have made important contributions to the development of this book. They include Karl D. Hawver, MD; Elahé Mir-Djalali, Ph.D.; David Guttman, DSW; Letitia Lundeen, Ph.D.; and Dale Miller, Elizabeth Ticknor, Susan Llewellyn, Edith Lewis, and Joyce Seltzer. The most essential contributions, however, have come from the hundreds of people who participated in the jealousy studies and tests and were exposed to the psychotherapy methods described herein. These people have learned, often the hard way, how to deal with jealous partners. They, more than any psychotherapists or social researchers, are the experts—the real authors of this book. They, more than any others, want to help people in similar circumstances by teaching them what they know, to spare them of some of the pain they have had to endure. I hope their wishes are granted.

Robert L. Barker
Catholic University
Washington, D.C.

THE

GREEN-EYED

MARRIAGE

Surviving Jealous
Relationships

Prologue: A Green-Eyed Marriage

The young woman was clearly frightened and confused as she entered the therapist's office for the first time. Her medical record said her name was Joan, and that she was the wife of an Air Force sergeant, the mother of two small children, and a person who had a problem with overweight and depression. It said she was being referred for psychotherapy after her physicians could find no organic cause for the terrible headaches, stomach cramps, nausea, and anxiety with which she also suffered. She spoke in a voice so quiet that she could scarcely be heard.

"I know I should've come here before now," she whispered, "but I was afraid Lennie—that's my husband—would get mad. I kept hoping my problem would go away by itself. I thought maybe the pills would help, but it seems like I tried them all and nothing works."

Indeed she had. Her medical record was thick with entries by various doctors who, at different times, had prescribed nearly every drug that seemed remotely relevant to her condition—sleeping pills, minor tranquilizers, antipsychotics, pain remedies, antidepressants, hormones, vitamins, and mood elevators. "I finally had to admit to myself that I'm getting sicker," she said tearfully. "It's because things are so terrible at home."

"Lennie should be here too, but he would never go for counseling. No one can tell him anything. He's the jealous type, and I think he's getting worse. I can't get him to change, and I can't talk him into getting help. He won't let me out of his sight. He always accuses me of seeing someone. I've never cheated on him, ever, and I never will. But how can I get him to believe that?"

They had met in high school, and she was in awe of him from the

1

beginning. He was handsome, charming, and very popular with all the girls at school. Joan, on the other hand, was something of the opposite. Shy, self-conscious about being overweight, and feeling unattractive and dull, Joan never dreamed she could have a boyfriend like Lennie. Yet somehow he became more interested in her than in the others. He deluged her with attention, constant phone calls, notes passed to her in school, dates, and unending conversation. Never had she felt so important, so loved and wanted. Never had she felt so happy. She would do anything for him, go anyplace, be anyone he wanted. She wanted nothing more from life than to please him.

The pregnancy wasn't well received by her parents. They wanted her to have an abortion. They wanted her to remain in school for at least the two years until her graduation. And most of all they wanted her to stay away from Lennie.

But he was more persuasive. He wouldn't permit an abortion. He was graduating soon and planned to join the Air Force. They would marry and get away from her family. They could make it. He seemed so confident, even if she wasn't. She agreed with him. She would stay with him no matter what. It would be difficult, but their love would somehow get them through.

She had no idea how difficult. It wasn't their many financial problems that made it hard. And it wasn't because of the birth of another child, which came soon after the first. Nor was it having to move from one Air Force base to another every time they would just get settled. What made it really bad was Lennie's possessiveness. What had once seemed so important to her—Lennie's intense attention and apparent devotion—had become a prison.

Occasionally she worked as a waitress to supplement Lennie's meager military pay. He could barely tolerate it. "Did you see any interesting people today?" was his standard greeting on her return from work. Often it would be followed by interrogations and accusations. He frequently made unexpected visits to the restaurant. He asked his friends to stop by the restaurant and report back to him about her behavior. "Joe said he had a burger in your place today," Lennie would say, "and he told me you were acting pretty friendly with the manager."

How was she supposed to respond? She believed she had tried everything. Mostly she told the truth: "I only love you, Lennie, and I'm not interested in the manager or anyone else." Sometimes she would ignore his ill-concealed charges and simply walk away. Sometimes she would try to counter his accusations with some of her own: "You're a fine one to talk, Lennie. I know you've been flirting with the new secretary in your section." Sometimes, in her frustration, she would offer sarcasm: "Yes, Lennie, you finally found me out. I *have* been friendly with the manager, but we can't get married because the manager is a woman."

No matter what she tried, the outcome was the same. First there were accusations, then threats, then arguments, fights, tears, apologies, and finally promises to do better next time. Then the same pattern began again. Only it was getting worse. Lennie was becoming increasingly violent. He began to slap Joan. Then he started using his fists. Then came the severe beatings. Yet, as his ferocity increased, so did his subsequent remorse. He would always cry, ask for forgiveness, plead for another chance, and promise to do whatever he could to make the family happy. The only thing he would not do was seek professional help. He claimed his status as an Air Force sergeant would be jeopardized with that on his record. Meanwhile, the tension increased, and Joan's depression and anxiety magnified.

It was on a bitterly cold February day that a near tragedy occurred. Lennie had become convinced that Joan was up to something. In the previous few days she had been coming home from the restaurant later than usual. She explained that for a few days she was driving home one of the other waitresses, whose car was unreliable in such weather. She would stop if it bothered him so much. But Lennie was uncharacteristically charitable. It was all right with him, he said. Actually he had a plan to expose her infidelity once and for all.

He had followed her many times before and had been embarrassingly unsuccessful. This time he had a foolproof strategy. He had come to believe that Joan was carrying on her affairs in their car. Looking the car over, he learned he could fit into its trunk and open it from the inside with a screwdriver. He would conceal himself there and wait. When she and her lover were together, he would emerge and catch them. Then his suspicions would be confirmed at last.

He got off work early and walked to the restaurant, which was nearby. Her car was in its usual spot at a far corner of the restaurant parking lot. It was getting dark by now, and a heavy snow was falling. Visibility was so poor he knew he wouldn't be seen. Quickly and quietly he got in the trunk and waited. Her shift would be over within thirty minutes, and soon thereafter he expected his confrontation.

What he didn't know was that Joan had already left. Fearing the driving conditions in such bad weather, Joan and other waitresses had been driven home in the owner's truck, and the restaurant was closed. Joan had picked up the children from her baby-sitter neighbor, and they were all waiting in the warm house for Lennie.

Knowing nothing of her change of plans, Lennie was determined to wait in the trunk as long as it took. The storm continued and the temperature dropped. It was becoming unbearable. After waiting an hour, Lennie finally decided to try his plan on a warmer day. His hands were numb from the cold, and he could hardly hold the screwdriver to release the latch. He twisted at it, pushed it, pulled it, and even hit it with the screwdriver, but it wouldn't open! Perhaps the coldness caused it to stick. Perhaps it was his numbed hands. Whatever it was, Lennie realized he was trapped.

He would need help to get out. It would be embarrassing to explain his predicament to his rescuer, but he had no choice. He began screaming, "Help me! Help me! I'm in the blue car. In the trunk. Help!" Then he would listen for a response. Nothing. A person would have to be crazy to be walking around in this weather, but it was his only hope. He called for help again, as loud as he could. The car and the storm muffled his sounds. His voice was weakening. The cold was sapping his strength.

Joan had grown worried. Lennie was long overdue from work. The bus he usually took home had passed by two hours ago. She had called his office and learned that he had quit early for the day. She called everyone they knew. No one had seen him. Where could he be? Maybe he had slipped on the ice and was lying unconscious in a snowbank. No one could survive outside very long in this weather. She called the police. They began searching the area, assisted by Joan and Lennie's friends and neighbors. Hours passed in the bitterly cold night, and no one could find any sign of Lennie.

Eventually a police officer asked about the family car. Had Lennie possibly driven it away? Perhaps there were some clues in it that could help locate him. The police found the car at the restaurant and looked it over. No sign of him there. Maybe something was in the trunk. No, it wouldn't open. Might as well look someplace else. But where? There was no other place *to* look. Well, then, maybe the trunk should be forced open. The lock was frozen. A lighted match was held to the base of the inserted key. Finally the trunk door opened.

There was Lennie, unconscious, his skin gray, huddled pathetically, having tried to protect himself from the cold. He was rushed to the hospital, where he was in critical condition for the next few days and where he had to stay for several weeks. The frostbite and shock were serious but did little permanent damage. Joan was at his bedside daily, as were his friends and coworkers. Everyone knew what he had done. He was humiliated with no pride left to salvage.

He had ample time in the hospital to consider his situation. During his recuperation he thought of the pain he had inflicted on his family and of the energy he had wasted in his futile effort to learn something he didn't want to know or believe anyway. His wife and friends had stuck by him through this latest fiasco. He was more open to help, and in any event, he was too weak and too grateful to be very resistant.

Through therapy and the help of his wife and friends, Lennie was able to cope more successfully with his jealousy problem. He found better ways to release tension than by fighting with or accusing Joan. He learned to communicate better with her. Therapy for Joan also helped her to cope more effectively. As their relationship improved, her physical and emotional symptoms became less serious. But both of them have had to keep working hard to control the problem. They found that as long as they continue these efforts, their relationship can be relatively healthy.

Of course, not all jealous relationships are so severe or lead to such serious consequences. In some people jealousy problems are not even evident, while in others they may be so mild or of such brief duration that the discomfort they cause is scarcely noticed. And for others, the suffering is even worse than that experienced by Joan and Lennie.

To many people, especially those who have never been close to a victim of jealousy, Joan and Lennie's experience seems incomprehensible. After all, how can such behaviors be explained? What induces people to go to such extremes? How can a person seem so normal and responsible in every other way and yet act so bizarre in this one area? How can a person devote so much time and energy to trying to learn something about a loved one while dreading that the suspicion might be true? How can jealousy lead people to harm the very individuals they love most?

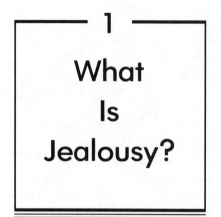

1

What Is Jealousy?

Nearly everyone experiences jealousy at times. It happens to all types of people—men as well as women, the very young and very old as well as people in between. It happens to heterosexuals as well as gays, to members of all racial and cultural groups, and to those who are basically stable and emotionally healthy as well as to those who are mentally disturbed.

We first become aware of jealous feelings when we sense the possibility of losing someone or something to a rival. It most often occurs when someone we love seems unusually interested in another person. Yet there are many other situations where it also occurs. It may happen when one's employer is impressed with a fellow employee, when a best friend starts spending more time with another person, when a teacher gives more recognition or higher grades to a classmate, when a minority group member gets less opportunity for social acceptance or advancement than is available to others, or when a parent gives more attention or privileges to a sibling.

Most people don't consider jealousy to be a serious problem or a debilitating disease. Some individuals even think of it as a positive emotion, something to encourage as a demonstration of love. It is so common it isn't usually thought of as an abnormality.

Nevertheless, jealousy can cause much pain and suffering. Social researchers find that it is related significantly to divorce, spouse abuse, and even murder. No one can estimate how much it has contributed to such elusive phenomena as unhappiness, the loss of productivity, and lowered aspirations.[1]

How can jealousy be considered at once a common and harmless human trait and a source of misery for so many? How can it evoke amusement in most people but also be seen as a monstrous affliction? It was Shakespeare who called it "the green-ey'd monster," the emotion that drove Othello to murder his innocent wife. Nevertheless, Shakespeare also used jealousy as a humorous theme in many of his other plays. It is the multifaceted nature of jealousy that accounts for this—the fact that it comes in many forms and disguises, has a wide range of intensities, and affects people in varied ways.[2]

Jealousy may be seen as existing on a continuum. On one end is apathy. On the other are intense anxiety and overwhelming suspicion. Only the middle range of this continuum contains what could be called "normal jealousy." This is the kind that most people occasionally experience. When it is in this middle range, it is usually identified as a slightly bothersome but basically harmless human trait, the kind people think of when they find jealousy to be amusing and rather insignificant.

Normal jealousy feels like a mild form of anxiety and fear. People experience it by worrying a little about something they possess, want to possess, or imagine possessing. They think about the possibility that someone or something is going to take their possession from them or prevent its acquisition.

Most often this "possession" is a loved one—a spouse, intimate friend, or close relative. However, the possession can also be an important object, such as a desired job, promotion, money, or property. Or it may be something more abstract or symbolic, such as the respect of one's peers, fame, or prestige. Those with normal jealousy worry that there is only a limited supply of this respect, prestige, or love and that whenever any goes to someone else, there is that much less available for themselves. The great fear is that the desired object will be lost to someone who appears to be more deserving. When or if this happens, the individual feels less deserving and thus less adequate.[3]

Fortunately, people with normal jealousy get over this uncomfortable feeling fairly rapidly and easily. They soon realize that their fears are groundless and that they are in no danger of losing what is important to them. They may learn, on their own or with the help of others, that there is an ample supply of what they want and that they will get their share. People with normal jealousy can readily understand that they didn't have any special rights to the possession in the first place and will have to work all the harder to get it later. Or perhaps they have enough self-confidence to believe that they can hold their own against potential rivals.

When the jealousy is not normal, the people afflicted with it aren't so fortunate. For them, jealousy is intensely and endlessly painful. Typically, they become obsessed with the idea that someone is going to take away the person or object they believe they need so desperately. Guarded and suspicious, they look for signs that what they fear the most—the loss of what they want—is about to happen. They find it difficult to concentrate on anything else. Consequently, their work suffers, and they are less effective in meeting their responsibilities. Many of the people who are closest to them becoming increasingly annoyed by their behavior and begin trying to avoid them.

For those who experience abnormal jealousy, the emotion sets up a self-fulfilling prophecy. As their associates try to avoid them, their worst fears of losing love and respect are realized. Rather than improving in the behavior that led to their rejection, they become even more vigilant, more distrustful. They strive harder to gather evidence to confirm their suspicions in the hope that this will prevent the loss. Yet, they remain highly vulnerable to the loss of everything they most desire—lovers, spouse, family, job, friends, and, especially, self-esteem.

This was true in the case of Vincent, a brilliant and articulate young lawyer whose professional competence concealed a high degree of personal insecurity and self-doubt. Because of his outstanding performance in law school, he was able to get a position with his city's most prestigious firm. Within months he had established a reputation in the firm as an excellent professional, and soon he was being considered for promotion. His future seemed assured and his hidden insecurities diminished.

Then the firm hired another recent law school graduate with an equally impressive background. Marian was a young black woman who demonstrated rapidly that she, too, deserved to be considered for promotion. Vincent noted that she started getting as much attention and respect as he alone had been receiving before her arrival. Now he had to share the firm's admiration with Marian.

Vincent found himself studying her intently, waiting for her to make mistakes or errors of judgment. He started acting more nervously around her, and seemed less confident in meetings they attended together. As his preoccupation with her increased, his concentration on his own work diminished commensurately. Older lawyers in the firm told him they had recently noted a decline in his performance. This caused Vincent's insecurity to grow, making him even more self-conscious and less effective. But, because he could only think about his rival's work, it didn't cause him to think about improving his own. He called the other lawyers' attention to her few deficiencies. He implied to them that he felt victimized by reverse racial and sexual discrimination. He became convinced that Marian would get the promotion he coveted and felt he deserved. When the promotions were announced, he was not surprised that she got one and he didn't. What did surprise him, however, was learning that he would have been promoted, too, except for his poor recent performance. It was his own work, not hers, that led to his failure.

The condition that leads to such troubled behavior is known as "pathological" or "morbid" jealousy. The most important difference between pathological and normal jealousy lies in their degrees of intensity. The symptoms of pathological jealousy are stronger and appear much more frequently. These symptoms usually include serious insecurity, strong feelings of inadequacy, and often considerable suspiciousness or paranoid thoughts. Severe anxiety and depression are also often observed. Pathologically jealous people seem very rigid and stubborn and tend to be zealous about people's adherence to rules. They are overly concerned with such seeming superficialities as their own and other people's appearance and possessions. They often lack the ability to empathize or see things from the viewpoints of others. They are more inclined to imagine that threats exist when they don't. Finally, they often have difficulty controlling their anger and can be violent and destructive.[4]

Pathological jealousy can be an incurable, even fatal condition. Through suicide or self-destructive behavior, many die from its consequences. Others don't die but are in such emotional pain that they wish they could. For many it is a lifetime malady that saps them of their energy, drains them of their spirit, and keeps them from reaching their potential. It is no wonder that the Bible (Song of Sol. 8:6) says that jealousy is as "cruel as the grave."[5]

Although jealousy has been studied, discussed, and explained at least since the beginning of recorded history, humans have not reached much consensus in defining it. At various times and in different cultures, the term has been equated with envy, covetousness, zeal, passionate ambition, paranoia, selfishness, and even love.

When the ancient Greeks referred to this concept, they used the word *zelos*, which meant both "jealous" and "zealous." "Jealousy" was considered to be synonymous with "zeal," or passionate ardor in pursuit of something. As their mythology shows, the Greeks were fascinated by *zelos*. Almost all their gods were incessantly embroiled in conflict based on jealousy. Zeus, the chief god, is a philanderer. His wife, Hera, is the prototype of the jealous spouse. Obsessed by his affairs, she accuses him, follows him, and tries to trap him in his indiscretions. Nevertheless, her efforts have no effect in making him change his ways. The countless jealous spouses who have emulated Hera through the centuries have almost always obtained the same results.[6]

The Romans used the word *zelosus,* but it meant more than "zealousness," also referring to competition for a love object. Much of the existing Roman literature and history read like soap opera, with countless anecdotes centering around one person's efforts to arouse feelings of jealousy in another. Such episodes are commonplace even in Roman mythology, as when Cupid, the Roman god of love, is smitten by the charms of Psyche, the goddess of the mind. Cupid's mother, Venus, who has more than a maternal interest in her son, is consumed by jealousy and does everything she can to thwart the affair, without much success.

The Old Testament reveals that the ancient Hebrews often equated jealousy with envy and covetousness. (As such, it was a violation of the Tenth Commandment.) In its earliest pages, it tells how jealousy destroyed Cain and Abel, the firstborn sons of Adam and Eve. Cain is a hardworking farmer who offers the best of his harvest to God, but God prefers the sheep that Abel has contributed. Cain is bitterly disappointed and jealous of his younger brother. In his bitterness he kills Abel and denies his misdeed to God. God marks Cain's immorality for all to see, thereby making unbridled jealousy a sin against God and man.

Ambiguity and confusion about jealousy are deeply rooted in Western consciousness and are reflected in numerous biblical passages. For example, the Creator declares, "I the Lord thy God am a jealous God" (Exodus 20:5). Later, according to the New Testament, "God is love" (1 John 4:8), but then it says that "love is not jealous or boastful" (1 Cor. 13:4).

In contemporary times, the ambiguity and confusion remain. Everyone seems to have a unique interpretation of jealousy, and often the same person will offer two or more contradictory definitions. In one recent study, a group of 175 graduate students was asked to define "jealousy." Half of them thought it was synonymous with "envy," and a quarter thought it was a form of suspiciousness. Others had widely disparate descriptions, ranging from a sick possessiveness to a healthy indication of love and from a learned pattern of behavior to an instinctive human trait. As the students compared their ideas, their definitions continued to change. One finally ended the discussion by applying the late Supreme Court Justice Potter

Stewart's famous line about pornography to jealousy: "I may not know how to define it, but I sure know it when I see it."[7]

The definition that will be implicit hereafter seems simple at first but contains several elements. *Jealousy is defined as a group of uncomfortable emotional reactions to the perceived threat of losing a possession.* However, this definition needs further elaboration in order to clarify and understand a complex pattern of feelings and behaviors.

The first thing to remember is that jealousy is not a single feeling or emotion but a combination of emotional reactions. It is not included on the familiar lists of single emotions, such as anger, joy, fear, or sorrow. These feelings are the ingredients, the bricks that are laid to make up the whole structure called jealousy. Jealousy is better included among the more complex conditions, or combinations of emotions, such as love, hate, ambition, and insecurity.

To love someone is to experience many different single emotions. It is the combination of these emotions that comprises the totality called love. The ingredients that make up each individual's love keep changing. If Mark is in love with Cathy, his love may consist of three parts joy, five parts pride, one of greed, and so on. Later, after Mark learns more about Cathy or sees her behave differently, his love for her changes. It now consists of three parts pride, five of greed, ten of lust, one of joy, and so on. Of course, the single emotions may number in the hundreds. The relative influence of each emotion keeps changing as Mark's needs and experiences change. What is important to him at this moment may not be so important in a different context or at a different time. Whatever its ingredients, it all adds up to love. This is why each person's love is unique.

It is this way with jealousy, too. Each jealous person has a unique combination of feelings that constantly fluctuates. The ingredients that make up one person's jealousy will probably differ from those that make up jealousy in another. Two people may be considered equally jealous; they may feel it and show it identically. But the components of each person's jealousy are unique. Mark's jealousy may be made up of ten units of fear, five of anger, two of lust, and so on. Cathy's jealousy, on the other hand, may consist of five units of fear, six of anger, six of lust, and so on. The numbers of different feeling components may be in the hundreds, but they add up to the totality we call jealousy. And the ingredients that constitute each person's unique jealousy keep changing with the experiences, values, and circumstances of that person's life.

In its normal as well as its pathological form, jealousy can be uncomfortable. Usually, the more severe the jealousy, the greater the discomfort. Even when jealousy is only momentary and mild, the individual is less happy, stable, and healthy. The jealous person immediately strives to correct the uncomfortable feeling and get back to the prejealous state, whether in a constructive way or not. Every flash of jealousy is accompanied by feelings of anxiety, fear, and anger, even if only mildly felt. If the jealousy is a little more intense, the person may also feel nauseous, dizzy, enraged, and mobilized for conflict. If there is no respite from these feelings, the incessant stress eventually contributes to other physical and mental disturbances.

Looking at many jealous people, it is hard to imagine that they are uncomfortable. In fact, they sometimes seem to enjoy their jealousy. At least they seem more invigorated and in command of their faculties. Moreover, they don't seem to want to avoid the feeling. Because most people usually try to avoid anything that causes discomfort, this is confusing. However, some pathologically jealous people actually seem to go out of their way to activate it. They look for the threats; they store up the grievances; and they appear to want to perpetuate the jealous feelings.

But jealous people aren't doing this for enjoyment. Rather, it is because jealousy seems to them to be a less unpleasant feeling than something else. They believe that jealousy, painful as it may be, will protect them from some greater pain or unpleasantness. It is a price the jealous person feels must be paid to avoid an even greater hurt, such as rejection, abandonment, or humiliation.

In the example of the young lawyer, Vincent was in great pain as he sensed that Marian was usurping his place in the law firm. He knew that his jealous feelings were not going to help his cause and were not going to give him the ability to fight back. But he couldn't get rid of them because of his growing fear that he would be humiliated. His failure to get the promotion would expose him as inadequate. His jealousy made him seem more alert and effective, but in fact he was distracted, ineffective, and discomforted.

The discomfort felt through jealousy comes from the sense of being threatened. To feel threatened is to sense danger, to fear that you will be harmed. If a very attractive and popular person proclaims a desire for the person you love, you may feel at risk. You fear that your lover could be taken from you. You do not feel threatened, however, if you are confident in your mutual love and attraction.[8]

Perceived threats come in many forms. What you might consider to be threatening may seem innocuous to someone else. You could feel threatened by the potential loss of prestige or control over others as well as by the possible loss of a loved one. For example, when a man finds that his date at a party is spending an inordinate amount of time with his rival, the perceived threat may not be over the potential loss of the woman. Instead, the man could feel threatened not so much by the loss of the date as by the fear that others will think him less attractive or capable than his competitor. It is his reputation that appears jeopardized, not his relationship.[9]

Many studies show that women tend to feel jealously threatened for different reasons than do men, at least in our culture. They attach greater significance to physical attractiveness in other women, feel more threatened by it, and look for flaws in other women. Men tend to be less threatened by outward appearances and more by the demonstrated capabilities of other men. Both experience challenges to their own nature and abilities but tend to be aroused by different stimuli.[10]

A person can feel threatened, and thus jealous, even when no true danger exists or no apparent change of circumstance has occurred. For example, a woman may feel very secure about her husband's love for her. One day they take a pleasant stroll through their neighborhood. Even though her husband has said or done nothing unusual, her feelings suddenly change. Inexplicably, she feels jealously suspicious of him. She soon realizes why. She notices that they are walking in the same place where she was once rejected by her former fiancé.

Because people perceive threats from so many different sources, it is difficult to predict what will trigger a specific person's jealous reaction. And it is equally difficult to predict what the reaction will be, even after the jealousy has been set off.

Jealousy is manifested as a defensive reaction to a perceived threat. This reaction may appear in many forms of overt or unobservable behavior. It may be seen in verbal accusations, overprotectiveness, attention-getting activities, and even violence. Reactions may also include responses that are not detectable by outside observers or perhaps even by the individual himself. The jealous person may respond only with clenched teeth, an increased flow of adrenalin, or private thoughts or fantasies that some danger is imminent.

Each person's jealousy reactions are unique. This is because all people learn through their own early experiences how to behave in specific circumstances. Even if jealousy is eventually proved to be an instinctive trait, the behavioral responses that come from it are the result of socialization and teaching. We are taught what to like and dislike, what to be concerned about, and what to value or disregard. If a man is raised in a household where everyone screams and fights whenever there is a risk of losing something, he is taught that screaming and fighting is "natural," or appropriate, behavior. If another man is raised in a household where everyone calmly discusses and negotiates about who owns something, he is taught a different version of "appropriate" behavior. Later, when these two men are exposed to identical circumstances, one behaves differently from the other.

Many people in our culture who share similar upbringings express their jealousy reactions in similar socially acceptable ways. Normal jealousy is often expressed so subtly that it is not noticed by others or possibly even recognized by the individual who feels it. Typically, the person with a mild jealousy attack will attribute those feelings to something other than jealousy and thus not even recognize it for what it is. When normal jealousy becomes more overt, it is commonly seen in rather innocuous behaviors. These might include

- Pouting when you are given less attention than your rival
- Gossiping about or revealing your rival's faults
- Manipulating others into paying you compliments
- Dressing or behaving to get more attention than your rival
- Developing your skills or abilities so you can overcome your competition
- Repeatedly asking your loved one such questions as, "Am I still the only one in your life?"
- Becoming more watchful and vigilant about the activities of your loved one

If the jealousy, however, has gone beyond the normal range, either temporarily or permanently, the reactions may be anything but innocuous. They may include

- Accusations made in a loud and hostile way
- Confrontations and threats made to the real, suspected, or potential rival
- Secretive attempts to uncover evidence that the relevant other is slipping out of the commitment
- Activities designed to control, intimidate, or occupy the relevant other to eliminate the possibility of losing that person
- Physical abuse or coercion

Because jealousy derives from fear of losing someone or something considered to be personal property, if no one had any sense of ownership, there would be no jealousy. But virtually everyone feels possessive about some things, no matter how little is owned or how communal is one's philosophy.

Although possessiveness is universal, each person is taught what kinds of things must be shared and what things are private property. Some societies teach their citizens that the money they earn is theirs, while others that it is to be shared. In certain less developed cultures, the people cannot understand the idea of having exclusive ownership of a piece of land, and the notion of having sole possession of a sexual partner might be incomprehensible. Some tribes have taught their members to share space and people. In some cultures, families consider it normal for the children to sleep in the parents' bed. For other families this is unthinkable. A young child may be taught that this teddy bear or this toothbrush or this coat belongs to no one else. At the same time the child learns that the contents of the refrigerator and the television set, and the attention from mother must be divided among many people. For most people, sharing some things and not others becomes taken for granted at a very early age. A child soon learns to accept being deprived of mother's undivided attention but is still permitted to be outraged if an older sibling removes the teddy bear from the crib.

Because each culture teaches its members what is to be owned exclusively and what is to be shared, what will cause one person to feel jealous may have no impact whatsoever on others. For example, Jake pays a visit to his old friend Hank and Hank's wife, Mabel, for a few days. One day, when Hank comes home early from work, he finds Jake and Mabel making love. Hank is probably appalled. He has been taught all his life that such activity is a bad thing. It is a risk to his happy home, a violation of his moral values and exclusive marital rights. On learning of this event, Hank's friends might scorn Mabel, comfort Hank, and cheer his efforts to fight back against his former friend, Jake, the cuckolder. This would be a fairly typical reaction in our culture.[11]

But if this scenario took place in an Eskimo village, where wife lending had been a common part of the culture, a different reaction might be expected. Hank would gladly offer Mabel to Jake. To do otherwise would be considered in poor taste. Hank would be proud if his offering went well and Jake was pleased with Mabel. Hank would only be angry at Mabel if she refused to cooperate or didn't please Jake. "How could you do this to me?" Hank might ask her. "Now everyone will think I am selfish and inhospitable."

One of the most important things we are taught to possess in our culture is the object of our affection or love. When we are in love, we want and expect exclusivity. Sharing certain intimacies is unacceptable. But this view is something that other cultures do not always teach their members. For example, in polygamous cultures—those that accept one man having several wives or one woman having several husbands—jealousy is unusual between the spouses who must share. They are taught to believe that this type of sharing is acceptable and not a threat to preserving one's possessions. Sharing a spouse with other wives or husbands may be no more of a jealousy producer in such cultures than sharing food from the family dinner table would be in ours. Some of us may want the biggest portion, but we accept sharing as the norm.

In polygamous cultures wives have been known to encourage their husbands to acquire additional wives. Doing so tends to add to the first wife's prestige. It divides the work load and childbearing and -rearing responsibilities. Not many years ago, a woman in one such culture took her husband to court because he had not yet taken any other wives. She was dissatisfied because this meant she had to perform all the domestic chores without assistance. The court ruled in her favor, and her husband was ordered to obtain a second wife within six months.

Jealousy problems may exist in every culture but are probably not expressed so conspicuously in cultures that encourage sexual sharing. Sociologist Kingsley Davis compared those that stress sexual fidelity and monogamy and those that do not. He found significantly fewer examples of jealousy problems in societies that endorsed wife trading. A tradition in some cultures has been the *jus primae noctis*, or "right of the first night," to which few, if any, jealousy problems attach. In these cultures, when a young woman marries, someone other than her new husband takes her virginity. Often this man is the tribal chief, village priest, or some other esteemed person. Neither the bride nor the groom seems jealous or troubled by the tradition. They expect it, are gratified by it, and are honored. It is not a threat because there is no risk that the new spouse will be lost to the other person.[12]

While jealousy doesn't occur without possessiveness, the object we seek to possess can be anything. A lover is only one kind of "possession" and perhaps not even the one that is most often associated with the jealousy response. A more likely candidate is one's sense of self-worth, security, prestige, or "face." To lose face and the love and respect that accompany it may be the greatest threat of all.

We know this is true when we see how very jealous people behave with their loved ones. If love were the sole motivator, one would expect the jealous person to be more concerned about the other person's happiness and fulfillment and do everything possible to help achieve them. Yet, the opposite is more often the case. Very jealous people cannot tolerate it when their lovers want to grow, learn, or become more successful. They often react with displeasure when their lovers want to go to school, try to get new jobs, receive promotions, or do anything that establishes more independence. Instead of being happy about such developments, very jealous people typically distrust their companions and make accusations and issue ultimatums. This may be followed by interrogations, threats, and violent abuse. They often have their partners followed, try to trap them, and look for signs of deceit or indications of dishonorable intentions.

What are they trying to accomplish with such behavior? Clearly, it is not to achieve greater love or happiness in the relationship. The answer is apparent when asking jealous people why they treat their lovers this way. The answer is almost always the same: "Because I don't want to look like a fool." When this is the motive, the possession they hope to retain is not love but their own self-esteem.

Feelings of personal worth and integrity are very much at the core of jealousy problems. People who feel good about themselves, who have self-confidence and emotional security, are rarely, if ever, troubled by pathological jealousy. There is more consensus about this among social scientists and mental health professionals than about any other aspect of jealousy. In one survey of psychiatrists, 90 percent of them believed that jealous people had low self-esteem. It is exceedingly rare to find that proportion of psychiatrists agreeing about anything.[13]

Conversely, people who suffer from feelings of inadequacy or inferiority are most vulnerable to experiencing jealousy problems. Some scholars say this is the major or only cause of serious jealousy. It is not a new idea; more than 250 years ago, Benjamin Franklin wrote in *Poor Richard's Almanac* that jealousy was caused by a person's inability to feel competent or adequate.

It is the feeling of inadequacy that is ultimately behind the fear of losing a possession to someone else. The dominating fear is that the rival is more deserving or more capable of acquiring the valued object. The inadequate person can't obtain or retain the valued object through intrinsic merit. It has to be done through manipulation or intimidation. This person thinks, "I may not be able to keep your love, but if I continue to guard you, I can keep you from having the opportunity to leave me."

Those who feel inadequate tend to seek reassurance by gaining superficial approval from others. To get it, they often observe what others seem to like and then behave accordingly. They make disparaging remarks about their rivals while extolling their own virtues. They are concerned with material possessions and personal appearance in the belief that this will gain them the admiration of others. They try to be loved or respected for what they have, because they doubt that they can be loved or respected for what they are.

People suffering feelings of inadequacy are at the mercy of others. They have so little sense of self-worth that they seek it in recognition from others. Though they are frequently devastated when the others withhold it, this only makes them try harder to get it. They get more possessions or belittle their rivals or improve their appearance even more.

The jealousy problem occurs when people who feel inadequate sense that others are gaining the love and approval for which they have worked so hard. They compare themselves to these others and fear that they don't really measure up. Their only recourse is to hold onto whatever it is they already have. They feel they can only do so through manipulation, coercion, vigilance, or abuse. But the jealousy doesn't end when control is achieved or when people say they approve. It ends only when the jealous person achieves an inner sense of self-worth and doesn't have to rely on others for it.

This is what happened with the young lawyer who failed to get promoted. After Marian was advanced, Vincent became very depressed and ineffective in his work. Eventually his employers recommended psychotherapy. Vincent concurred and worked in therapy for over a year, concentrating primarily on changing his low self-esteem. When he accomplished this goal, he was once again able to do highly skilled legal work. When a new group of capable young law graduates was hired, he found he could help them rather than feel threatened by them. He eventually received his promotion and is now a senior partner in the firm. He has a well-deserved reputation for being able to help his colleagues and rivals for the good of the organization.

In order to understand jealousy better, it is also necessary to analyze and correct some of the most common misconceptions that have persisted about it for many years. Some people believe that showing jealousy indicates how much love there is. Some people believe that envy and jealousy are the same thing. Some believe there is no such thing as jealousy outside sexual competitiveness. Many people think jealousy occurs only among young people or that it is less likely to occur in shy or passive people. Many people believe that jealousy happens mostly to women, and many others believe it happens mostly to men. Many people believe that jealousy is bad or has no redeeming attributes, while others think it is highly beneficial to humanity. All these commonly held views are based on incorrect assumptions or faulty data. They are either wrong or overly simplistic and obscure our understanding of the nature of jealousy.

The greatest misconception about jealousy is that it is an indicator of love. This view is often expressed this way: "I *want* my lover to be jealous of me. How else can I know if my lover really cares?" Such people try to test their partner's "love" by provoking jealousy. They might act suspiciously or leave threatening clues—anything to lead the partner to believe they are interested in someone else. Then, when the partner acts jealous, perhaps becoming hurt or even violently angry, they are assured that the love continues. It is an assurance based on a falsehood.[14]

Somehow, this idea that jealousy indicates the depth of one's love for another person has persisted for centuries. As long ago as A.D. 400, the philosopher Saint Augustine wrote, "He that is not jealous is not in love." And, more recently, a poll of thousands of spouses showed that a majority of Americans believe this, even though most behavioral scientists do not.[15]

Because so many people hold this to be true, they are flattered when their partners behave jealously toward them. They tell their friends who hold the same view and are further encouraged. They derive ego-gratification from their assumption that they are important to and loved and desired by the other person.[16]

It is surprising that, with so little evidence to support it, this myth has endured for such a long time. In fact, jealousy is no more a sign of being in love than obesity is a sign of being a good cook. Anthropologist Margaret Mead put it another way when she wrote, "Jealousy is not a barometer by which the depth of love can be read, it merely records the degree of the lover's insecurity." And psychiatrist Otto Fenichel wrote, "Jealous people are those who are not able to love but who need the feeling of being loved." More recently, one psychotherapist wrote, "It is possible to feel jealousy toward someone you don't love, whom you don't like, and even toward someone you heartily dislike."[17]

Some studies indicate that there is a negative correlation between the degree of jealousy and the presence of love. In other words, the more jealous a person is, the less is the likelihood of love as we generally know it. Of course, these ideas depend on how one defines "love." Most people want to think of love as a state of caring and giving to another person. It is wanting and striving for the other person's happiness and well-being. Jealousy, on the other hand, is self-centered. Jealous people are more concerned with their own happiness and well-being than those of their partners.[18]

The "love" one sees in jealousy is based on feelings of dependency. It is the kind of love that humanist-psychologist Abraham Maslow called "D-love." He identified D-love (dependency-based) to distinguish it from "B-love" (being in love), which seeks the happiness and well-being of the other. He concluded that both types generally exist in all of us. We can hardly avoid feelings of dependent attachment, but they are not one of our more noble virtues. Jealousy doesn't exist in B-love, and it doesn't fail to exist in D-love. Jealousy doesn't care about the happiness or well-being of the other; holding onto the person for one's own sake is the goal. Thus, jealousy comes from depending on the partner, from feeling inadequate to cope without the presence or possession of the other.[19]

Other scientists have extended Maslow's theories about love and consider that it contains three components: intimacy, passion, and a decision to commit. Each element can be depicted as one side of a triangle, with each side ideally being of approximately equal length. In a healthy love relationship, both partners' triangles would be similar and well matched.

But if one person has more or less passion than the other, or more or less of the other elements, a distortion occurs. The partners are not well matched and their respective versions of "love" are not synonymous. This results in each partner wanting to give and receive something different in the relationship. In other words, each person may be interpreting "love" from his or her own perspective and it may not be the same as the interpretation given to it by the partner.[20]

Generally, people who attempt to test their partner's love by provoking jealousy feelings aren't testing what they think they are. For example, a man says to his wife, "Wow, I sure saw a beautiful woman on the bus tonight! She sat next to me and we had a good talk." Then the man studies his wife's reaction. If she is upset, insecure, or angry, he may feel gratified. Knowing that she is disturbed may suggest to the husband that she loves him because she is threatened by the possibility of losing him. If she weren't upset, the husband might imagine that she doesn't care whether she loses him or not. Supposedly, she passed his test.

But, in fact, the husband might have wanted his wife to pass his B-love test, and she only passed the D-love test. It wouldn't prove she is interested in his well-being or happiness but only that she wanted to preserve her own selfish interests. The husband's ego is not gratified, and ultimately he is not made to feel more secure. He has thus accomplished very little in his attempt to prove his wife's love through jealousy. It doesn't tell the husband that his wife cares about him. It only says she is being selfish.

This kind of thinking is seen more frequently in pathologically jealous people than in those with normal jealousy. As a person's jealousy intensifies, the inclination to give to the other person diminishes. Jealous people become obsessed with the need for reassurance, seeking guarantees that they will not be abandoned, that they will be forever loved. The giving in the relationship becomes more one sided. A relationship with mutual giving and caring cannot flourish in a jealous atmosphere. It may not even survive.

Another misconception about jealousy is that it is restricted to sexual competitiveness. For many people, jealousy seems to pertain only to male-female relationships. It seems to them that rivalries between members of the same sex for desired members of the opposite sex are the cause of jealousy, or the only cause that really matters. Some writers have even theorized that human jealousy is the result of the same genetic drive that causes animals to compete for their mates. It is pointed out that certain male animals try to outdo other males of their species by preening or fighting rivals to win the attention of and sexual rights with the desired females. The females compete with one another to acquire and retain the best location for attracting the rivals for their attentions. Once the pairing has been established, the animals will often do anything they can to preserve these rights. This view holds that jealousy is the human manifestation of this natural drive to procreate.[21]

Yet, while male-female sexually oriented possessiveness and competitiveness may be the most important sources of jealousy, they are not the only ones. There are well-documented reports of jealousy that exists in infants, between younger siblings, between older siblings, among young children, and between homosexuals. There are even analyses of mothers and fathers being jealous of their young children. Perhaps it exists between any two people who vie for the same thing.[22]

Three examples illustrate jealousy without overt sexual competitiveness.

• Clarissa is dining alone in a restaurant, and her waitress is attentive and pleasant. Soon another woman arrives and is seated at a nearby table. The waitress becomes far more attentive, warm, and humorous with the new diner and relatively less interested in Clarissa. The time and attention the waitress devotes to the other party are at Clarissa's expense, and this causes her a mild and momentary unpleasant sensation. Clarissa later reports that she felt jealous of the other diner, having apparently lost the waitress's favor to her.

• Harold works in an office with several other employees, all of whom have equal rank, pay, and formal status. The boss, a tight-fisted man who will soon determine which worker will get a pay raise, has seemed to like Harold and has complimented his work. Soon one of the other workers begins to go out of his way to curry favor with the boss. He tells him the latest jokes, brings him newspaper clippings on the boss's favorite subjects, and gives him tickets to sports events. Harold notices that the boss is spending more time with the other employee and enjoying his company more than anyone else's. Harold soon recognizes that he is no longer his boss's favorite. He begins to feel uncomfortable and insecure around the boss and develops hostile feelings toward his colleague.

• For years Sally and Kim have been best friends as well as next door neighbors. Then another young woman moves into the neighborhood, a woman who is warm, outgoing, and charming. Kim begins to spend more time with the other person and less with Sally. When Kim is with Sally, most of the talk is about the new neighbor's many accomplishments. Sally has never met the other person, but she feels jealous nevertheless. She believes that her friendship is threatened and that the primacy of the relationship no longer exists.

There is no overt sexual connotation in any of these common occurrences. Nevertheless, the feeling of jealousy exists. Someone felt the risk of losing a positive relationship with a waitress, an employer, or a friend. It is not that these people were owned by the jealous ones, but their attention and devotion had been possessed, at least for the moment. When others entered the scene, these possessions were jeopardized.

In many, if not most, jealousy situations, it isn't overt sexuality but attention that is coveted. This is most readily seen among young children in a family. They are inevitably going to have conflicts over the attention rights to "*my* mom" or "*my* dad." They compete not for total possession of the parents but for their immediate attention, demonstration of affection, or apparent love. If they argue over who gets the most privileges, often they are really trying to decide who is the parents' favorite. The child's response when the parents say no is likely to be, "How come you like him best?" And the response when given a privilege is often, "Ha ha, *my* mom likes me better than you."[23]

Psychoanalysts may continue to see sexual overtones in many places, including the strivings of young children to gain parental favor. Freud, for example, said that the child who has a new sibling feels "dethroned, despoiled, prejudiced in its rights; it casts a jealous hatred upon the new baby and develops a grievance against the faithless mother." If this view is accurate—and at most it is an unproved hypothesis—it still wouldn't support the commonly held misunderstanding that equates sexual competitiveness and jealousy. Most people who see this as a cause of jealousy are thinking only about overt sexuality between sexually mature humans.[24]

Perhaps jealousy is not even an exclusively human characteristic. The behavior of some animals surely resembles jealousy. Most dog owners are well aware of this. When the owner of a dog pets another dog, his own dog is likely to get very excited and attempt to regain the favor of its master. The dog nuzzles between its owner and the rival or otherwise tries get the owner's attention.[25]

Other animals may be unconcerned about human responses toward them, but many of them seem to be very threatened by the possibility of losing their possessions to another animal. A mother bird keeps an eye on her nest or favorite food source and chatters away the other birds who might want to be there. Some writers and zoologists see this as a basic instinct and call it the "territorial imperative," but its behavioral manifestations seem identical to those associated with jealousy.[26]

Are women more jealous than men? Or is it men who are the more jealous sex? There are many who argue that men are much more inclined toward jealousy than women, just as many others claim that women have this distinction. Often the claims are made by the jealous person him- or herself, as a justification for the behavior.

"Well," such a man might say, "I'm just acting normally. Men are supposed to be competitive, and jealousy is just a form of that. It's our way of keeping our women in line. That's just how we are, and you just have to accept it if you want a man in your life."

A woman who espouses this argument might say, "I'm just acting normally. All women are jealous. That's why we aren't friendly to attractive or single women, especially when our man is around. We weren't raised to have 'buddies' and to cooperate on teams like you men. So you'll just have to make allowances for me."

Neither argument has much validity. As is true about many other "gender myths," both are based on stereotypes rather than objective evidence. The fact is, no scientific data support either hypothesis. Men are not more jealous than women. Women are not more jealous than men.[27]

There is, however, a considerable amount of evidence that men and women show jealousy traits in different ways. This is probably why the misunderstanding occurs. The evidence is still tentative because no large-scale studies have yet taken place to determine the differences in male-female jealousy behavior but many interim studies have led to some interesting conclusions:[28]

• Men are more likely than women to blame their jealousy on others. They will attribute their jealousy to the woman's behavior or to a third party. They, more than women, blame jealousy on "the nature of men."[29]

• Women, on the other hand, are more likely to blame themselves when a conflict about jealousy arises. They tend to think that if they had done something better, they would receive more attention from the other person. Women also are more likely to acknowledge their feelings of jealousy, while men are more likely to deny that they have such feelings.[30]

• Women attach more significance than do men to physical attractiveness. In the presence of attractive women, other women are more inclined to feel jealousy than are men in the presence of attractive men. Women, more than men, will look for flaws in the appearances of other members of their sex.[31]

• Men are more likely to confront a third party about some real or imagined threat. And they are more likely than women to confront their partners with demands or ultimatums. Women, on the other hand, tend to avoid such confrontations with third parties when they feel jealous. They are more likely to act dependent and cling to their partners with greater tenacity.[32]

• Men are more inclined to express jealousy through rage and violent behavior. Women are more likely to express their jealousy in a passive-aggressive way, by tears and attempts to provoke guilt. After the violence, the man tends to become despondent and self-incriminating. Women seem to get despondent and self-incriminating after their jealousy flash without the intermediate step of rage and violence.[33]

• Men, more than women, become jealously upset when their mates engage in outside sexual affairs. For example, if a man discovers that his wife is infatuated with the mailman he may well shrug it off. Only if his wife had sexual intercourse with this man would he be upset. In that case he would be more inclined than a woman in a similar situation to demand revenge. He would be more likely to confront the postman with anger and violence. He would demand that his wife spell out all the details of the affair and possibly never forgive her.[34]

• A woman, on the other hand, would become more upset if her husband were infatuated with another woman. Women don't like it, but they are more accepting than men of their spouses' sexual infidelities. If a woman discovers that her partner had sexual intercourse with another woman, she is as likely to be concerned about the potential emotional involvement as the sexual activity. This is not to imply that women accept extramarital sex or involvement by their partners, but only that they are more likely to be forgiving than are men.[35]

How are these differences explained? Some say that genes or hormones are the cause. Some say, as Freud did, that "anatomy is destiny." These factors are relevant, to be sure, but even more important is that the two sexes are taught to react differently. Behavioral differences have much to do with the way society condones or disapproves of certain actions that are deemed "male behavior" and "female behavior." Boys are typically encouraged to act aggressively when threatened, while many girls tend to be encouraged to find a protector. Thus, an adult male is more likely to express jealousy feelings by aggression, rage, and possibly confrontation with the suspected rival. If he merely accepts his fate, gives over his "possession" to his rival, or expresses no feeling at the takeover of his territory, he is accorded little respect in society. But if a woman in the same situation behaved identically, she would have less social respect than if she were to seek help. If she flew into a rage, confronted her suspected rival, and engaged in a fistfight, she would probably be viewed as a low-class, undesirable harridan.[36]

The "double standard" continues to have influence, too. Both men and women still accept a man's sexual infidelity more readily than a woman's. In contemporary society, people have become more tolerant about a woman's sexual behavior but are still not as tolerant as they are of a man's. Consequently, men show less acceptance for their unfaithful women than women show for their unfaithful men.[37]

The differences in the way men and women show their respective jealousies are not as great as they once were. This is primarily the result of the recent and welcome social trend away from sex-role stereotyping. It is becoming more acceptable, indeed even mandatory, for women to behave more assertively. Society is becoming less tolerant of helpless women who passively resign themselves to whatever fate men have in store for them. More than ever in our society, men are expected to renounce their double standards and demands for exclusive control. Increasingly, men are expected to show warmth, empathy, and sensitivity to the needs of others. As this trend continues, it seems probable that few if any differences will remain in the way men and women express their jealousy feelings.[38]

Does jealousy change with age? Many people believe that jealousy occurs in people primarily during young adulthood. Even most psychiatrists who were polled said that spouses in their twenties were more likely to be jealous of one another, with less jealousy seen in each succeeding decade. This notion may be encouraging to those who suffer from jealousy problems. It implies that the problem will go away as one grows older and becomes more mature.[39]

Unfortunately, there are no such certainties. As we have seen, the problem is also quite common among young people, old people, and those in between. Most people know of older men or women who act quite jealously. They can be possessive about their spouses, the time and attention they receive from their children, their clergymen, their doctors, and their friends. Clearly, there is no guarantee that the problem will go away by itself. One case illustrates jealousy in an elderly person:

In the ward of a psychiatric hospital lived an eighty-seven-year-old man who, because of his senile dementia, required total care. He seemed to the staff members to be virtually oblivious to his surroundings. He needed to be fed, clothed, and bathed. He spent his days strapped into a wheelchair, babbling randomly and incoherently whether anyone was there to hear or not. He seemed unaware of his surroundings, other patients, or staff.

One orderly was in charge of his care, dressing and feeding him daily. The orderly would talk with the old man, or rather they would talk at each other simultaneously. The orderly was unable to tell if the old man was even aware of his caretaker's existence. One day, when the ward had more patients than usual, a new patient was assigned to the orderly's care and the orderly fed the new man first.

The old patient, who had been babbling in his wheelchair nearby, looked directly at the orderly. For the first time he seemed clear eyed and well aware of his surroundings. He suddenly became enraged. He launched into a torrent of foul language and vituperation, such that the ward had never before heard. He screamed at the orderly that he was being disloyal and, between cursing insults, accused him of liking the new patient best. He swore that from then on he wouldn't care if the orderly lived or died. Shortly thereafter he resumed his incoherent babblings and again seemed unaware of his surroundings.

Jealousy had not diminished in this man. He felt that his exclusive possession, his hold on the orderly's undivided time and attention, for that moment at least, was being threatened by the new patient.

One reason for believing or hoping that jealousy will diminish with age is that it is associated with sexuality. Although it rarely goes away completely, sexual drive diminishes as one gets older. It would seem, then, that jealousy would diminish commensurately. But this is true only when the jealousy is derived from sexual rivalry. When it is not, there is no special reason to expect it to lessen.[40]

It is true, however, that there is a relationship between the aging process and people's jealousy behavior. Several studies have shown that older people, as a group, have less concern about jealousy issues than younger people. The Kinsey reports, for example, said that older people are more accepting of extramarital sex. One researcher tested groups of people by describing jealousy-provoking situations and found that virtually everyone under thirty-one would become somewhat jealous, while only 60 percent of those over thirty-one would feel jealous in the same situation.[41]

These changes don't just happen automatically. As some people get older, their jealousy feelings actually do go away. For others they may remain as they always were or may even intensify. Others who have never before been particularly jealous may develop such feelings.[42]

Many older people act out their jealousies differently than when they were younger. A man who was once prone to jealous rages might later feel just as jealous but might lack the energy to lose his temper. Thus, he only appears to have mellowed. Some people still have the energy to act out jealousy feelings but have lost the catalyst that once set them off. If a woman was once very jealous of her now deceased husband, she hasn't really changed. Her changed situation is the only difference. Some older people seem more mellow only because they believe their partner no longer constitutes a threat. They know the partner now lacks the energy or interest to cause them problems.

It is not aging or reduced sexual interest but emotional maturity that reduces jealousy. Maturity, of course, is not necessarily a product of chronological age. It has more to do with the ability to postpone immediate rewards and gratification in order to acquire something more significant in the long run. Maturity often, though not always, comes from experience, from learning, and from acquiring new values. Older people, with their greater range of experiences, have the potential for more objective appraisals of themselves and others. This equips them with opportunities to be more tolerant of differences in individual behavior.

If an older person doesn't grow in emotional maturity or is so closed off from the environment that the range of experience does not increase, there is little reason to believe that jealousy feelings will diminish. There are not many ways to determine which people are going to get over such feelings as they grow older. The best clue, however, is a person's relative maturity compared to others of the same age and the relative tolerance for new ideas, experiences, and other people's value priorities. If a person is able to look at other viewpoints, is interested in what's going on in the world, and is eager to learn new things rather than simply maintain current views and stereotypes, there is a greater likelihood that jealousy will diminish as that person gets older.

Another misconception about jealousy is to equate it with envy. Many people use the terms "jealousy" and "envy" synonymously. However, while they are closely related and have the same origins, they are not the same. Envy is based on the strong desire to have something that belongs to another person. Jealousy is based on the desire to keep something from being taken away by another person. Nonetheless, jealousy grows out of envy and could not exist without it.[43]

Experiencing envy is commonplace. Spencer watches his neighbor Nigel drive up in a new car. He feels envious, not jealous. He would like such a car himself but can't afford it. He resents Nigel, who has just made him feel inferior—at least with respect to financial matters. Martina stays up all night studying for the final exam, while her brainy roommate Joyce spends the night partying. Even so, Joyce gets a higher grade on the exam, and Martina envies her roommate's abilities. A young child is given a cookie and is happy. Then the child notices that her mother has given a slightly larger cookie to her big sister. The child is less happy than before any cookies were handed out and angry at her sister for having more.

Envy is less mature, less developed, and less healthy than normal jealousy. Normal jealousy is a useful extension of envy because it can cause one to anticipate potential threats—it can be a warning to be alert. Envy, on the other hand, is more passive. It usually leads to the conclusion that one cannot have the desired object. The envious person is often hurt and unhappy because of some real or imagined deprivation. Envy might lead someone to pout and whine or to rationalize about other people's possessions. While normal jealousy says, "I've got to be on the lookout for anyone who might try to take this away from me," envy says, "Poor me. Everyone else has this except me."[44]

Envy is also motivated more by material possessions or personal talents, while jealousy is more concerned about what possessions and talents can bring—affection, attention, recognition from others, and being loved. Jealousy issues revolve around the symbolism of a thing, while envy is more concerned with the thing itself. For example, a jealous child is concerned about who gets the biggest cookie or most privileges because it seems to symbolize more parental love than the brother or sister gets. The child's interpretation is that "Mom likes me best because she gave me this cookie and lets me stay up later than you." With envy it is the cookie, not the parental love, that is important.[45]

Of course, a person can be envious and jealous simultaneously. Because both traits stem from immaturity, from a sense of fear and deprivation, as well as from unreconciled conflicts about sharing, it is common to find both in the same person. For example, a three-year-old child is happily playing with a set of blocks. Then he notices that his big brother is building a model airplane. He wants an airplane model too, even though he has no idea what it is for and was happy with his blocks. He both envies and is jealous of his brother. He envies the brother's model plane and feels deprived and inferior because he lacks one. However, he is also jealous. He fears that his parents will give more of the limited supply of love to his brother and commensurately less to him when they see what the brother has accomplished.

Another mistaken assumption about jealousy is that only very aggressive or passionate people or those who are very extraverted in the way they express themselves are prone to jealousy. This idea stems from the fact that more aggressive or more verbal people show their feelings openly, clearly, and sometimes dramatically. In other words, when extraverts are jealous they show it more visibly than do introverts. It may be harder to observe expressions of jealousy in quiet people, but it is quite visible when expressed by assertive ones.[46]

This mistaken assumption also comes from the way many people define "jealousy." If they equate it with "zealousness," as the ancient Greeks did, then by definition it is associated with assertive people. Those who do not equate the two terms do not hold this view.

Jealousy is no more likely to exist in aggressive, dominating people than in passive or shy people. It is just expressed differently. A person who is withdrawn, quiet, and inarticulate can certainly be just as threatened by the possibility of having possessions taken as anyone else. Many quiet people are more likely to be jealous because their passive natures make them feel they are easier prey for others. Introverted people may be more likely to suppress their fears, keep them hidden from others, and perhaps even from themselves. They may find outlets for these feelings that are indirect and seemingly unrelated to jealousy feelings.

For example, if an introverted person who is jealous comes to believe that someone else wants his girlfriend, he may not confront the potential rival or say anything to his girlfriend. Instead, he may displace or sublimate his feelings by devoting more of his energies and interests to his hobby. The hobby might be something like golf or bowling or wood carving or drawing. But whatever it is, it allows the person to express his feelings indirectly. In golf or bowling the introverted person may unconsciously be hitting his rival or girlfriend every time he strikes the ball or pins. In carving or drawing, he may be asserting his control over the situation and shaping it to conform to his own ideal.

Concealing jealousy feelings in such activities may or may not be healthy. Activities can be healthy for a passive person who is otherwise unable to express much outward anger or concern directly. Displacement may be a necessary and healthy way to get rid of unhealthy jealousy feelings. However, there are occasional risks. People who are not up front about their feelings, who displace them in indirect ways, can be unpredictable. This makes it hard for others to anticipate problems or eliminate behaviors that cause distress to the jealous person.

A final misunderstanding about jealousy is the assumption, made by many people, that it is invariably a negative, harmful, or unhealthy phenomenon. Such a belief is easily acquired by those who observe or experience some of the unpleasant consequences that seem to come from jealousy. They might ask, "How can there be any good in a trait that leads people to commit murder, spouse abuse, and countless other cruelties?"

Not all jealousy leads to such problems, and not all jealousy is pathological. Some is normal and can be useful and necessary to survival. Some other jealousy may not be an asset, but at least it is not debilitating.[47]

Every trait that humans possess, and every behavior that we continue to exhibit as a species, has a function, whether we recognize what it is or not. The function of jealousy, in its normal state, is to mobilize us for necessary action. It can cause increased adrenal activity and more rapid breathing. Our sympathetic nervous system responses are energized. These physiological changes increase the sugar content of the blood, which in turn tones up the striated muscles to prepare them for action. We become more alert, readier to compete, and more active in striving to fulfill our needs.[48]

Why is such mobilization necessary? Consider the young child who does not actively strive to gain some of the limited attention and affection her teacher has available. The nature of her plight would be similar to that of one baby robin in a nest of active siblings. All the babies thrash about actively to attract their mother's attention. They are seeking to be the one to consume the worm she has brought. If the baby robin does not actively struggle to get a share of the mother's attention, death will occur. Some say human infants had to have jealousy in order to generate the necessary motivation and activity to survive. Like the baby robin, some early humans would have been ignored in their caves, left to wither and die, while their more demanding siblings would have survived to become our ancestors.

Those who believe jealousy is a learned pattern of behavior, rather than an instinctive remnant of our survival mechanisms, must also regard it as having some utility. Learning theorists tell us that we learn to retain those behaviors that have worked for us and discard those that do not. Thus, any jealousy-induced behavior that has been retained has been reinforced. We learned that a certain action worked. We remember that, and eventually, when we encounter a similar situation, we remember to use it again. It is only there because it has proved to be useful.

It is when jealousy turns pathological that it no longer has useful or positive elements. Pathological jealousy is learned in the same way as is normal jealousy. It is acquired through experience, trial and error, and through imitating others. But eventually something goes askew, and the mechanism that teaches us to be somewhat actively possessive gets out of control. The person gets an inordinately positive experience from the jealousy flash. Perhaps the person was finally regarded more seriously by others. Possibly it proved to be a way of controlling others.

Jealousy can turn pathological in many ways. Sometimes what was learned at a younger age is no longer useful, but the person hasn't found a suitable replacement for the behavior. Temper tantrums worked at the age of three, so why not now, decades later? Rage causes one's spouse to act contrite, humble, or more supportive, so the rage reaction has been rewarded. Rage sometimes gains the person what is wanted—control, attention, and the illusion of love.

The pathologically jealous person cannot be happy and ultimately causes unhappiness for others, too. The best outcome one can hope for in dealing with these people is to identify the jealousy, understand the mechanisms that perpetuate it, and help them to manage and control it effectively.

2

Is It
Harmless
or
Destructive?

How can one recognize the difference between "normal" jealousy and the kind that is sick and destructive? The ability to do so can be crucial to those who are about to make serious commitments to others. If they choose people who turn out to have major jealousy problems, their chances for future happiness and emotional security are greatly diminished.

Distinguishing between normal and pathological jealousy may be of even greater importance to one who is already committed to a jealous person. To live with anyone who is pathologically jealous is to increase greatly the risk of being harmed physically, emotionally, economically, and socially. Not only are the partners of jealous people subjected to so much stress that they are vulnerable to serious emotional problems themselves, but they are also much more likely to be involved in separations and divorces. In addition, the wives of pathologically jealous men, in particular, run a high risk of being physically abused and even of being murdered.

In fact, many sociological and criminological studies show that there is a significant correlation between pathological jealousy and homicide. Recent FBI statistics show that around 25,000 murders are committed every year in the United States. Of those that are solved, just over one-third (34.5 percent) of all the victims were spouses, mistresses, lovers, or rivals of the offenders, with real or suspected sexual infidelity a major precipitating factor.[1]

Although most pathologically jealous people do not kill, many do inflict serious injury on those to whom they are closest. Some demographic and sociological studies show that violence occurs in one-fourth to one-half of all American homes. For some husbands the marriage license is considered a "hitting license."[2]

For the 1.8 million American women who are abused by their husbands every year and show up at shelters, clinics, hospitals, and doctors' offices where the causes of their difficulty can be studied, jealousy appears to be a primary factor. An evaluation of seventy recent surveys of wife abuse found that extreme jealousy was present in most of the husbands, ranging from 66 percent in some samples to over 95 percent in others. The problem may even be worse than these statistics indicate. Most victims don't report abuse to the authorities or go to shelters. Social researchers estimate that only one case of spouse abuse in 270 becomes known to the authorities. Even when the spouse abuse is very damaging and recurrent, according to these researchers, only about half of the cases are reported.[3]

While abuse, divorce, and murder are the most serious of the risks facing individuals who become involved with jealous people, they are not the only ones. Virtually all people in this position also experience being continually distrusted, being compelled to account for their time and thoughts, having to avoid certain friends, losing opportunities to get better jobs and educations, and facing a virtual end to any sense of freedom and autonomy.[4]

Given that these risks are inherent in becoming involved with a pathologically jealous person, there is ample incentive to determine in advance how serious the problem is or is likely to become. Unfortunately, the characteristics that reveal pathological jealousy are difficult to detect. Even experienced professional psychotherapists, psychiatric diagnosticians, and social researchers aren't in agreement on how to do it. And, unlike individuals who live with jealous people, the professionals don't have to make such assessments while facing constant belittlement, ridicule, denials, and physical assaults. The following cases testify to the difficulties involved in determining the seriousness of the jealousy problem:

They were newlyweds, but they already had so many conflicts that they were deeply immersed in marital therapy. The wife had a long list of grievances about her husband and was reciting them to the therapist. Chief among them was his jealousy, which she described as "unreasonable," "unjustified," and "sick."

"What makes you think his jealousy is so bad?" the therapist asked.

"Oh, he always questions me when I have lunch with a guy in the office—we go out every week or so; we're just friends. But when I get home it's like an interrogation. He asks if I like the guy. Then he gets all bent out of shape when I tell him I do. He's pretty old-fashioned, too. He doesn't like it when I get dressed up to go out with the girls. One time I told him I believed in taking separate vacations, and that really sent him into orbit."

"How does he show you he doesn't like it?"

"Well, he doesn't beat up on me or anything, but he gets pretty bad. He gives me that look. He gets an attitude. He looks mad, rolls his eyes, gets quiet. Mostly, though, he just pouts and acts like a martyr. I think he's trying to put me on a guilt trip, trying to make me feel like I'm doing something wrong. It would be easier if he just yelled or cussed or something."

"How do you feel about what she's saying?" the therapist asked, turning to her husband.

"Hell, no, I don't like it when she goes to lunch with some dude. And she wants to go out without me *all* the time. Who'd like that? Sure I get jealous. But I don't have to yell or throw stuff around. I get quiet because we've already tried talking, and it only leads to arguments. We just don't agree about some things. I don't think that makes me sick with jealousy like she says."

Was the husband pathologically jealous? Even though the wife thought so, it is likely that problems other than jealousy lay at the root of their difficulty. His jealousy was rather normal, the kind everyone occasionally experiences. He had the jealous twinges that come from recognizing a realistic threat, a risk that something important might be lost.

Eventually it was learned that the wife had other reasons for thinking her husband was abnormally jealous. She had not had extramarital sex but had started actively fantasizing about it. This made her feel guilty. The resulting discomfort had no place to go, so she attributed it to her husband's reaction. For her, his relatively calm manner was almost as painful as physical violence would have been. Understandably, she perceived his behavior as excessively cruel.

Another couple interpreted jealous reactions very differently. The man explained to the marital therapist that his wife was "a little possessive, probably a little more jealous than average, but nothing to worry about." He felt confident he could handle any problems of that nature. Then he described how he handled them. He said his wife expected a detailed accounting of his whereabouts whenever he was away from her. He knew she was terrified that he would have an affair with another woman and abandon her. So he coped with her anxiety by reassuring her regularly of his fidelity. He told her everything, even before she asked. He avoided women whenever possible. When they couldn't be avoided, he made sure other men were with him. He told his wife about each of his acquaintances and invited her to call them to verify any of his claims. Even so, on the rare occasions when his actions appeared even slightly suspicious, his wife would become enraged. Tears would be shed, blows struck, dishes smashed, and threats made. Yet his response to this remained supportive. He would comfort her, praise her for her love and interest in him, and swear his continued faithfulness.

This man, it was later learned, concealed many angry feelings. He had suppressed his anger and negative emotions for so long he had become afraid of losing his self-control. To let even some of it go might release his entire accumulation—the residue of years of unexpressed feeling. He feared an avalanche of unchecked, unpredictable, and unlimited rage. To keep it controlled, he would not permit himself to see anything that might result in his expressing negative feelings. So, to him, his wife was "pretty normal." In fact, she was suffering from a high degree of pathological jealousy, and he remained consciously oblivious to it.

These two cases illustrate how easy it is for one person to misinterpret another's jealousy problem. In the first instance someone was seeing pathological jealousy where it didn't exist. In the second, someone was not consciously seeing it where it did exist.

Misinterpreting the nature of jealousy is easy, because people who are jealous tend to conceal their problem. No seriously jealous person is going to admit being one, knowing that the disclosure would lead to rejection or negative responses. Most jealous people are ashamed of their condition and tend to deny its existence to themselves as well as others. In a classic psychiatric study of jealousy, a researcher called it "the most common human emotion but the most concealed and disguised. It is present when no one suspects its presence."[5]

Truly jealous people are inclined to conceal these tendencies from others as well as from themselves. This reflects the nature of their insecurities and self-doubt. Confident people are more inclined to disclose some of their own unflattering characteristics. Those without confidence, on the other hand, want to conceal such characteristics—as though they will be more acceptable and lovable to others if their faults are not revealed.[6]

Jealous people frequently conceal the problem by not saying anything about the intense fear and anger contained within. Because they have experienced others' lack of tolerance for such behavior, they learn, sometimes the hard way, to refrain from accusations, threats, and violence. Then they let the feelings out later, often in the privacy of their homes or with people who are less able to defend themselves.

As Lord Byron wrote in *Don Juan*,

> *Though he was jealous, he did not show it,*
> *For jealousy dislikes the world to know it.*

Such people also frequently hide their jealousy through the use of such defenses as denial and projection. In denial they insist, and actually believe, that they have no problem. No matter how much pain they cause themselves or others with their jealousy, they do not relate these outcomes to their jealous reactions. They have done nothing wrong, they insist, and believe that they were only protecting what is or should rightfully be theirs. When others tell them they have a jealousy problem, their typical response is, "You're wrong. No one else ever said that about me."

More often they hide their jealousy by projecting the problem onto others. "It's you who have the problem," they will say. "If you'd quit flirting with all those people, I'd be okay." Jealous people usually believe their violent or intense jealous reactions are justified by the unreasonable behaviors of those nearby rather than attribute them to any inherent problem.

Because jealous people conceal their condition as much as possible, those who become involved with them often find out about it after it is too late. The jealous person imposes a serious deception on others with harmful consequences to everyone involved.

Another reason it is so difficult to determine whether someone has a jealousy problem or not is that so many jealous people are otherwise quite attractive. They can be so productive and capable that their problem is less noticeable to others and is often disregarded or forgiven.

Sociologists have long noted the phenomenon that permits this to occur, calling it the "halo effect." When someone has one quality that is important or valued by others, those who value this quality will have a higher overall impression of that person and tend to overlook his or her less desirable attributes. For example, an athlete can be successful and much-admired even though he or she is addicted to drugs. An actor can be idolized for looks and style even though he or she is vain and insensitive. Recent studies reaffirm, for example, that people who are more attractive are rated higher in job performance than are less attractive people whose work is just as good.[7]

If a person who is famous or idolized has a serious jealousy problem, the resulting halo effect will often keep it from seeming so serious. However, if the same jealousy problem existed in a skid row alcoholic, it would be much more noticeable.

Highly successful people may also have more at stake in trying to conceal their problem and control their jealous tendencies. They may divert their attentions to other activities, or they may keep their jealousy from becoming overt through inner fantasies about committing destructive acts on themselves, their love objects, or on those who seem threatening.

One example of such reactions may be found in the life of Sigmund Freud, the progenitor of psychoanalysis. When he was a young man and engaged to Martha Bernays, he learned that she and her teacher, artist Fritz Wahle, seemed to enjoy a mutual affection. Freud came across and read some of the warm letters his fiancée had exchanged with Wahle and was consumed by jealousy. He cried, tore the letters to shreds, and threatened Martha and Fritz. He wrote Martha that this made him suffer so much that he wanted to sink into eternal sleep. By the next day his sadness had been replaced by rage, and he wrote to Martha, "When the memory of your letter to Fritz . . . comes back to me I lose all control of myself, and had I the power to destroy the whole world, ourselves included . . . I would do so without hesitation."[8]

Freud's jealousy was nearly as great as was his genius, and because of his awesome contributions he is not so well remembered for his jealousy. Most people who are severely jealous lack Freud's brilliance, so their problem is not so easily hidden. But other jealous people are very capable in many ways. They are included among the leaders in every field and have made unparalleled contributions to society. Their gifts predispose others to overlook their jealous traits, forgive them, or pretend they didn't see the signs.

Determining how serious a jealousy problem is is also complicated by the fact that jealousy may become pathological only in isolated instances. A person can remain normal for years and then unexpectedly—given a particular set of circumstances—become uncontrollable. After the single but severe jealousy reaction, the person may never again show such behaviors.

Another reason for the difficulty in determining whether or not a person has a jealousy problem is its cyclical nature. Because jealousy is not a static entity, a person with this problem will often behave inconsistently and thus unpredictably. The person may act unreasonably jealous for several weeks, then go for months acting maturely, and then return to the jealousy phase again. Even though the circumstances seem to remain the same, the person's jealousy comes and goes. It may be more pronounced during certain seasons of the year, times of the month, or hours of the day, regardless of external events or provocations. In many people these changes seem spontaneous; that is, they seem to occur not because of different conditions in the environment but because of something that goes on within the person. Another person trying to determine the extent of the problem can easily get confused trying to determine which personality is the representative one. The case example of Winston illustrates this pattern.[9]

On most days, Winston was a very pleasant person. He was a highly respected member of his community and a good provider for his family. He worked hard in his job as manager of a grocery store and always seemed to be courteous and efficient with customers. He had little interest in socializing outside of his home, preferring to spend his evenings with his wife and children. Only they had to deal with his serious problem.

Winston had always been very jealous, as his wife knew all too well. She had learned to be careful around him. She knew, for example, that she had to avoid developing friendships with other men. She learned that it was unwise to tease Winston or do anything that would cause him to feel ridiculed. And she found that it was better not to argue with him about anything. Winston could be very hostile when angered, and he didn't care who in the family was hurt when he lost his temper.

The most difficult part of the problem for Winston's wife was dealing with his inconsistency. She considered him a sort of Jekyll and Hyde personality and never knew which face would be revealed next. If he were always possessive and jealous, she felt she could handle it, but Winston was more complicated. Sometimes, if she wasn't home when he expected her there, he would subject her to angry tirades. On other occasions when she wasn't home to receive his call, he acted nonchalant about it. When she tried to get him to look at his jealousy problem, his defense was to point out all the times he did not act badly. Winston's wife was so confused that she couldn't be sure what his problem was or if he had one. Maybe the problem was all in the way she interpreted things.

Research has not yet been able to explain this phenomenon completely. Some studies suggest that the changing patterns of jealous expression are due to physiological, hormonal, and developmental changes in the body. One investigator reported that there is a correlation between biorhythms and conflict between people. Couples whose biorhythmic patterns fall out of sync are more prone to arguments, misunderstandings, and accusations.[10]

Other studies show that when social harmony and sense of emotional well-being exist in certain areas of a person's life, there is less likelihood of a jealousy reaction regardless of provocation or circumstances. In other words, when a person feels personally contented and happy and secure in relating to others, it would take more to provoke a jealous reaction than if the person were otherwise distressed. A jealous person who has a satisfying marriage is less likely to feel threatened than one who does not.[11]

Cyclical patterns in jealousy reactions are also explained by the mood swings that occur in depression. Jealousy is more likely to occur in depressed people than in those who feel relatively content. It seems more prevalent among mildly depressed people than among those who are deeply depressed. One who is severely depressed might feel so worthless and unloved that apathy is the only emotion left. However, a mildly depressed person is less apathetic and might still fight to hold onto possessions.

Nearly every depressed person has ups and downs. If jealousy accompanies depression in some people, it follows that there will be ups and downs in its expression. In the case example of Winston, it was eventually learned that his underlying problem was depression. His jealousy came and went as did his depression. His wife noted the connection and persuaded him to seek medical help. His doctor administered antidepressants, and Winston supplemented the treatment with psychotherapy. As his treatment for depression proved successful, his jealousy was no longer a problem for himself or his family.[12]

The severity of a person's jealousy is also hard to determine because it is related, to some extent at least, to the provocation. Thus, a jealousy problem may not become evident until provocation occurs. For example, a jealous person will not usually act possessively during the courtship phase of a relationship, but once a commitment has been made, a sense of ownership may develop. Then the behavior of the relevant other may provoke a jealousy reaction, even though it is the same behavior that occurred before the commitment.[13]

For example, a woman became very angry at her husband every Saturday as he left to play golf. She accused him of using golf as an excuse to see his girlfriends. She threatened to leave him unless he stayed home. She threw dishes and food around the house as her rage intensified. Nevertheless, he left. If the husband had never done anything to suggest that he was a philanderer and had been typically kind and supportive to his wife, it might be easy to conclude that she had a severe jealousy problem. However, such was not the case in this example. The husband actually had a long history of infidelity. He frequently returned from golf days with lipstick or perfume on his clothes and was often caught in lies about his whereabouts. He even brought a venereal disease home to his wife.

In this context, the wife's behavior is less likely to be seen as pathological jealousy. It was jealousy, to be sure, and it may not have been the healthiest or most effective response she could make. But it was qualitatively different from pathological jealousy.

Is it really jealousy if suspicions about a loved one are confirmed.? This question is similar to the old saw that says, "It's not paranoid thinking if they really *are* out to get you." Jealousy exists whether or not the fear is valid. For example, if a loved one really is interested in another and is overtly provocative, it is jealousy, just as if the emotion stemmed entirely from one's own fantasies. A jealousy reaction may be appropriate to the circumstances or not; it is still jealousy. Whether it is unhealthy or not depends on whether the reaction is destructive or productive. If the reaction is violence against the supposed loved one, with or without provocation, it is unhealthy. If the reaction is a rational attempt to dissuade the loved one from leaving, or if it is a systematic attempt to let go of the possession in the face of insurmountable efforts to the contrary, it is healthy.

In any case, determining how jealous a person is means considering the circumstances in which the reaction takes place and the type of reaction that results. If such information is unavailable, it is virtually impossible to make an accurate assessment of the degree of jealousy. It can't be done solely by looking at the person's reactions.

Psychiatrists and other mental health professionals haven't been very helpful in showing people how to distinguish between normal and pathological jealousy. Most psychiatrists think of pathological jealousy as a symptom of other mental illnesses rather than a disorder in its own right. Jealousy, even the pathological kind, is excluded from the emotional disturbances officially identified by the American Psychiatric Association. The association's current (third) edition of the *Diagnostic and Statistical Manual of Mental Disorders*, better known as *DSM-III*, attempts to describe all the mental diseases and their symptoms. Many conditions rarely found in humans are included, such as psychogenic fugue, functional encopresis, and Tourette's disorder. Better-known conditions are also listed, such as phobia, paranoia, and schizophrenia. When these disorders are given official recognition, they are listed along with the distinguishing criteria for making accurate diagnoses. The criteria are established by panels of experts who determine the exact symptoms that exist for each mental illness. But American psychiatry's *DSM-III* contains only one reference to jealousy. It is in the section on alcoholic problems, and it says only that too little information exists to document the existence of a condition called "alcoholic jealousy."[14]

Its virtual omission from the psychiatric classification system suggests that jealousy is not considered an entity on its own but that it is considered symptomatic of other disorders or that jealousy should be diagnosed under conditions other than its own name. Thus, anyone trying to assess the extent of the problem would have difficulty trying to determine if certain behaviors are caused by jealousy or by some other personality characteristic. In practical terms, anyone who wants to determine how serious his or her partner's jealousy problem is would not get much help from the experts.[15]

Even if we could get the experts to tell us who is jealous or not, we would still find it necessary to rely on our own judgment. This is challenging because we can't be totally objective. Objectivity requires some detachment and an opportunity to look at things without personal involvement. Even professional psychotherapists, who are uninvolved and presumably objective, find it difficult to assess jealousy properly. Moreover, they are able to confer with their colleagues, share ideas, and compare viewpoints. But people in the situation usually remain isolated. Little wonder they are vunerable to misinterpreting their companions' degree of jealousy.

Self-confidence is typically lost by virtue of being around someone who is very jealous. Regular subjection to accusations, ridicule, intense scrutiny, and distrust leads to self-doubt. Severely jealous people have a way of bringing down those with whom they share lives. They drain them of their feelings of adequacy and self-worth. They contribute to their guilt feelings and create an environment in which stress often leads to symptoms of anxiety and depression.[16]

Living with a jealous person is not usually a great confidence-builder. People in this position are often corrected, challenged, or ridiculed for their conclusions. Friends question their taste, relatives think they have taken leave of their senses, and professionals wonder if they are masochistic. Everyone asks, "What does my friend see in that person?" To cope, they develop excuses and blind spots for their companions. Then others wonder how they could be oblivious to such a blatant problem. Eventually these people can't help but doubt their ability to judge things accurately.[17]

How, then, can anyone be sure of making accurate assessments? What are the yardsticks for measuring a loved one's degree of jealousy? One tool that has been found to be useful is the Jealousy Rating Scale. Developed over a period of several years by extensive interviews with many people who had jealousy problems, this test consists of 100 questions to be answered about the potentially jealous person by someone who knows him or her very well. Each item characterizes a behavioral trait that is frequently found in people with jealousy problems. If one is found to have many of these traits, the person is considered to have the problem.[18]

The test is given mostly to people who are concerned about a companion's possible jealousy. They are asked to take it home and complete it within a week, thinking about each answer but writing their responses in ink. This reduces the chances of their changing their minds. Those who live with jealous people are so often filled with self-doubt that they are inclined to change their minds frequently. Most test designers have found that the first answer committed to paper is usually the most accurate one.

Though the test is designed to be completed by someone other than the possibly jealous person, it often works well as a self-assessment device, too, and is sometimes given to the person who is thought to be jealous as well as to the companion. Used in that way, the instructions are modified and the subjects are told to answer the questions about themselves. If they answer the questions about themselves and see the results, they can sometimes have a more objective estimate of their own problem. What follows is the questionnaire, with instructions and explanations for interpretation.

HOW JEALOUS IS YOUR COMPANION?

Is it serious? Is it nonexistent? Or is it just about average? To find out how your companion compares with others, fill out this questionnaire. Remember, each item applies to your companion, not yourself. If you think a statement accurately describes this person, write "true" in the space provided. If the statement does not accurately describe this person except in rare instances, write "false" in the space provided. If you are unsure whether the statement accurately describes this person, write a "?" in the space. Answer every item, using ink.

_____ 1. Often seeks compliments about appearance.

_____ 2. Has had a very jealous parent.

_____ 3. Is inclined to be moody.

_____ 4. Believes it is safer to trust no one.

_____ 5. Finds it difficult to express sympathy to someone in sorrow.

_____ 6. Often seems jumpy or edgy.

_____ 7. Is easily discouraged by criticism.

_____ 8. Is worried about getting old.

_____ 9. Frequently misinterprets what others say or do.

_____ 10. Has feelings of inferiority.

_____ 11. Often feels life is unfair.

_____ 12. Has had sexual problems.

_____ 13. Is not considered easygoing.

_____ 14. Had a parent involved in an extramarital affair.

_____ 15. Often acts violently angry.

_____ 16. Is easily embarrassed.

_____ 17. Often feels something dreadful is about to happen.

_____ 18. Sometimes tries to make loved ones jealous.

_____ 19. Is worried about what others might think.

_____ 20. Was once hospitalized for mental illness.

_____ 21. Frequently accuses loved ones of wrongdoing.

_____ 22. Is prejudiced against some racial groups.

_____ 23. Has had an extramarital affair.

_____ 24. Is not easily moved to feel sympathy for others.

_____ 25. Is often saddened by memories of childhood events.

_____ 26. Does not want to take chances.

_____ 27. Prefers being alone or with only one other person.

_____ 28. Is accident-prone.

_____ 29. Is slow to sense other people's feelings and moods.

_____ 30. Sometimes carries a grudge.

_____ 31. Seldom pays compliments to others.

_____ 32. Starts quarrels with loved ones more than once a week.

_____ 33. Seems restrained or inhibited in sexual relations.

_____ 34. Frequently feels misunderstood.

_____ 35. Doesn't like groups in which people joke around.

_____ 36. Doesn't tend to help people in trouble.

_____ 37. Complains about rather than accepts unfair situations.

_____ 38. Has fewer than three friends.

_____ 39. Fears being taken advantage of by others.

_____ 40. Sometimes thinks of committing suicide.

_____ 41. Has been previously rejected in a love relationship.

_____ 42. Has been diagnosed as paranoid by a doctor.

_____ 43. Tends to be argumentative.

_____ 44. Often wants reassurance about sexuality.

_____ 45. Insists on prompt obedience.

_____ 46. Had a relative (not a parent) involved in an extramarital affair.

_____ 47. Has been diagnosed as "schizophrenic" by a doctor.

_____ 48. Is not optimistic about the future.

_____ 49. Frequently daydreams.

_____ 50. Has secretly followed loved ones.

_____ 51. Is often accused of being illogical.

_____ 52. Sometimes likes to ridicule people.

_____ 53. Is not deeply concerned about the welfare of others.

_____ 54. Is not considered capable of deep feeling.

_____ 55. Is easily bothered by noise and confusion.

_____ 56. Doesn't like to talk about sex.

_____ 57. Sometimes talks about getting revenge.

_____ 58. Has a drinking problem.

_____ 59. Often feels rejected by others.

_____ 60. Has had someone secretly follow a loved one.

_____ 61. Has nightmares every few nights.

_____ 62. Frequently looks in the mirror.

_____ 63. Experiences the feeling of being watched or followed.

_____ 64. Believes most people are basically dishonest.

_____ 65. Doesn't like speaking before groups of people.

_____ 66. Often questions loved ones closely about telephone callers.

_____ 67. Has fantasized about getting revenge.

_____ 68. Often dreams about sexual matters.

_____ 69. Is considered very jealous by others.

_____ 70. Often tries to get sympathy or pity from loved ones.

_____ 71. Does not like to share things.

_____ 72. Believes people are out for whatever they can get.

_____ 73. Is lacking in self-confidence.

_____ 74. Has had relationships end because of jealousy.

_____ 75. Is attentive to movie or TV love scenes.

_____ 76. Frequently accuses loved ones of being unfaithful.

_____ 77. Often doubts loved ones' explanations of their whereabouts.

_____ 78. Believes most married people commit adultery.

_____ 79. Is interested in gossip about people's sexual activities.

_____ 80. Sometimes enjoys hurting people.

_____ 81. Easily becomes impatient with people.

_____ 82. Often seems preoccupied.

_____ 83. Has had periods of prolonged depression.

_____ 84. Self-conscious when meeting strangers.

_____ 85. Often suspects being the subject of other people's gossip.

_____ 86. Doesn't rely on others in making decisions.

_____ 87. Tends to be secretive.

_____ 88. Has destroyed household objects in anger.

_____ 89. Doesn't usually give encouragement to others.

_____ 90. Is prejudiced against certain religious groups.

_____ 91. Has often wanted to be dead.

_____ 92. Feels like a failure when hearing of others' success.

_____ 93. Fears being criticized by others.

_____ 94. Is bothered by thoughts about sex.

_____ 95. Fears being murdered or kidnapped.

_____ 96. Is uncomfortable discussing personal problems.

_____ 97. Is self-conscious with members of the opposite sex.

_____ 98. Is less generous than most people.

_____ 99. Has more worry and anxiety than most people.

_____100. Fears the possibility of being ridiculed by others.

SCORING

—— Number of responses marked   × 2 =   ———
    "true"

—— Number of responses marked   × 0 =   _0_
    "false"

—— Number of responses marked "?"   × 1 =   ———

(100)

——   TOTALS   ———

                                            (degree-of-
                                            jealousy score)

Scoring the test is easy. First, be sure you have answered all the questions. Then count the number of responses you have marked "true" and enter that number in the top left space. Then count the number of responses marked "false" and enter that number in the second left space. Finally, count the number of responses to which you have responded with "?", and enter that number in the third space on the left. If you have answered all the questions, the three numbers on the left should total 100.

Now put numbers in the spaces on the right. To get the first number, multiply the number of "true" answers by two. Answers marked "false" get no points, so put zero in the second right space. Answers marked "?" get one point each, so write your number of unknowns in the third space on the right. Then add the numbers in the column on the right. The total is the score.

The scale has a range of from 200 to no points. Each question item is often found in jealous people. But some jealousy is normal. Therefore it is normal for everyone to fall somewhere near the middle of this scale. There is no definite cutoff line between being normally jealous and very seriously jealous, but the scale suggests degrees toward or away from the problem.

It is important that those who take this test use it appropriately. The test-taker must recognize that the test and its results are just guidelines and only clues pointing to possible problems. The results are only aids in help-

---

JEALOUSY RATING SCALE

200–180	Serious disturbance indicated.
179–160	Pathological jealousy probable.
159–140	Pathological jealousy possible.
139–120	Borderline. Further assessment needed.
119–100	Borderline. High degree of normal jealousy.
99–80	Normal jealousy.
79–60	No jealousy problem to be concerned about.
59–40	Less jealousy than average.
39–20	Borderline. Possible problem.
below 19	Abnormally low. Great apathy indicated.

---

ing to make more objective evaluations. Keeping this in mind, the scores are clues to determining the degree of jealousy.

Scores that fall in the extremes in either direction indicate the greatest cause for concern. It is easy to conclude that a high score suggests serious pathology. However, it is less obvious but just as true that a low score indicates a potential problem. Those considered most healthy in this dimension are those who fall in the middle, with scores between 40 and 120. Here's how some other scores may be interpreted:

Scores over 180 are rare and almost always indicate that a serious problem exists and should not be ignored. If the answers are completed accurately, those who live near this person may be in a risky situation. Though people who receive such scores might be highly averse to receiving outside or professional help, it is strongly indicated. Until professional help is obtained, anyone living with such a person might do well to minimize further contacts except in the presence of others.

Scores between 160 and 179 also suggest a serious problem, and the same precautions apply as in the higher scores. However, there may be less risk, and the subject may be somewhat more flexible. When jealousy problems occur at this degree it will be very difficult and unlikely for the person to overcome the problem without professional help. Thus, if such help is refused, the loved ones may seriously have to contemplate separation, at least temporarily. A reunion can occur when symptoms abate or there is consent to professional help.

In the 140–159 range, there may be cause for concern, but the person is probably more amenable to getting help from professionals or at least from loved ones. And, with help, the prognosis for improvement is much better. Those who are close to the person can be effective in helping, so they are especially advised to learn everything they can about the problem, read everything available, and be rational in dealing with the person. They may also find that they can start therapy for themselves without so much resistance. The jealous partner might eventually volunteer to come along, even without much prodding.

Those rated between 120 and 139 are in a gray area. Certainly jealousy is an important ingredient in their lives, but they may be able to control it without much unpleasantness. Some people at this level may be experiencing the beginnings of pathology. For them the problem is not yet urgent but could become so. If they have understanding and perceptive loved ones, they can learn to control or overcome the problem even without professional help. Their partners can be effective toward this end by being understanding, supportive and communicative. They can be effective if they apply the techniques described in this and other writings about jealousy.

Scores below 40 can suggest a different set of concerns. By no means are people who score low on this test necessarily to be considered free of emotional problems. Showing so few overt signs of jealousy in our culture could imply that some feelings are being suppressed or concealed from others. Possibly the subjects who receive this score have found other outlets for the expression of some feelings. Some people who have very few of the emotional traits of a jealous person may be seriously disturbed. For example, in some forms of schizophrenia, such as the catatonic kind, there is a virtual absence of any demonstrated strong feeling. Of course, this is not to imply that a low score on this test indicates such serious mental illnesses. There are many other tests and procedures to determine if this is so. But many people are so detached emotionally, so jaded, indifferent, or insensitive to others that they would score low here.[19]

This test has been given to more than 300 people. Some were clients in marital therapy, while others were college students and helping professionals. Many clients who have expressed concern about their jealous partners have found it helpful. They say it makes them look at many different aspects of the partner that they might not otherwise have considered. It helps them avoid giving too much attention to certain aspects of their partners' behavior while excluding other equally important parts. It is not the definitive assessment, but it provides a more objective basis of comparing individuals' situations and determining the degrees of risk involved.

The test has some acknowledged limitations. Like all instruments that purport to categorize people according to some standard, it has less relevance to people who might have different standards. As we have already seen, people are taught by their cultures how to behave in possibly threatening situations. Each cultural group has its own views about what is threatening and how one is supposed to react. Thus, what is considered normal or pathological by one group may not be so considered by another. A score of 150 might suggest serious problems about jealousy for a middle-class white but something entirely different for a less affluent Hispanic. A score of 30 may be abnormally low for a middle-class white American, but if the test had been given to a nineteenth-century Eskimo a score of 30 might indicate a seriously high degree of jealousy. Thus, while members of any cultural or minority group can take this test, the resulting scores might not be interpreted the same as indicated in the above scale.[20]

In using the test one should note that a person's scores can change from one time to the next. Sometimes people take the test when they are depressed or have just been treated badly by a jealous partner. The score on such occasions could well be different than if the test were taken during happier times. Or sometimes those who are being assessed were unusually charitable or more suspicious than ever at the time the test was given to their companions. Variations in resulting scores can be minimized when the test-taker is instructed to answer the questions with the long view in mind. It should not be based on the behaviors or feelings of just the past few days or weeks. Some people find it helpful to take the test several times to get a better perspective and to measure any possible changes.

The Jealousy Rating Scale is only a guide. Its purpose is to objectify what one already senses. It is to alert people to factors they might not otherwise have considered. It is to list, in a simplified way, the different traits that are often found in jealous people. The test gives people some "balance" by distributing components of the problem. This means that assessments will be based on many factors rather than just a few that are given excessive weight. The test can provide some rough ideas about the relative seriousness of the problem.

Each of the questions used in the test is related to a characteristic that is frequently found in jealous people. Thus, another use for the test is to look at each item as an element to describe characteristics of a person with this problem.

Once a person has a more objectively based opinion about the degree of jealousy that exists in the loved one, it is desirable to consider several questions: How does the problem begin? What keeps it going? What is the role of relevant others in perpetuating it? What can be done about the problem? How can the jealous person be helped? What self-defense strategies can be used to deal with the jealous person? What is the best way to protect the children of jealous relationships? How can one get out of such a relationship if all attempts to help or improve the situation have failed?

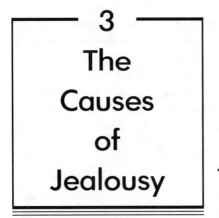

3
The Causes of Jealousy

Jealous people are inclined to attribute their condition to those closest to them. "The only reason I'm jealous," they say to their loved ones, "is because of the way you act! If you'd stop flirting with everyone, I'd be okay!" The jealous people making these—and similar—accusations believe them. Unfortunately, so do many of the people who are being accused.

Their response is understandable. Most people who are subjected to repeated charges of this type will begin to wonder if they are indeed the cause. They see enough clues to suggest that they are at least partly responsible. They note that their partners' jealousy reactions always seem to follow something they themselves have done. Sometimes, when they try to act differently, their jealous partners act less suspicious, at least for a while. This makes it natural for them to wonder: "If I can sometimes set it off, and if I can sometimes keep it from happening, how can I not be the cause?"

Actually, a spouse or loved one may have *something* to do with setting off the flash of anger, *sometimes*. The jealous person's relevant other *may* have some influence on the severity and frequency of the expressions of jealousy. Some may want to make their partners jealous in the mistaken belief that this will prove or demonstrate love or devotion. Some partners may have self-destructive tendencies and behave in ways that encourage angry behavior in their partners. But to infer from these possibilities that the partner is the *cause* of the other's jealousy is misdirected and overly simplistic. It would be like saying a match lighted in a room full of gas fumes is the cause of the explosion.

The gas fumes in the room, not the match, are the problem. Matches serve a valuable function and are lit all the time with no harm. The gas-filled room could have exploded even without that particular match being lit. Another match could have been lit. Sparks or intense heat or a fire in an adjoining room could also set off the explosion. The problem is the enclosed gas, and the solution is to dissipate the gas and stop the source of the fumes.

The same kind of cause and solution exist with the pathologically jealous person. Eventually and inevitably this person will see or interpret something in another person's behavior and feel threatened by it. No matter how the other person behaves, it is just a matter of time before the jealousy flash occurs. The "cause" lies within the jealous person, not within the jealous person's companion.[1]

It is necessary to look into the mind and body of the jealous person, rather than of the partner, to locate the source of jealousy. Indeed, it is necessary to go deeper and farther back in the jealous person's development than one might imagine. When jealousy first becomes pathological, it is not easily distinguishable from the common expressions of jealousy that exist in everyone. In order to determine when someone's jealousy crosses the line from normal to pathological, one must review its full progression in the individual.[2]

The origin of pathological jealousy is somewhat analogous to that of cancer. Cancer begins with a single cell, one of such inconspicuous dimensions as to be imperceptible. By itself it is of no importance to its host; some scientists even hypothesize that everyone carries some cancer cells without being bothered by them. However, when certain other conditions are also present, the cancer cell multiplies, and the mass grows and begins to crowd out the healthy cells around it until it can become life threatening. The growth has passed some point between a normal living phenomenon and a life-threatening problem. To effectively understand, prevent, and treat cancer requires an understanding of the conditions that permit it to become a problem.

In a similar fashion, the seeds of pathological jealousy exist in everyone. Germination and growth depend on certain conditions that may or may not permit the development of pathological jealousy. It is not yet certain why the jealousy seed exists, however. Various investigators have offered hypotheses and thoughtful speculation but no proof. Many biologists believe, as Charles Darwin did, that humans are genetically programmed for jealousy. He wrote in *The Descent of Man* that jealousy was normal in humans as well as animals and was based on the hunger response. The healthy infant is immediately aware of the need for nourishment and is threatened whenever the source of food is absent. In mammals, this source is the mother's breast, but the mother cannot always be available. She needs some cues to tell her when the infant is in need of food. These cues come from the infant's hungry behavior—expressions of discomfort, anxiety, and fear and demands for attention. The infant's hungry behavior seems to have the same basis as the adult's jealous behavior.[3]

Psychoanalyst Melanie Klein reached similar conclusions. Jealousy is a later manifestation of envy, she wrote, and envy occurs almost at birth. The newborn (neonate) soon comes to recognize that the mother's breast is the all-powerful source of food and thus has life-or-death control. The infant is totally helpless and dependent and resents the fact that there is a superior being that has such power. The infant envies the mother's possession of the breast and wants it always to be available. Since it is not, the infant becomes angry and sometimes expresses that emotion by biting the breast.[4]

These infantile expressions of envy and jealousy change as the child develops and becomes more aware of the environment. Some children feel less vulnerable and more secure as they grow, and thus they do not retain or develop significant problems with envy and jealousy. Others continue to feel vulnerable and insecure as they grow, and jealousy becomes serious.[5]

The development of serious jealousy problems in early childhood can be illustrated by comparing the childhoods of two fairly typical people. Steve and Alicia had been married for five years before they sought professional marital therapy. Their marriage was jeopardized primarily by jealousy problems. Steve would rarely let a day go by without accusing Alicia of inappropriate behaviors. He accused her of flirting every time he saw her talking to a man. He berated her when she was particularly attentive to a male newscaster on television. He would even start fights about her clothing and makeup, saying she was trying to attract men. Alicia, who loved her husband, was losing patience with him. She wanted the marriage to survive but knew it could not if his jealousy problem persisted.

What had gone on in Steve's life that contributed to his jealousy? What was different about Alicia's prior experiences that kept her from becoming just as jealous? While not all jealousy problems, or their absence, have identical origins, Steve's and Alicia's backgrounds are fairly representative.

Alicia had a relatively secure childhood. Her parents were apparently warm, loving, and reasonably self-confident. She had an older brother and a younger sister. Everyone in the home learned to share and to give one another needed attention. When Alicia accepted the need for sharing, she found that she got a sufficient amount of attention for her own needs. When she fussed or acted selfishly and demanded exclusive attention, she was more likely to receive a response she didn't like. When she let her little sister play with her toys (although unwillingly at first), she was praised and encouraged for her generosity. Though she actually had no choice but to share, as she grew she came to learn that doing so was advantageous in the long run. It meant that not only did she have her own possessions, but she also had greater access to enjoyable things that belonged to others. As she entered adolescence, she developed close friendships. Her friends enjoyed and rewarded her, in part because she was a giving person. She began dating, learned to have nonpossessive relationships, and was able to tolerate the ending of relationships with several of her dates. Of course, not everything was perfect in her life or she would not have had to endure the problems she did encounter. But she wasn't unreasonably jealous.

Steve, on the other hand, had a rather different childhood. He was an only child, and his parents were not close to one another. Both of them had apparently competed for the attention of their infant son, and both had lavished attention on him. When the infant Steve cried, there was a race to be the first one to take care of him. To little Steve it must have seemed as if there were no limits on the sources of comfort and attention and that there was no need to do anything particularly complicated in order to get more than enough. There were no rivals—no one to compete for the limited resources. When he was in the company of other youngsters, his mother—who hated to see him unhappy—would remove him from any squabbles or conflicts and compensate him by giving him a toy or a snack. His world was devoted to pleasing himself, with scant recognition of the needs of others. He learned none of the pleasures of giving.

As Steve grew older and was away from his parents, he was confronted by the fact that others had different priorities. They didn't always like giving to him without reciprocation. He frequently had conflicts with other youngsters; he was a school tattletale, often trying to ingratiate himself with teachers and other adults. When he began dating, his relationships were unsuccessful. He expected girls to meet his needs, and it really did not occur to him that they might have needs as well. Girls who were originally attracted to him were soon repelled by his narcissistic, self-centered orientation. As a young adult he sought a wife who would be his possession, whose purpose would be to make him happy. Thus, in marriage too, he was ill equipped to tolerate the meeting of needs other than his own.

Steve's development illustrates only one of the many conditions that can permit pathological jealousy to grow. Not learning the value of sharing at an early age can be very relevant for some people. However, parents would be ill advised to conclude that they must withhold attention from their young children to prevent something like this. Far more jealousy problems spring from the absence of sincere and consistent attentiveness than from its overindulgence.

The theories that Darwin, Klein, and others offered about the inherent nature of envy and jealousy are still debatable. But there is now widespread consensus among social and behavioral scientists that a considerable part of jealousy reactions is learned. This learning process begins at birth and, to some extent, even before birth. Learning continues throughout life, and at each developmental stage a person has many opportunities to learn to become pathologically jealous. The normal neonatal brain is fully developed at birth, and the baby lacks only experience and information to provide a frame of reference. Though the infant hasn't yet acquired enough information to make intelligent decisions about what behavior is or is not effective, this is soon remedied.

The neonate immediately becomes aware of changes, of different sensations—of discomfort and comfort or danger and security. Soon thereafter the infant shows signs of attempting to influence these conditions by various behaviors. At first the behaviors consist of random, impulsive, free-floating, trial-and-error responses. Then there seems to be an awareness that some movements are more effective than others in influencing conditions. If, for example, the sensation is the feeling of cold or hunger, the infant learns that squirming or crying often results in desired improvements. Getting fed or held or wrapped in a blanket after such behaviors tells the infant to behave that way again.

Infants then begin to learn that certain behaviors improve their chances of getting other privileges. They also become aware that their caregivers won't always be available on demand. This can be very threatening because, after all, survival itself is at stake. The threat is reduced when the caregivers find the right balance between immediate attention and teaching the infants that waiting is sometimes necessary and will not result in death.

Human infants are activated by the needs for intimacy, affection, and a sense of safety, as well as for food. Before it was generally understood that such needs existed, many institutionalized children who were not held, fondled, and comforted had inexplicably high death rates even though they received adequate nutrition. This serious infant disorder is known as maras-mus, which derives from the Greek for "wasting away," and it can occur when babies are not touched or held. In other words, the presence or absence of physical intimacy can be a life-or-death matter for some infants.[6]

Given that infants have this need, it is understandable that it is pursued as actively as food. However, the parent, the primary source of intimacy, is not always available. So the healthy infant must learn to share the care-giver's time with others, eventually learning to overcome its innate fear that sharing may have life-or-death consequences.[7]

Babies who later become pathologically jealous haven't learned this satis-factorily and dread the idea of being deprived of the needed amounts of food or attention from their caregivers. At some point in everyone's early life comes the awareness that only a limited amount of attention is available and that much of it is going elsewhere. Some babies react to this threat by attention-getting behaviors. They learn, possibly inaccurately, that atten-tion comes only as a result of their actions and that their very survival depends on their own efforts. They fear they may be inadequate or unable to live up to such demands. They may become excessively possessive and have tearful outbursts whenever left alone; they may feel overwhelmed, simply withdraw, or develop serious illnesses.

This scenario is not intended to suggest that all jealousy problems should necessarily be attributed to improper parenting. Parents can't completely control whether their children will become very jealous or not. Too many other factors, over which parents have no control, contribute to the devel-opment of jealousy.[8]

At best, parents can only reduce the odds. They can do so by giving enough time and attention to their children, particularly during the first weeks after birth. It helps to be fairly prompt in meeting a child's needs for physical and emotional nourishment. Yet parents must also acquaint their babies lovingly with the reality of having to share the parents' time. When parents are consistent in their behaviors toward their children, and especially when they show that they are happy to be with their children—even when such demonstrations haven't been demanded—the odds are fur-ther improved.[9]

Once babies have advanced beyond their earliest months, they are still vulnerable to developing pathological jealousy. Through a variety of cir-cumstances, they can acquire such emotional problems as feelings of inadequacy, insecurity, depression, or even paranoia. Or they may be deprived of healthy role models and thus not learn to behave in maturely effective ways. Each of these conditions has influenced pathologically jealous adults to some degree.

Everyone has occasional self-doubt. Most people question their worth or effectiveness in certain circumstances. But those with serious feelings of inferiority or inadequacy carry these doubts to the extreme. Their feelings are intense and omnipresent. They may deal with them through a variety of reactions, including overcompensation or concealment by striving to achieve power and dominance. They may use avoidance—keeping away from any challenges that might reveal potential inabilities—or they may become highly possessive, so that in their perceived inadequacy they have to work hard to retain the possessions that might otherwise be taken by their many "superiors." Or they may become pathologically jealous.

Psychoanalyst Erik Erikson concluded that a major stage in human development was the individual's effort to overcome feelings of inferiority and replace them with a sense of industry and self-competence. When children reach early school age, Erikson said, they are exposed to the larger world while still incapable of much independent activity. In many ways children fear being inadequate. If this fear is not balanced by a growing awareness of their abilities, children could carry it throughout their lives. They need encouragement in knowing that, through their own efforts, they can have some impact on their surroundings. When children have opportunities to explore, to try, and to test themselves, they can overcome this potential sense of inferiority and achieve the deeply rooted sense of industry that will remain with them through the rest of their lives.[10]

Not all people who feel inadequate develop serious jealousy problems; feelings of inadequacy can lead to many other problems instead. However, most people who have problems with jealousy also have feelings of inadequacy. This is why anyone who wants to help a jealous person does well to start by helping them feel better about themselves and striving to enhance their sense of self-worth.

Closely related to feelings of inadequacy, or perhaps other manifestations of them, are feelings of insecurity. Feelings of insecurity are a person's sense of unprotectedness and helplessness in coping with the unexpected, with the uncertainties of life. Like feelings of inadequacy, they, too, emerge in early childhood. They derive largely from a lack of consistency or stability in the child's environment. Children who become secure have been able to count on their environments to remain relatively constant. Insecurity, however, arises when the people and situations in a child's life are rather unpredictable and the rules and methods for daily life are unclear. With this unstable foundation, the child lacks inner resources to encounter unusual events or unexpected occurrences.[11]

Jealous behaviors can also originate in a youngster's identification in early childhood with an older person who is very jealous. It is probable that a person with jealousy problems had parents or parent surrogates with similar tendencies. This is similar to findings about the parents of spouse abusers. Virtually every study confirms that abusers tended to be abused when they were children or frequently witnessed such activities between their own parents.

People learn their behaviors largely by seeing what their elders do and imitating it. When they are very young, they usually choose parents to imitate. As they grow older, they emulate the behaviors of others—often an older sibling, then a teacher, then a teenage idol, and so on. They may want to behave the way they perceive their role models behaving. No matter how unhealthy or destructive that behavior seems, it becomes the standard against which they measure themselves.

If the role model's behavior contains pathologically jealous traits, the younger person will imitate them, too. If a father said, during his child's first few years of life, that he was going to beat up anyone who even looked at the child's mother, the child would find that appropriate and acceptable. By the time an individual has developed alternative references and potential role models, the traits he or she emulated during the most formative years are likely to be deeply embedded in the personality.[12]

As children who are insecure get older, they tend to look for stability outside themselves. They have learned that they can't depend entirely on their own abilities to maintain stability but must look to others. If the others are stable and consistent, there is likely to be less difficulty with pathological jealousy. Conversely, if the others are unstable and cannot be relied on, the probability of pathological jealousy increases.

Many children nowadays have to move from one home or neighborhood or school or even from one parent to another. Even worse, they may have to contend with homes in which the rules keep changing, so that they cannot count on past experiences to predict which behavior will lead to agreeable results. If what a child is permitted to do today depends not on what was permitted yesterday but on whether the parent is in a good mood, has had a hard day at work, has not had too much to drink, or has just read the latest newspaper article on child training, then the child is unlikely to grow up feeling very secure.

Without consistency in their environments, children cannot easily develop confidence. They can't learn to make sound decisions because the outcomes of their choices depend on factors over which they have no control. They can't learn how to cope with the environment if it keeps changing regardless of what they do. They feel forced to seek the approval of others for any sense of security or confidence that is available.

Many children in these circumstances learn that the only way to gain the approval of others is to rely on material possessions or superficial characteristics, such as having the best toys, getting the highest grades, or looking more attractive than others. If this same motivation remains into adulthood, security will probably be sought in the acquisition of wealth, good looks, social position and contacts, and a desirable spouse. Yet, with little emotional stability and consistency in early life, the individual will remain insecure no matter how many material possessions are subsequently acquired.

This is an important reason why affluent people are as likely to be insecure as very poor people. It is hopeless to depend on possessions to overcome inner insecurity. Any possession can be lost at any time, leaving one at perpetual risk and inevitably far more insecure than those who rely only on themselves. Thus, security and insecurity have nothing to do with what a person has. They have everything to do with what a person is.

Many children start to get jealous as they become more aware of their peers. They compare themselves and their possessions and abilities with those of other youngsters. When they think they compare unfavorably, they are threatened. They fear that the other, more capable children will receive all the available respect and love, thus depriving them of the amounts that they need. They feel so threatened by this prospect that they may try to hurt their rivals or cause them to seem less desirable to others. This may take the form of bullying, ridiculing, or attempting to get other children into trouble with parents or teachers. Jealous children don't actually receive more love or respect when their rivals are harmed, but they believe that their chances for receiving it in the future are improved. Such was the case with Billy, a boy who was severely disturbed by pathological jealousy.

Billy had lived in foster homes nearly half his eleven years. His father had abandoned the family when Billy was an infant, and his mother had been in and out of mental hospitals with paranoid schizophrenia. Social service agencies tried to make permanent adoption arrangements for Billy but were rebuffed when his mother would not agree to lose him forever. Whenever she was released from the hospital, she would take legal action to regain custody of her son. However, she had no financial resources and few social skills and was incapable of providing a stable home for herself or her son. She mismanaged her welfare payments and Supplemental Security Income (SSI) so badly that they frequently had no food and were often evicted from their rented rooms. She encouraged Billy to shoplift, and both of them basically lived on what he could steal. On one occasion, the police found them living in an abandoned car near a city park.

Billy's life in foster homes was not much more successful, though he spent time in twelve of them, never staying in one for longer than six months. Some of the problem was that his mother kept returning and causing his removal from the homes. But most of the problem stemmed from Billy's behavior. He was filled with anger and insecurity, feelings that intensified in the presence of other youngsters. He was severely handicapped by uncontrollable envy and jealousy feelings involving the other children and the foster parents. Most of his foster homes included other children, often the natural offspring of the foster parents. Fighting with these children, stealing and breaking their toys, and disrupting the household were his major pastimes. The foster parents were often understanding and sympathetic about Billy's problem and tried to show him love and attention. But they had to show these feelings to their other children, too, and when they did, the trouble would begin.

As soon as Billy sensed that he was loved and respected in these homes, he began to fear that he would lose these feelings. Inasmuch as he had lost them so many times before, it was an understandable fear. He coped with these anxieties in a destructive way, directing his destructive impulses toward the other children. They were the ones who were loved, he concluded, and they had taken that love from him. The solution would be to get them out of the picture.

Among Billy's interests were matches and fires. He was often apprehended by foster parents lighting matches and burning paper. On several occasions he burned the plastic dolls and toys belonging to other children in the household. Twice his activities led to serious fires in which fire fighters had to be called.

Starting fires, abusing other children, and being removed by his mother kept Billy from achieving stability. His inevitable insecurity contributed to his pathological jealousy, which in turn prevented him from achieving any semblance of order in his life.

Fortunately for Billy and his mother, they were able to be reunited in a program that provided treatment and halfway-house care for families in similar circumstances. Both have lived in this setting for several years now, and Billy has been able to control his disruptive behavior. He no longer has to share his mother or to experience losing needed love and respect. Nevertheless, Billy is likely to have jealousy problems throughout his life. The scars of his insecure childhood are too great to expect anything else.

Adolescence is the next life stage in which jealousy problems may originate. The major developmental task of adolescence is to achieve a sense of autonomy so that independent living is eventually possible. The parents' major challenge during this time is to help the youngster achieve it gradually. This is done by giving the adolescent the right balance of supervision and self-reliance. Too much or too little supervision can contribute to the youngster's developing feelings of inadequacy and insecurity. And too much can also result in an inability to make independent decisions and sound judgments. In either case, there is greater likelihood that jealousy problems can occur.[13]

Immaturity also plays an important part in the adolescent's development of jealousy. Emotional immaturity relates to the inability to postpone immediate gratification for more significant rewards later. No one can always get what is wanted immediately, but it takes experience to learn how to deal with this. Younger people, thus, tend to have lower tolerance for frustration and delay. Mature people on the other hand, are able to delay gratification. They have learned to share and find rewards in the process. So maturity is not often seen with pathological jealousy, but immaturity often is.[14]

Sexual jealousy first becomes apparent during adolescence. Teenagers begin to measure their sense of worth by their apparent attractiveness to members of the opposite sex. They are more concerned with the approval of their peers at this age than at any other time in their lives. Those who enter puberty with relatively high degrees of insecurity and doubts about their worth find it more difficult to compete fairly. Thus, when they develop relationships with members of the opposite sex, they rapidly become more possessive and distrustful of potential rivals.[15]

Insecure adolescents may be even more preoccupied than jealous children with material possessions and superficial characteristics. However, because they are now struggling to achieve autonomy, they are confronted with a curious dilemma. On the one hand, they feel the need for possessions to keep them protected against their feelings of insecurity. On the other, they can feel approval only when others see and appreciate these things. Therefore, the insecure adolescent needs others but fears them at the same time. If they were not insecure they wouldn't feel so compelled to hold onto valued objects or wouldn't be so threatened when others covet them. This was the dilemma that confronted Denise, a sixteen-year-old girl who felt threatened by her attractive younger sister.

Nearly everyone believed that Denise would achieve great success in life. Her family, her teachers, her boyfriend, and her classmates expected that she would become a great scientist or statesman. But Denise herself was secretly not so sure. She concealed massive insecurity, self-doubts, and low self-esteem. She worked hard to get those perfect grades because they caused others to give her the respect that she couldn't give herself.

Her sister, Sandra, didn't seem to have conflicts like this. Though she was not a very good student, she was beautiful and charming and exuded self-confidence. Everyone, especially boys, liked Sandra and wanted to be around her. She dressed provocatively, strutted sensuously, and flirted shamelessly with all of them. Eventually, this included Denise's boyfriend.

Denise tried to appear casual about it at first. But she couldn't help noticing how her boyfriend wanted to spend increasing amounts of time near Sandra. Denise tried to keep them apart. She discouraged her boyfriend from calling or coming to her home, where he might encounter Sandra. She warned Sandra to leave him alone. She obsessively thought about the possibility of the two of them together. She felt desperate and knew she would do anything to keep her boyfriend.

A few months later, Denise still had her boyfriend, but she had lost everything else that was important to her. No one believed any longer that she would become a great scientist or statesman. They weren't even sure she would return to high school. She had dropped out because of her pregnancy. Sex was the only way she felt she could keep her boyfriend and divert his attentions away from her sister. The plan worked, somewhat, but only temporarily.

Years later, Denise was living on Aid to Families with Dependent Children (AFDC) in a public housing project with her three children. She had never returned to school. She had married her boyfriend, but he had eventually abandoned her and the children. Her sister Sandra had completed college, was happily married, and no longer flirted as she once had. Denise still had dreams and ambitions, but now they were for her children. Her own chance had been wasted when adolescent jealousy changed the course of her life.

A person's likelihood of developing adult jealousy problems has generally been determined by adolescence. However, not all pathologically jealous people reveal their condition until they are adults. With many adults it shows up for the first time as a form of mental disorder such as depression, paranoia, or schizophrenia.

Depression is now the most common emotional disorder in our culture and is a major factor in the development of many jealousy problems. Mental health professionals believe that depression arises from physiological or chemical imbalances, from internalized anger, or from the sense of having lost something of value. More often than not a person's depression comes from various combinations of these elements rather than just one.[16]

The depressed person can have some physiological, systemic, or hormonal imbalance that causes the symptoms of sadness. This type of depression can trigger jealousy if the victim feels so despondent that his or her self-esteem is diminished. The preferred treatment is medication, such as antidepressants or lithium, sometimes supplemented by psychotherapy.

Depression that stems from anger turned inward is also a significant factor in some jealousies. Anger is a normal, necessary, and universal emotion, but when social conditions prevent it from being expressed directly there may be problems. With no acceptable outlet it may become internalized and result in another form of depression. Often, jealous people try to control their tempers and anxiety by concealing their anger. Depression is a result.

Internalized anger is sometimes quite visible in very jealous people. When they have temper flashes or make accusations, they are letting out some of this anger. When they finally control themselves, they are deprived of this outlet. The anger hasn't dissipated and has nowhere else to go. As a result these jealous people often become very sad and remorseful. They also become sad because of the loss of face their behavior has cost them. They typically believe, as we have seen, that love and respect come from being acceptable to others. Because the outburst has made them look bad, they sense a loss of the respect that is so vital to them. For those with this kind of depression, the usual recommendation is catharsis or opening up about feelings in order to find an acceptable outlet that will permit symptom reduction.

The other source of depression is a sense of loss of something valued. The loss may be real or imagined, and it may already have occurred or it may be anticipated. This form of depression may, in fact, be what many jealous people are struggling to avoid. They may fear losing their loved objects to others who seem more deserving. People with this source of depression are sometimes relieved when they find substitutes for the lost object. They may also find relief by reassessing the value of that possession and realizing that they can do well without it.

Jealousy is often thought to be a form of paranoia. Many people who are jealous are inordinately suspicious. Paranoid thinking occurs when people believe that there is a conspiracy to cause them harm or that others are secretly ridiculing or talking about them.[17]

Paranoid states come in many different forms. In most people who have occasional experiences with paranoid thinking, the problem is not serious nor long lasting. But in others it is seen in a type of schizophrenia, the paranoid type, in which the victim has psychotic delusions or hallucinations that such conspiracies are taking place. It is also seen in the deeply embedded character pattern known as "paranoid personality disorder." Victims of this disorder do not have hallucinations but are extremely suspicious, guarded, secretive, and overconcerned about the hidden motives of others. The American Psychiatric Association considers pathological jealousy to be one of the diagnostic criteria of paranoid personality disorder.[18]

One of the more serious manifestations of paranoid thinking is a form of psychosis. The psychotic person is not always able to distinguish between reality and what is internally imagined. One of the four kinds of paranoid psychosis is based on jealousy. Incidentally, the others, which won't be discussed here, are erotic, grandiose, and persecutory.[19]

The jealous type of paranoid psychosis is the delusion that one's possessions are being threatened. What makes this a form of psychosis is that the reasons for feeling threatened are not apparent to others. One might imagine that other people are planning to cause harm by taking away one's spouse or love object and leaving one bereft. Yet there seems to be no actual threat other than the one that is imagined by the individual.

Jealousy reactions that are associated with psychoses are treated in the same way as other psychoses. Antipsychotic medications—especially when supplemented with individual or group psychotherapy, social supports, and a natural helping network—have proved to be very effective in the treatment of paranoid schizophrenic people. With such help the symptoms of the psychosis, including pathological jealousy, are often controlled so that the victim can have a fairly normal life.

Overt mental disorders such as psychosis, paranoia, and depression do not account for all adult jealousy problems. In fact, most jealous people are otherwise mentally stable. They have developed jealousy problems because they learned that such behavior provides them some immediate advantages. They have learned through repeated experiences that their jealous behaviors can be rewarding to them. It seems beneficial to them, even though there may be long-term troublesome consequences.[20]

How does one learn that jealousy is rewarding? It usually happens when others do what the jealous person wants in order to stop the jealous behavior. For example, a small child may act violently possessive when the mother pays more attention to a sibling. If, whenever this happens, the mother ignores the sibling and comforts the child, the child will believe that the temper tantrum is a good and valuable technique for achieving desired results. With growth, the temperamental behavior may continue and become integrated into the personality. The child may think it is normal to act that way. By the time this child is exposed to other priorities, situations in which no one is rewarded for showing such behavior, it is too late to change easily. Further experiences will tend to reinforce the jealous behavior and contribute to the additional development and perpetuation of jealousy.

Behavioral scientists conclude that all behaviors, including jealousy reactions, are perpetuated because they are of some perceived benefit to the individual. When a behavior is rewarded, it is reinforced. The reward may not be apparent to observers or sometimes even to the jealous individual. It may take place entirely within the jealous person's mind and unique value system. It may not even look like a reward and sometimes may even appear to be the opposite. And the reward may be of short duration, followed by offsetting negative consequences.[21]

What is considered a "reward" can be deceiving. If, for example, a child feels deprived of attention, then any attention might be preferred to being ignored. If he learns his mother ignores him when he conforms to her expectations but spanks him when he doesn't, he starts behaving badly. The spanking doesn't appear to be a reward because it hurts, but it gains the reward of parental attention. The child wanted the attention so much it was worth the pain to get it. Most parents recognize that this trait is common in children; far fewer people consider that the same phenomenon exists with adults.

Adults do many things that are immediately rewarding, even though harmful in the long run. For example, a person may enjoy smoking even though knowing that there is long-term risk of lung cancer. The pleasure is immediate and the risk is not.

For the jealous individual, the same reinforcement systems operate. This person derives some immediate gratification from his or her behavior. It may not be apparent to anyone what this gratification is, and it does little good to point out the negative consequences that follow. To the jealous person, these consequences are not immediate and may not happen anyway, but the gratification from showing the jealousy comes immediately and with certainty.

Because everyone has a unique conception of what is rewarding, it is not possible to describe all the rewards that people have derived from jealous behavior. However, we can look at the three most common types of rewards. One is that the jealous behavior defends the individual against other emotional disturbances that may be more painful and serious or that are less acceptable to the individual. Another reward of jealous behavior is that it provides an opportunity to release pent-up emotions that can find no other acceptable outlets. And finally, the expression of jealous behavior can be rewarding because it provides a sense of power and control over others that might not otherwise exist.

The most common reward that perpetuates jealous behavior seems to be the defense it provides against more painful emotional experiences. Many people conceal more serious emotional disturbances by expressions of pathological jealousy. They usually do this by attributing discomforting impulses or painful thoughts that exist within themselves to others. In other words, they relieve their pain by projecting it elsewhere. This idea was first described by Sigmund Freud, who hypothesized that projection was among the most important elements in jealous behavior. This explanation was personified in the relationship between Pierre and Jeanne.

Pierre's jealousy probably saved his marriage. He had been very active sexually before settling down with Jeanne, his new wife. However the wedding ceremony did not constrain his libido. For months, although he tried to devote his exclusive attention to Jeanne, and even though their sexual relationship was good, he found it difficult to keep from thinking of possibilities with other women. Jeanne sensed his conflict and did everything she could to keep him happy and sexually fulfilled. She knew he had once been promiscuous and wanted to make sure he had changed his ways. She read about various sexual techniques and was always eager to try out new things with Pierre. That, she believed, was the best way to keep him happy at home.

One day the thought occurred to Pierre that Jeanne might have similar obsessions. Possibly she also had strong urges for sexual experiences with others. She denied it, of course, but he wasn't convinced. He began to wonder where she had learned all these sexual techniques. He wondered why she was always so eager to have intercourse, as though she was trying to hide her true feelings. Soon he seemed to forget about his own desires for other women, as his thoughts increasingly centered around Jeanne. His suspicion and possessiveness of Jeanne were strong enough to distract him from his desires to have affairs. His jealousy rewarded him by making it possible to project his own discomforting and painful desires onto his wife. It was less painful for him to be jealous than to endure the sexual frustration.

According to Freud, some jealousies are rewarding because they provide a defense against a thought that is even more intolerable. Many people, he thought, had latent homosexual tendencies but would be quite distressed if the idea were permitted into their consciousness. They keep it from becoming conscious by combining the defenses of projection and denial. A man who has an erotic interest in another man, Freud thought, would deny such a feeling in himself and then project it onto his wife. He would think, "It is she who wants that man, not me." Freud's speculation could not be proved, but it was based on several of his cases that seemed to confirm the idea.[22]

Jealousy is also rewarding for some people by providing a mental defense against feelings of worthlessness. Jealous people fear losing their prized "possessions," but they usually have a more horrible fear. They are afraid that their inadequacies are so great that they don't deserve the continued affection of their loved ones. Such a fear is powerful, and the idea won't go away by itself, even by consciously thinking about something else.

But it does go away if another compelling idea can be put in its place. The idea of worthlessness in the jealous person is usually displaced by the idea that someone else is involved, someone who is manipulating the situation and attempting to take the loved one away. The individual thinks, "Someone is trying to steal my lover. This person is manipulating my loved one, who now has no choice but to go along with it. It's not that my loved one dislikes me; it's just that the other person is so cunning and powerful." Painful as this idea is, it is less so than thinking of oneself as unworthy. This jealousy is rewarding in that it defends against the more painful idea of worthlessness.[23]

A similar defense mechanism commonly used by jealous people is known as "reaction formation." In this mechanism, one idea is also substituted for a more painful one. However, here the new idea is the exact opposite of the idea being concealed. Presumably, when a reaction formation is necessary, it is because the idea is so abhorrent that the only escape is to get mentally as far away from it as possible. The farthest one can get from an idea is its opposite.

Most theorists of human behavior have their favorite examples of this phenomenon. There is the man who voyeuristically wants to see unclad beauties, but the idea is so unacceptable that he becomes a movie censor or crusader against pornography instead. There is the woman who doesn't really like her children and doesn't want them in her life. However, because this idea is intolerable to her, it is concealed by her lavishing time, attention, toys, and expressions of unequaled love on the children. And there are the do-gooders who hide their contempt for people, the workaholics who can't admit that they are really lazy, and the daredevils who keep cowardly tendencies secret by attempting heroic feats.

Jealousy can be a reaction formation for the individual who is basically apathetic or antipathetic toward a loved one. For example, a woman doesn't really care about her husband or has grown contemptuous of him. She wishes she would never see him again. However, she has been raised to believe in the sanctity of marriage and the duty to honor commitments for life. She can't acknowledge her true indifference to her husband to herself or anyone else. So she hides it by experiencing the opposite feelings—she fears losing him; she feels threatened that he will love someone other than her; she wants to know about his every move; and she listens closely to him, trying to find if there are any discrepancies in his stories that would indicate that he has interests elsewhere. She has such an intense preoccupation with her husband that no one would suspect that it is based on indifference.

All defenses against more painful ideas are unconscious. That is, the jealous person is not aware of the true motivation behind the jealousy. Because it is unconscious, it does no good simply to tell them that they are using defense mechanisms. They simply wouldn't believe it.[24]

In fact, telling them might cause them to have more difficulty in solving their problem. Instead of using the information to enhance their under-standing or insight, they would be more likely to think, consciously or unconsciously, of ways to justify their positions. This would make it even more difficult to help them recognize their true feelings and thus eliminate the reasons for this kind of jealousy. It is usually more effective to do what professional psychotherapists try to do. They are supportive and gently ask questions that lead these people to look at themselves and their deeper motivations. If they can look inward and don't have to be defensive, they will be more likely, eventually, to see for themselves what underlies their jealousy.

Another reward that people often get from jealous behavior is the op-portunity to release emotions that would otherwise be suppressed. It is a fact of our modern culture that we are often expected to conceal our feel-ings. There are social pressures against being very demonstrative, angry, or even quiet, except in well-defined circumstances. Some people still look askance at men who cry in public or kiss other men. They raise their eyebrows at women who show anger in aggressive ways. People are not supposed to show their displeasure about visiting in-laws, their disapproval of someone's attire, or their joy at the funerals of rivals. But when these feelings exist and we are taught to conceal them, a certain amount of emo-tional pressure results.

We have to find more acceptable outlets for these emotions. Anger, for example, can be dealt with indirectly. Outlets for anger can include going to sports events and howling at the officials, booing the other team, or criticizing members of the home team for their deficiencies. One can also silently curse the reckless drivers encountered on the roads, engage in politi-cal debates with the gang at the office, and chew one's own fingernails.

One of the healthiest outlets for pent-up emotions is their direct verbal expression to others who are accepting and understanding. This is essen-tially what happens in most forms of psychotherapy. Since they first began practicing their craft, therapists have found that people feel better and elimi-nate many of their symptoms of emotional dysfunction when they talk out their feelings.[25]

The word therapists use for this experience is "catharsis." It usually occurs when the client is encouraged to say anything that comes to mind. The client is given the opportunity to describe inner feelings and thus rec-ognize what they really mean. When the feelings have had a proper airing out, the person can see them more objectively and can see how they have been influencing him- or herself and others.

Of course, catharsis is not the exclusive domain of psychotherapists. Much more of it goes on outside therapists' offices than within—in fact, between friends, marital partners, and intimate family members. It also goes on in bars, churches, car pools, and everywhere people gather. It even takes place when a person is alone and able to write thoughts in letters or diaries or to talk into a tape recorder. If a person is able to ventilate feelings regularly, there is less likelihood of experiencing the emotional distress that comes with unexpressed feelings.

Unfortunately, not all people have equal access to this opportunity. Some people don't have anyone with whom they can talk. Others have developed such self-contained personalities that they can't easily let their feelings show, even to themselves. They have been taught to believe that such demonstrations will cause them some painful consequences. They fear they will be ridiculed or exploited.

As a group, men may yet be more inhibited about expressing their feelings than are women. Our culture still seems to encourage women to discuss their feelings openly and to discourage such behavior among men. Men are supposed to be more self-contained and to take care of themselves. They don't feel so comfortable describing their fears and deficiencies, even to their wives. They are trained to think of themselves as the protectors, the ones who can solve their problems without help. They feel they shouldn't burden their loved ones with such concerns.[26]

Those who can't release these emotions directly or indirectly can be vulnerable to emotional distress. In such situations they may lash out with violently jealous behaviors as a way of unconsciously discharging their pent-up feelings. For these people the jealous reaction is a form of catharsis. Their feelings have been building and, without opportunity for release, can cause unbearable psychic pressure. The jealous provocation can trigger an explosion of accusations, and they can criticize and demand explanations and apologies for hours. When they eventually stop, it is not because they are satisfied with the alibis or secure that the threat has passed but rather because they have discharged some of their stored emotional energy.

Such people are rewarded for their expressions of jealousy. They get rid of some emotional tension, they feel better as a result, and they associate the improved feeling with the jealous reaction. This feeling is remembered as new tensions develop and there are no healthy releases. They need to have another jealousy reaction. However, for the outlet to exist, there must be something about which to be jealous. Thus, they may set up situations that can lead to jealousy confrontations. A man may invite a friend home to visit his wife and then leave for a while on some contrived excuse. A woman lawyer constantly mentions a new colleague to her architect husband and then notes how he pays attention to it. Jealous people aren't usually aware of setting up such situations, even though it may be quite apparent to those who are set up.

When a discharge of emotions is the motive for a person's expression of jealousy, it obviously does no good to provide airtight alibis or valid justifications. At best, this will only cause the jealous person to stop ventilating for the time being. This means that additional emotional energy has to be stored, meaning that even more needs to be released later. When the explosion comes, it may be stronger and more violent than it would have been otherwise. In dealing with this kind of jealousy, it would probably be better for all concerned to encourage regular jealousy-based arguments. If they are frequent, they may not be so explosive or dangerous. They may provide a necessary outlet that would not otherwise exist, as in the case of a young man called Ray who used jealousy in this way.

Ray was what most people would still call the "macho" type—big, strong, not very verbal, easily prone to anger, and emotionally constricted. Ray believed that men who confided their troubles to others were "wimps" or "queers." He rarely talked to anyone, including his wife, except when berating her about the attention she gave to others. He was unlikely to have entered therapy if his wife had not preceded him. The problem for which he finally sought help was his sexual impotence.

Naturally, he couldn't bring himself to talk about it with any of his acquaintances. It was too embarrassing for him to discuss it even with his wife. The frustration experienced by Ray and his wife made their relationship explosively tense. His wife, however, had an advantage. She was not inhibited about discussing her problems and had people with whom to talk. She talked with her sister, her clergyman, and her gynecologist. Even then, her frustrations and tensions were severe. The situation must have been much more so for Ray, who didn't have these opportunities.

He used jealousy as a form of catharsis. It was a convenient outlet, permitting him to get rid of tension, anger, and feelings of inadequacy. He launched periodically into violent accusations about his wife's supposed infidelity, often punctuated by physical abuse as well as prolonged lectures about how she was to conduct herself in the future. She was understanding and sympathetic and realized that he was tormented by feelings of inadequacy about his erectile dysfunction. She also realized that he was projecting his own problem away from himself and onto her.

Her response was to deny his charges, remain quiet, and say anything she could think of to pacify him and get him to stop. Yet stopping was the last thing he needed to do. His need to vent emotional pressure was equaled by her need to feel safe with him. She faced a real danger of harm if his outbursts continued.

Ray always seemed to feel better after his jealous tirades. This was the clue that suggested that he used the jealousy reaction as an excuse to let off steam. He remained good-humored, relaxed, and trusting for several days after each outburst. The good times seemed to last longer if his tirades were longer and more intense, and there was even a slight improvement in their sexual situation. When he was more relaxed and self-confident, he could occasionally maintain an erection.

Of course, this couple had many other problems to resolve before they could achieve the relationship they sought. But central among them was their need to learn how to permit open communication. In marital and sexual therapy, Ray made remarkably rapid improvements with both problems. The reduced sexual frustrations and the newfound appreciation for more open communication with his wife led to a significant reduction in his jealous reactions.

Another reward that encourages some people to behave jealously is the sense of power and control it sometimes generates. The low self-esteem found in many people with jealousy problems often results in their having rather docile and passive personalities. This frequently causes them to be exploited or deprived of the same advantages available to others, or at least they perceive this to be the case. They are often ignored in groups and seem almost invisible in restaurants and stores. Their inability to command much attention further erodes their diminished self-esteem and contributes to their feelings of powerlessness and vulnerability.

To cope, they may try to find ways of asserting some control over others. They may associate with those who have less power. They may choose as marital partners those who are even less assertive. They may be physically abusive of their spouses. They may be tyrannical with their children. Some may choose employment in institutions or schools where they are able to dominate young people, patients, or prisoners. And sometimes they may not do much but sit back and criticize others, claiming that if they were in charge things would be done much better. All of these behaviors can provide some people with illusions of power and control.

Another way they achieve this is through jealous behaviors. They may discover the effect of this by accident. For example, a woman may feel that her husband never listens to her. She remains frustrated about this for several years. Then one day she discovers lipstick on his shirt after he has returned from a business trip. She explodes with rage. She has had outbursts and temper tantrums before, but because of her basically passive temperament she hadn't been taken very seriously. But this time it's different. The jealousy has triggered something deeper within her. She is afraid now, and her response is that of a cornered wild animal. She is hard to ignore.

As she continues her accusations and admonishments, she becomes aware of a new and unfamiliar experience. Her husband is listening. He seems humble and contrite and will do anything to make it up to her. She is in control. She has power. It is almost inevitable that she will find another reason for a future outburst, no matter how circumspect her husband remains. She has just been rewarded for her jealous behavior.

The reason her behavior commands such attention is that she feels it so strongly and sincerely. It is not an act. If she decides later that jealousy was a good way to get attention or control and "acts" jealous, she will not get any more attention than usual. Her newfound power can only come from her honest fear. She may be more vigilant and confrontative, and she may remain dominated except when there is reason to suspect that her marriage or possessions are at risk. Otherwise she uses jealousy to assert some control over her circumstances.

It can be argued that jealous behavior is, for some, a healthy and appropriate reaction, and that it is perpetuated because it is an effective way to retain one's relationships and possessions. This argument says that jealousy exists in some people because it is justified. A person's partner may be unfaithful or at least be acting suspiciously. Others really might be trying to usurp someone's position. To behave jealously can help a person stay on the alert for any possible threats. Alertness makes it more difficult for potential rivals to get close, and it makes it impossible for one's partner to get away with anything.[27]

Those who offer this argument suggest that jealousy serves a purpose similar to that of a smoke detector or a "Star Wars" defense shield. It keeps an individual alert to real danger. It assures some advance warning so that proper defensive measures can be taken. It serves early notice that the situation is getting out of control so that action to reestablish authority can be taken. And, finally, it provides a deterrent. The partner of a very jealous person knows about the vigilance and may decide that any independent behavior is not worth the problems it would cause. The net result seems to be that one's possessions are retained and one's home continues intact. What greater rewards could there be?

There is nothing particularly unhealthy about competing with rivals to acquire or retain something or someone of value. There is nothing inherently unhealthy about watching out for situations in which such losses could take place. If the jealous feeling is confined to such feelings and reactions, it is not unhealthy. Unhealthy or inappropriate jealousy comes from the way the reaction is expressed. For example, if one attempts to hold on to a loved one through constant vigilance or by threatening all potential rivals, the jealousy is unhealthy. If one attempts to hold on to a loved one by working at being more lovable, kind, and considerate, then it is healthy.

Essentially, there is no healthy excuse for having temper tantrums or abusing one's partner because of suspicions, whether they are well founded or not. Suspiciousness and possessiveness are ultimately ineffective. They obstruct opportunities for communication and expressions of affection. While it is understandable that a seriously jealous person can be afraid of losing a valued possession, this feeling is never a license to react in destructive ways.

Jealous behavior can be perpetuated by an infinite variety of perceived benefits. Every individual has unique needs and unique ways of meeting them. Whenever a need is met, however unattractive it might appear to others, the individual's behavior is reinforced. In helping a person with a jealousy problem, it is useful to look for the rewards to be derived from jealous behavior. Finding them makes it easier to help overcome the problem. It follows that if the jealous behavior is rewarding, finding a way to withhold the reward could help extinguish the behavior.

The partner of the jealous person is the one who has the most to gain by locating the reinforcer and eliminating it. However, it is not always so easy to find. The partner may be too close and too involved to see it. Or sometimes the jealous person compels the partner to provide such rewards. It is even possible that the partner gets some kind of gratification from the jealousy, so that he or she consciously or unconsciously encourages the jealous behavior.[28]

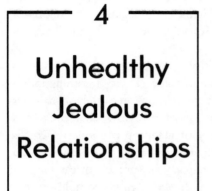

4

Unhealthy Jealous Relationships

Love and devotion are not the only reasons people marry or maintain committed relationships. Some people do so because they obtain neurotic gratification from their alliances. People in such relationships often have unhealthy elements in their personalities. They often need or want to be with others who tolerate or encourage the continued expression of these problems. Both people, by unspoken agreement, provide each other with the necessary emotional or behavioral supports for the perpetuation of the problem. An example of such a relationship is seen in the case of Paula and Leo.

Paula had a deep contempt for men but nevertheless wanted the social benefits of marriage. As a young girl she had been repeatedly sexually molested by her father and had never recovered from the trauma. She transferred her contempt for him onto all other men. As a result her relationships with them were unsatisfactory. She was very assertive and angry and found herself getting into intense arguments with most of the men she dated.

Eventually she met Leo, a man who didn't argue. He was extremely passive and submissive and had almost no interest in sex. He had found that most women didn't care to be with him for long; they got bored and lost interest. But the new relationship provided for their mutual well-being. Both felt comfortable that she was dominant. Both accepted her need to express her anger regularly. It made her feel better and it made him feel that he was holding her interest.

Some people meet many unhealthy as well as healthy needs in the relationships they form. They become attracted to one another even though they appear to have little in common and seem totally unsuited to each other. They stay together even though their relationships seem to outsiders to be unhappy. Some people are most comfortable being married to spouses who are cruel or indifferent. This pattern is sometimes seen between alcoholics and their spouses when the drinking partner tries to stop while the spouse is secretly encouraging the drinking to continue. The spouse without the drinking problem derives some sort of reward or pleasure from the existence of the alcoholic spouse's problem.

There is nothing inherently wrong or unhealthy about people with problems wanting to be together and wanting to help one another solve them. It is only unhealthy when one or both of the partners have neurotic elements in their personalities that are encouraged by the other. If two people are together to meet their respective unhealthy needs, they preserve and perpetuate the unhealthy parts of their respective personalities. This makes it much more difficult for either of them to develop normal or healthy patterns of thinking and behaving than if one alone tried to resolve his or her problems.[1]

Jealousy can be encouraged and perpetuated in unhealthy relationships. Usually this occurs when one member of the relationship has a jealousy problem and the other secretly encourages it. One person acts jealously and the other person provides a reward for the behavior. The nonjealous person has some neurotic personality characteristic that derives unconscious pleasure or satisfaction from the other's expression of jealousy.

What would cause anyone to feel satisfaction when being accused or victimized by jealousy? It might be that the nonjealous person has a desire to be treated badly, which happens whenever the jealousy is provoked. It might be that the person feels neglected or ignored and incites some jealousy in the partner to stimulate some apparent interest. Perhaps the partner believes the myth that jealousy is a sign of love and is testing the jealous person's feelings. Maybe the partner has a neurotic need to be maintained in a childlike role and finds that this is achieved when the other is jealously possessive. One example of such a relationship concerned the case of a jealous husband and his agoraphobic wife.[2]

The husband was abnormally jealous and extremely possessive, especially with members of his family. He demanded complete accountability and insisted on knowing where they were at all times. Most wives wouldn't have been able or willing to tolerate such scrutiny for long, but such was not the case with his wife. She suffered from agoraphobia. She became terrified of being in public places or away from her home. She became increasingly constricted in her activities until her primary goal was simply to avoid situations in unfamiliar environments from which escape would be difficult.

Most spouses are sympathetic or irritated or at least want the phobic person to recover from this painful condition. They usually work to help solve the phobic person's problem. But in this case, the jealous husband was gratified by it. He was relieved that he didn't have to worry that his wife was going to be lost to a rival. She was always home. She too was gratified by his jealousy. She could attribute her constricted life to his problem and avoid having to face the problem within herself.

The serious mental disorders suffered by both the husband and the wife were much more difficult to treat because of the symbiotic nature of their relationship. The more he overcame his jealousy problem, the more he frightened his wife by encouraging her to get out into the world. The more the wife overcame her fear of the outside world and wanted to become a part of it, the more threatened and abusive her husband became. Had either been alone there would have been more incentive and support for overcoming their respective illnesses.

This is not to say that jealousy is the fault of the nonjealous partner. While this may be true of some jealous relationships, most jealousies have originated long before adult relationships begin. Most marriages and committed relationships that experience jealousy problems are not the fault of the partner but rather the result of long-standing and deep-seated psychosocial and behavioral problems within the jealous person.

However, a small percentage of jealousy-based relationships do support these unhealthy patterns, and it is important to define and determine their circumstances. Inasmuch as these dynamics are usually unconscious, it is not easy for the nonjealous partners to be aware of their participation or contribution to the problem.[3]

One way the nonjealous partner can recognize if culpability exists is by reviewing all the known ways that relationship patterns keep jealousy patterns in motion. With such knowledge, the nonjealous person can see if such patterns are present and if they are being encouraged unconsciously. This information will also suggest ways to discontinue those behavioral patterns that are found to exist.

There are countless unconscious reasons why people provoke jealousy in their partners. Scientific studies have identified the more common motivations. They show that some people try to provoke jealousy in their partners because they are:

- Masochistic, so they derive pleasure from the pain inflicted upon themselves when their partners become jealous[4]
- Angry and embittered because of past grievances, so they strive to make their partners jealous as a way of reciprocating their pain[5]
- Frustrated at their partners' indifference or lack of love, so they provoke attention-getting jealousy reactions[6]
- Enjoying the feeling of power over their jealous partners that they get when they have induced jealous behaviors[7]
- Trying to conceal other problems, so they provoke jealousy-based arguments to divert attention[8]
- Sexually stimulated by arguments, so they encourage jealousy feelings, knowing that an argument will result[9]
- Engaged in a game-playing ritual

The case example of Darryl and Lucy illustrates some of these patterns.

Darryl and Lucy were fighters. They had battled almost constantly through their ten years of marriage. Yet neither had yet shown any sign of giving up or any proclivity for ending the relationship. Sometimes their arguments became physical, and they were occasionally punctuated by mutual accusations, foot stamping, face slapping, vase throwing, and door slamming. They were always contrite after the heat ebbed—apologetic and filled with intentions to make amends. But they never promised they would tone down their arguments. They were an even match and usually fought honestly and fairly but frequently and with some violence.

A typical interaction went something like this: Darryl would have been away on a business trip for a few days. Or Lucy would have had particularly discomforting menstrual cramps. In any event, circumstances would prevent their engaging in sexual intercourse for a long enough time so that sexual tension intensified. Darryl would start making overtures signaling that sexual intercourse was desired and Lucy would appear enthused. Then she would casually mention that she had bumped into an old high school sweetheart that day. Or she would say she had seen an old Clark Gable movie on television and found him so sexy. Or she'd say she had to go to a PTA meeting where she was on a committee with that handsome Mr. Jones. Darryl was very jealous, and she could anticipate his response, though somehow it always seemed to come as a surprise to her. He would demand to know more details, and then he'd berate her for her flirtatiousness.

Her response was to ridicule. But in her denials and clarifications she would leave doubts, little seeds of suspicion: "No, I'm not going to be alone with Mister Jones. There'll be a whole group of us on the committee. Besides, he's not the type to try anything—at least that's what he told me."

Darryl would explode. "What do you mean, *he* told you? Why'd he tell you something like that?" The argument would intensify and culminate with one of them sleeping on the couch while the other was alone in the bedroom.

What was the purpose of this relationship pattern, and why did it go on with such fervor and without much change for the decade Darryl and Lucy were together? Why did it go on without apparent conscious intent or recognition of its true purpose, even though they were obviously intelligent and psychologically sophisticated people?

They didn't see it because they both had something important to gain by keeping it going. If either had recognized the nature of their ritual, they might not have been able to continue with it. Both had long histories of sexual disturbances. Darryl was often troubled by premature ejaculation problems. He was often anxious about his "performance" during intercourse and feared that he was sexually inadequate. Lucy would once have been labeled a "frigid woman." Now that that archaic term has given way to more enlightened descriptions of the problem, she would be diagnosed as suffering from functional dyspareunia.

Her problem was a painful sensitivity to touching or pressure in the genital area. She had developed an aversion to sexual intercourse virtually all through her postpubescent life. On those rare occasions when she did have intercourse, it was preceded by dread, apprehension, and fear. Doctors could find no physical source of the intense pain she experienced but she could never convince herself that it was symptomatic of emotional disturbances. Her aversion to sex was further complicated by Darryl's premature ejaculation, and his problem was intensified by feeling that he contributed to her pain.

Lucy used her husband's problem with jealousy to minimize sexual contacts with him. When overtures were made, she simply stoked up his jealousy and fueled it with innuendo by leading him to believe she was losing interest in him for someone else. His typical response made the outcome predictable—they'd fight. Their argument would drown any libidinous impulses, and they would forget about sex. She would not have to engage in intercourse but would also not feel guilty about it. That was her payoff: guilt-free absolution from sex. *She* didn't refuse *him*. *He* started the fight with his unreasonable accusations. *She* was willing until he started acting jealous again. If only he would overcome *his* problem, they would be able to have sex like other people. Or so her rationalization went.

Darryl, too, wanted an excuse to avoid sex, and the jealousy-based arguments provided an acceptable way to avoid it. His feelings of inadequacy and inferiority were intensified because of Lucy's strong and volatile personality. His jealousy provided him with a feeling of control and authority over his wife. So their respective needs were temporarily satisfied in a mutually beneficial way.

This unhealthy relationship pattern might never have ended if Darryl and Lucy had not overcome their sexual problems. They began attending a sex therapy clinic, and through it they were able to help each other resolve their respective difficulties. When they became able to enjoy sexual intercourse, their persistent conflicts were no longer necessary. It was possible, then, for them to begin direct work on their jealous and combative tendencies.

"Frigidity" is the name given to interactions of this type by the late Dr. Eric Berne, the creator of "transactional analysis." In the early 1960s Berne discovered that people play many "games" that serve important purposes in relationships. Some games are healthy, he said, but most are symptomatic of attempts to avoid more painful experiences. The "frigidity" game occurs when both husband and wife collude to avoid their unpleasant sexual experiences. To avoid sexual contact, the partners in the transaction engage in some diversionary conflict until the pressure for sex has abated.[10]

Berne defined a game as an ongoing series of complementary ulterior transactions progressing to a well-defined predictable outcome. In other words, two or more people (called "players") outwardly think and communicate that they have one goal in an interaction, when in fact their goal is something altogether different.

For example, the first game Berne detailed in his book *Games People Play* was called "Why don't you . . . yes, but." The player who is "it" defines a problem to a concerned individual or group. The others respond with helpful suggestions designed to alleviate the problem. "It" ponders each suggestion before saying, "Yes, but. . . . " Then "it" explains why that suggestion can't work. The game continues until the others tire of it, and "it" triumphantly concludes that the problem is insoluble, worse than anyone else has ever had to face. The ostensible purpose of the interaction is to obtain information or solutions, but the real motive is to obtain attention and sympathy, not to get suggestions but to reject them. If information were really sought then ideas could be accepted and implemented.

All games have several elements in common. For one thing, the real goals are not consciously known or realized by any of the players, at least not while the game is played. Another common element is that one game player, the person who is "it," finds some personality trait or "weakness" in the other players to make the game work. The weakness, or "gimmick," as Berne calls it, might be the other players' concern, fear, sentimentality, greed, or even jealousy. In the "Why don't you . . . yes, but" game, it is the other players' concern for "it" that is used.

After the other player has become involved (or "hooked") in the transaction, "it" pulls a switch to get a payoff. The switch is when it is first apparent that an ulterior motive is sought. In "Why don't you . . . yes, but," the switch is the continued refusal to accept any suggestions, even though suggestions are what are supposedly sought. The other players are confused trying to figure out what happened to them, while "it" has won the exchange.

Winning consists of being gratified, having recognition of the seriousness of the problem, having others show interest and concern, and—most important of all—leaving an opening for the game to be played again with equally certain outcomes.

The concept of games helps psychotherapists interpret their client's patterns of behavior that inhibit treatment progress. When the therapist or clients identify a game and reveal its ulterior motive, they can find ways of changing its direction. They can find an alternative to the predictable response and eliminate the usual payoff. Without the payoff, the couple is more likely to change the pattern of the relationship and increase the possibility of growth.

Many people involved in jealous relationships are playing games of this type. In so doing they encourage jealous responses in themselves and their partners. One way to eliminate the problem of jealousy and to get at the underlying cause of the problem is to recognize the existence of the jealousy game being played, its ulterior motives, and its probable outcome. The following are some of the major games used in the jealous relationship; wherever possible or appropriate the names coined by Berne are used here, although the examples come from recent work with jealous clients.

The "Uproar" Game is a variation of the "frigidity" game and was also played by Darryl and Lucy. In "frigidity," the goal is to generate some disagreements so that sexual intercourse can be avoided in an otherwise acceptable manner. In "uproar," the goal is to have major arguments or fights in order to avoid any kind of closeness, intimacy, or supportive exchanges or to meet other needs. In jealous homes, uproarious behavior is commonplace and keeps the participants from getting close enough to really work on the problem. The case of Lisa and Mark illustrates the "uproar game."

Lisa was an attractive twenty-eight year old, with a vivacious, assertive, and rather dominating personality. Mark was twenty-seven, good looking and athletic but very shy and introverted. He was not very articulate and seemed content to let Lisa tell the therapist about their problems.

They had only been married five months and had known one another only a few weeks before that. They met in a singles bar, where Lisa initiated the introductions and subsequent courtship. She had been on the rebound when she sought Mark out. She had just ended a stormy, volatile six-year marriage and still had strong feelings about her first husband.

Lisa and her first husband had argued throughout their lives together, mostly about their fears of the other's potential infidelity. Lisa felt certain that her husband had involvements with other women, and he was equally sure that she was unfaithful. Their pattern was to accuse, deny, demand apologies, and scream at one another for hours, make up, and end the ordeal with prolonged lovemaking. Then the conflict would be renewed the next day. This might have continued indefinitely, but one day Lisa's husband stopped an argument at midpoint and simply walked out. Before long he was able to get a quickie divorce in a Caribbean nation, remarry, and relocate to another part of the country.

Rejection and isolation did not suit Lisa. Though she still loved her first husband, she made a rapid and conscious effort to find a replacement. Before long she had swept Mark off his feet and engineered the new marriage. Then she tried to make it a duplicate of her first one; she had learned to enjoy fighting and its ultimate outcome.

She would come home late without offering explanations. She would talk to men on the phone, ostentatiously in front of Mark, and she flirted with men in public. She kept comparing Mark to her first husband, always unfavorably. She wanted to make him fight in order to recreate the relationship she had had in her first marriage.

It worked. Mark, who had not entered the marriage as a jealous person or as an outspoken one, found that he was rapidly becoming so. He started demanding accounts of Lisa's whereabouts. He monitored her telephone calls, threatened men who called her, and forced her to hang up. When he started feeling jealous he began screaming at her. Unable to match her verbal argumentative skills, he started resorting to physical intimidation. Their marriage was in serious trouble.

Therapy proved helpful for both of them. The first step was to help Mark learn to express himself more openly and without resorting to physical action during arguments. Lisa was helped to realize that Mark's jealousy was not an indicator of love or respect and that provoking it was pointless. She also learned that there were healthier ways of expressing love and affection and that it could be done even if not preceded by a fight. Once they no longer needed an uproar in order to validate their relationship, it developed into a healthy marriage.

The "uproar" game is more typically played by people who are uncomfortable with close relationships and want to distance themselves from their partners. They use jealousy to pick fights. When the hidden purpose of this game is revealed the couple can work on their problem more directly.

"If It Weren't for You!" is another game commonly played in jealousy situations. Typically, the players consist of a domineering husband or wife and an insecure spouse. The more submissive player is afraid to do something but doesn't want to admit the fear. The insecure spouse blames the hesitation on the notion that the other wouldn't approve. Usually the game involves third parties who are called on to offer sympathy and to concur in the blaming of the domineering person. "If it weren't for my husband being such a male chauvinist pig, I would get a job," a housewife might say to her kaffeeklatsch friends. The friends might be in similar circumstances, agree, and say they have the same problem. Or a man might say to his lodge brothers, "If it weren't for my wife always nagging me to do the yard work on weekends, I'd have the time to run for the club presidency."

People who play "if it weren't for you" often marry domineering mates. Their lack of confidence causes them to be afraid of doing something, so their choice of partners gives them convenient excuses. The way to end the game is for other players to avoid providing the payoff. This would be done by complete permissiveness. ("But I want you to get a job, Mabel." "Why don't you spend more time at the lodge so you can run for president, Ralph?")

The jealousy form of this game is illustrated by a young couple called Harold and Tricia. She was the jealous one, while Harold was rather shy and socially inhibited. She was possessive and feared having to share her husband's time with others. She wanted him to be more interested in her than in anyone or anything, including their friends, their relatives, and his job. At first he didn't mind, because he wasn't too interested in being with others anyway, but then her feelings intensified. If he remained late at work he was interrogated when he came home. Once, after he volunteered to lead his oldest son's scout troop on a weekend outing, Tricia berated him so strongly that he vowed never to do anything like that again. Harold started to feel it was almost not worth it to have any outside interests. He found himself avoiding people. So whenever anyone would encourage him to join in some activity Harold could say to himself, "I would if it weren't for Trish."

When the two played the game they had a mutual aim. Harold's purpose was to blame his shyness and inhibitions on Tricia's jealousy. He used Tricia to avoid situations that caused him to face his fears or inadequacies. Tricia's purpose was to keep Harold in her control so that her fear of being left alone would be minimized.

Both Harold and Tricia received important payoffs in keeping the game going. If either stopped playing, it would expose their fears and make them confront situations they didn't think they could handle. Of course, if they could get out of the game pattern, they would have to face the fears and would come to realize that they *could* handle them. Harold was capable of doing much better in social situations than he had imagined, and Tricia could survive without having him at her constant beck and call. When the game and its intent were identified, they could discontinue it and begin to address their real problems.

"See What You Made Me Do!" is another game that accommodates itself to jealousy situations. Its purpose is to absolve oneself of guilt for mistakes. One player asks the other for suggestions on how to accomplish something. The suggestion is followed but not exactly as prescribed, and the results turn out badly. The player then says to the other, "See what you made me do!" The player thus avoids being blamed for the poor outcome and attributes the mistake to the other. The goal—avoiding mistakes and transferring responsibility to the other without feeling guilty—has been achieved.

In the jealousy form of this game, the nonjealous person benefits from the partner's jealousy by blaming all mistakes on it. Charges such as the following are made: "You made me so nervous when we were over at the Smiths last night, with you staring at me every time I looked at her, it's no wonder I got drunk and made a fool of myself." Or, "No, I didn't get the job because I was uptight when the interviewer asked if I could work late some evenings." Or, "I lost the case in court today because the jury foreman was good-looking, and I started thinking you would make something of it if I won."

The game provides a convenient way of avoiding responsibility for one's mistakes or failures. It serves the useful purpose of being able to make errors without feeling blamed or guilty for them. In this game the non-jealous person has a hidden motive for keeping the partner jealous—to keep some excuses handy.

Two people who played this game with regularity were twin ten-year-old boys who were extremely competitive. They were almost always competing for the parents' time, and both were unhappy when some of it went to the other boy. Each derived great pleasure from the discomfort the other one felt when not given as much attention, whereas, if they had shared with or supported one another, there would have been more than enough for each.

They were placed in weekly outpatient psychotherapy sessions together. In the sessions, the therapist would have one draw a picture, build a model house from snap-together parts, or tell a story. The other was quietly to observe this process. As the boy would near completion of the project, almost invariably a mistake would be made. The story would get told wrong, or the crayon would slip, or the pieces would disassemble and the structure would collapse. In a fury the boy would turn to his twin and shout, "See what you made me do?!" The other boy had presumably been making faces, sighing too loudly, or moving around in his chair at a crucial time. Both boys were so conscious of the other's attempts to take away the limelight that they became more preoccupied with the other's presence than with the task at hand. This was a recurring theme in their lives. They each needed more autonomy and a sense of uniqueness.

This is also true of couples who engage in some jealous games. Often they pay more attention to their partner and to the jealousy problem than to the task at hand. They don't concentrate on what needs to be done because they are thinking about the possible reaction from their jealous companion. Then, if they fail or make a mistake, they can conveniently attribute it to the other. This game permits the jealous person to maintain controls and the partner to have excuses for the perpetuation of unhealthy patterns.

The "see what you made me do" game usually has a much more serious and often tragic outcome than in the example of the twins. Too often the jealous person accuses the partner and asks for corroboration and alibis and proof from third parties. But the partner may eventually feel pushed by such behavior into action that validates the accusation. Often, if the accusations are about a particular person, that person begins to loom larger in importance to the partner. Sometimes the partner begins to justify getting close to someone: "Well, if I'm going to be accused of something, I may as well do it. What have I got to lose?" Then, when the inevitable discovery occurs, the convenient response is naturally, "You drove me to it." The unfaithful one often feels fully justified in the action because of the partner's accusations.

"Cops and Robbers" is another game sometimes played by jealous partners. In real life, robbers attempt to steal money from banks or stores. Their goal, if not their method, is honest—it is to acquire money. Game-playing robbers have a goal that may be more dishonest than the method. Their motive is not the acquisition of money or other material possessions but the thrill of the ensuing chase. The aim is to outwit authorities and to exercise some power over those who otherwise have control.

This type of game originates in the childhood game of hide-and-seek. Most children who play derive their pleasure from keeping the others interested, not from finding such foolproof hideouts that their hunters quit looking. Very young children reveal that this is the true intent when they call out, make sounds, or show a part of themselves to the hunter. If the hunter gives up, the child is disappointed. So clues are left to provoke the other and keep the search alive. It has the same objective as baiting a hook or placing a carrot on a stick to get the mule moving. It is an enticement that is just beyond reach.

The jealousy version of "cops and robbers" has the jealous person playing the role of cop and the partner playing robber. As in all cops-and-robbers games, the robber leaves enough clues to tantalize the cop and throw some suspicion in the appropriate direction. In this case the "robber" tries to keep in control by keeping the jealous partner guessing. For example, a man might receive an innocent kiss at the office party and leave the lipstick on his cheek until there is a confrontation at home. He truthfully explains how it happened but withholds key details in order to arouse suspicion. Then he changes minor details of the story with each retelling, looking more and more guilty, until he calls someone from the office who confirms his version of the event. The "robber" is vindicated and the "cop" is humiliated.

What makes the game suspenseful is that the jealous person is vigorous in playing the game. Most people without serious jealousy problems would not pursue it. Like the very young hide-and-seek player, the "robber" would not get much gratification from playing it with an apathetic person. But with the jealous person's intensity fueling the game, the partner has a handy vehicle for fighting back against being dominated or controlled.

The "Courtroom" game is especially popular among jealous couples and always involves a third party. Its ostensible purpose is to get an arbitrator to hear both sides of a dispute and make a clear ruling in favor of one or the other. This is a game commonly played between couples in therapy, and therapists have to be alert to avoid it. One player is the accuser ("plaintiff") who tries to convince a concerned third party ("judge") that the other person ("defendant") did the deed. The game has its origins in the childhood activity of tattling and may sound something like this:

"Mommy, Billy took my squirt gun. Make him give it back."

"Yeah, Mom, but Jimmy was squirting me with it. Make him quit."

The supposed goal is to get the objective third party to resolve the dispute between two relative equals by presenting facts in an objective manner. However this is not the real purpose. The game would not be satisfying if the "judge" simply took sides and ruled in favor of one or the other—that would end the game. The players would rather make the issue obscure enough so that no decision can be made. This permits a continuation of the accusations by the "plaintiff" and explanations or justifications by the "defendant."

In the jealousy version of the game, the jealous person might say to an objective third party: "Let me tell you what Mary did last night while I was home babysitting. She didn't come in until ten-thirty and she. . . . " The spouse of the jealous person then says, "Let me tell you how it really was. I had to work until. . . . " The jealous person enjoys the process of accusing. He would be appalled to get what he is supposedly seeking:

"Okay, you've finally discovered me. I was out with your brother last night."

Such a confession would make the accuser aware of having lost power and control. Instead, the jealous person wants the denials and alibis to continue. This is more likely to occur by telling the tale only to those third parties who are objective and not prone to side taking. Most third parties will not take sides (at least not in the presence of both of them).

Both players receive a payoff. The jealous person gets to punish the partner by continuing the accusations without respite. The partner of the jealous person benefits by presenting alibis or excuses that the "judge" doesn't refute, providing the partner with a sense of power and righteousness.

The "Guess What?" game also occurs with frequency among jealous partners, with power as its motive. The game consists of asking the jealous partner questions that cause insecurity or fear. For example, a wife who is writing a letter looks up at her husband and asks, "How do you spell 'cuckold'?" The husband will be curious and, if already jealous, he may feel threatened. His wife will feel powerful if he begins trying to guess why she was using such a word.

More typically, the jealousy variant of "guess what?" has the partner manipulating the jealous person into asking questions: "If you insist on going to that meeting tomorrow night, guess what I'm going to do?" Such questions, designed to wave a red flag in front of the jealous person, are posed to bring out the suspiciousness.

If the jealous person doesn't want to guess, the partner may volunteer some additional causes for concern. "Spending time with you isn't the only thing I have to do, you know. I want to be with someone else anyway." After the right clues, the jealous person is sure to begin playing with fervor. "Are you going out to that new disco?" "No, guess again." "Are you going to start messing around with that new neighbor?" "No, guess again." This goes on long enough to assert the partner's control and leave the jealous person frustrated.

Most people would not continue playing after a while, but the jealous person will usually be more willing to go on because it fits in with the needs of jealousy. Finally, when the frustration is intense and there is a risk of moving into a more serious confrontation or a return to the previous painful episodes, the partner reveals the answer: "I'm going to visit my mother in the nursing home." The jealous person is made to feel foolish by having implied that the other's motives and intentions were ignoble. The partner has asserted control and fought against domination.

The "Wooden Leg" game permits the players to avoid having to behave in a responsible adult manner. Avoidance of responsibility is supposedly permitted because of some handicaps or weaknesses that may or may not be relevant. If, for example, a person with only one leg fails to write checks for his monthly bills, he could say, "Well, what do you expect of an amputee?" Similarly, jealous people can inflict abuse on members of their families and avoid responsibility for their actions. "Well," they may say, "I have this emotional problem whenever you're out of my sight, so don't blame me if I acted like an ass at the party." (The most publicized form of "wooden leg" in recent years took the form of an insanity plea. The president of the United States, his press secretary, and two police officers were shot, and the man who did it was found not guilty of the crime. "What did you expect of someone who was insane?" society was asked. In various cultures and in certain social circles many kinds of behavior are excused because of problems: "She's really insecure. That's why she is so critical of others." "He's a juvenile delinquent because of poverty and social inequality." "Well, he was drunk, so he shouldn't be blamed for running over that child.")

In the jealousy form of this game, the jealous person's partner accepts constant harassment, accusations, and pain because of the recognition that the jealous person has an emotional disturbance. The partner thinks, Why should I expect any difference? I know it can't be helped. It's not her fault. She just has this problem.

Often the partner feels a strong sense of purpose in the relationship, one that becomes so important that he or she resists efforts to change the pattern. This is occasionally seen when some spouses of alcoholics or people with physical handicaps become irate with others who want to help. They may even attempt to get the handicapped person away from potential sources of assistance.

Jealousy games appear in so many variations that it would be impossible to describe them all. Nevertheless, it is possible to stop playing them even when they aren't specifically identified, by first recognizing that a manipulative game of some kind is being played. Once that is acknowledged, people can make abrupt changes in their expected responses.

The most important indicator that a game is being played is that the supposed objective of the encounter is never really achieved. For example, the jealous person may want to interrogate the partner, and the partner may want to be interrogated. The purported objective is to determine that no wrongdoing occurred and that there is no reason, this time, to feel jealously threatened. But the real purpose is to keep the interrogation process going to fulfill whatever needs it meets in each player. As long as it continues to benefit both players in this way, it will recur.[11]

Another indicator is that one or both players want to continue the pattern. The most obvious aspect of jealousy games is their repetitive nature. When two people keep going over the same material, making and denying the same charges, and having the same fight with identical outcomes, it is probable that a game is being played. Once the players become aware that they are in the process of playing a game, they are able to discontinue it if they want to. It takes at least two people to play games, so if one person stops the repetitive transaction, the game cannot go on.

If the behavior is similar to cops and robbers, a player could choose to get "caught" immediately. Instead of leaving suspicious clues to provoke the jealous person, the partner simply acknowledges or points out that the clue exists. If lipstick is on the collar, the partner doesn't wait for an accusation but says how it got there and offers whatever proof there is that no wrongdoing occurred. No further explanations or apologies are given. This closes the matter and ends the game.

Rather than playing "guess what?" games, the partner simply asks for the answer at the outset. If the answer is not forthcoming, the matter is dropped so that the game can no longer be played.

In "courtroom," either partner could stop the process of looking for a "judge" to make a ruling about any possible jealousy-provoking wrongdoing. If one person keeps trying to find a judge, the other behaves with indifference to any interpretations that the third party offers.

If the game is "wooden leg," one can recognize that jealousy is a problem but not let that or feelings of sympathy provide an excuse for the behaviors that often come from it. Rather than these reactions, which only result in a recurrence of the unhealthy behavior, the partner insists on doing something to cure the problem, such as demanding that they enter psychotherapy or that they terminate their relationship.

The other reason some people encourage jealousy reactions in their partners is that they are masochistic—they want to be hurt. Consciously or unconsciously, they encourage others to cause them pain. The pain may be physical or more often emotional, and it may come from one other person or several.[12]

Masochistic people find that their wishes to be hurt can be met when they form relationships with jealous partners. They conveniently become physically abused, humiliated, or emotionally traumatized when their partners begin to suspect them of infidelity. Because they want to be hurt, they learn which actions will provoke jealous confrontations and behave accordingly.

To provoke jealousy and subsequent abuse, they use the obvious devices. They try to make the jealous partner believe they are being unfaithful or desirous of becoming so. They are gone for unexpectedly long periods of time and then offer implausible excuses. They leave letters or notes addressed to, or received from, their partners' sexual rivals. They show undue interest in or flirt ostentatiously with certain members of the opposite sex. Sometimes they actually engage in affairs and permit their actions to be discovered by their jealous partners. Usually the masochistic person will go only so far as to provoke hurtful, abusive behavior in the relevant other but not so far as to result in a termination of the relationship.[13]

There are many theories to explain why people are masochistic. One explanation is that these people feel terribly guilty about some real or perceived misdeeds and seek expiation in being punished. Another is that masochistic people are unconsciously so angry at themselves for real or imagined failures that they can relieve the anger only by getting someone to hurt them. Another theory is that masochistic people have been neglected or treated with indifference during their formative years, except when being disciplined for unacceptable behavior. Such people are said to associate the punishment with some desperately needed attention. There are many other theories, too, and debate about which is the actual cause of masochism. In fact, there may be many different causes for different people, and thus, more than one of the theories may be accurate.

No matter which theory best explains the cause of masochism, there is no debate as to its widespread existence. Psychotherapists and family therapists see it daily and struggle to overcome its powerful hold on many people. Obviously, many of these people find jealous partners and encourage more of the problem. However, this does not necessarily mean that living continually with a very jealous partner indicates the presence of masochistic tendencies.

Nevertheless, many mental health professionals and laypersons believe that it is almost always a sign of masochism to go on living with anyone who is pathologically jealous and abusive. They don't accept the possibility that some people continue to live with their jealous partners only because they rationally decide they have no better alternatives.

The idea that some people enjoy the misery of living with jealous people persists even in the face of evidence to the contrary. Nonjealous partners are confronted with this idea all too often. It often takes the form of well-meaning questions, such as: "How can you put up with that?" "Why don't you leave?" "If you don't like it, why don't you kick him out?" "Admit it. You really must like it, or you'd split up, wouldn't you?"

Posing these questions isn't usually designed to be cruel or unsympathetic. They are usually asked to encourage some decisive action. Nevertheless, their implicit message is that the individual is free to leave the jealous person if his or her behavior is unacceptable. The questions imply that anyone who stays in such situations and continues to receive abuse either deserves or wants it. The following case example describes a middle-aged woman who had been asked questions of this type for many years:

Thelma entered psychotherapy because of problems related to her troubled twenty-year marriage. Thelma's husband, Rudy, was a pathologically jealous alcoholic who frequently abused her physically as well as emotionally. Understandably, she was despondent and could see no possible resolution. Early in the first session the therapist asked the obvious question: "Why do you stay with him when things seem so bad?"

She silently pondered the question for several minutes as though she had never heard it before. Finally, she answered, but it was obviously not the answer that had occupied all her immediate thoughts. "Because I love him, I guess." However, before the second session, she wrote the therapist a letter:

Dear Doctor,

I've been thinking some more about your question, "Why do I stay with my husband." I must admit it makes me angry at you for asking it. Everyone else asks me too, my kids, my friends, the people I see in Al-Anon, and at church, everyone. I thought you would be more understanding than they have been since you are a professional.

I guess I know the answer. You and they are right. I should leave. You all think I'm sick because I stay. Okay, I agree. I am sick. But there is more to it than that. If you can cure me of my sickness, maybe I'll be able to do something. But you have to cure me of a lot of other things too.

For one thing, you have to cure me of my upbringing. I'm very religious. I've been taught since I was six years old that my marriage was for all eternity. I was told it is a sin to get a divorce. I believe in my faith. It's one of the few things I've been able to count on in my life. I know lots of you therapists don't believe that marriages are forever. Most of you aren't very religious, I'll bet. You may know what you're talking about, but I think God knows a few things too. Jesus said, "If a woman leaves her husband and marries another, she is committing adultery." It's in the Bible. Mark:10:12. Look it up if you don't believe me. So you have to cure me of my upbringing, my belief in God and His Word. If I follow His Word, I might be able to get separated but I could never get married again. So you'd have to cure me of not wanting to live alone the rest of my life.

Then you have to cure me of my wanting happiness and security for my children. They are teenagers. They like their home and school and friends. Rudy would never leave, so if we separated, I'd have to be the one to go. Could I take the kids with me? We'd have to leave their home. They'd have to change schools and wouldn't be able to see their friends so often. I don't even know if they'd go with me, now. They love their father, too. He isn't usually bad to them. If I tried to take them, he'd fight for legal custody. He'd have a good chance of winning, too, because the kids might say they'd rather stay at the house. So if I left or didn't get custody of them what do you think people would conclude? Everyone would look at me like I'm a terrible person. Sure, now they say, "Why does she stay?" but then they'll say, "Why did she go?" Mothers aren't supposed to abandon their children. But people would think I did. So, doctor, you'd have to cure me of my need for approval and self-respect.

And speaking of self-respect, I don't have a lot of it now. I have lost a lost of self-confidence. I know another reason I stay is because I don't believe I can make it out there. It's hard to have self-confidence when you are told how rotten you are day after day. So you'll have to cure this too.

I would have to be cured of my fear of my husband too. You don't know about his temper. You don't know how he gets when he's been drinking and finds me gone. Do you imagine that he would just sit there if I left? Not Rudy. He'd come after me, wherever I go. But, you say, that's nothing to worry about. Just call the police. Ha. Have you ever tried to do that? I have. I've had the police over plenty of times. They come but they say they can't get involved in domestic squabbles. Maybe you should see a marriage counselor, they say. Or a lawyer about a divorce. So I'm right back where I started from.

If I could get over that fear I'd still have to get over another one. I'm really scared that if I left I wouldn't be able to support myself. I guess I need to be cured of my desire for food and shelter. I can't seem to break the habit of it. Would I starve to death or freeze, or die of humiliation in a welfare office? I'm not a young woman and I don't have marketable skills. I should have learned some, but I didn't. I worry that if I left my husband he would sue me for desertion and get everything we have. So you would have to cure me of poverty too.

And speaking of poverty, you'd have to cure me of all these things you think are crazy right away because I wouldn't be able to pay you. I suppose I can go to some free mental health clinic, but that sure gets you off the hook with your ideas about separating, doesn't it?

So, in conclusion, doctor, even though I want to resolve the problem I want you to know that there are more things to consider than just saying I'm a masochist for staying with Rudy. Besides, he's really a good person. I love him and if he didn't have this problem, he'd be the best husband there is. I'll see you next week. You have your work cut out for you. So do I.

Sincerely,
Mrs. Thelma Blank

Thelma's letter shows that there may be reasons other than self-destructiveness or masochism to explain why people remain in unhealthy jealous relationships. Thelma's and Rudy's situation turned out well, partly because he eventually consented to participate in therapy with her. She gave the therapist permission to call Rudy to ask to discuss some of his wife's problems. He was apprehensive but finally agreed to a meeting. Before long and of his own volition, he acknowledged his role in her troubles. He recognized his emotional problems and said he wanted therapy. So both of them were included in a group therapy program for couples with similar problems. Both Thelma and Rudy could see that their difficulties were not unique. They eventually became "stars" of the group, as they effectively taught their fellow members how to avoid some of the problems they themselves had undergone.

Helping the others had a positive effect on Rudy's and Thelma's perceptions of themselves. Eventually they learned to understand, communicate, and support one another more effectively and to control jealousy-based conflicts. Rudy also started going to Alcoholics Anonymous and with its help has remained sober for the past few years. They now believe their marriage is fairly sound and that together they can successfully cope with any subsequent problems.

Unfortunately, the results they achieved don't happen for everyone. Their key to success was Rudy's willingness to work on his problem. It is difficult enough to resolve these problems when everyone is motivated. It is immeasurably more so when one is not motivated. How, for example, could the issues raised in Thelma's letter have been addressed without Rudy's involvement? If he had avoided therapy, no one could really have been sure that he even had such a problem.

Not all people who read Thelma's letter would agree with its objective. Despite her arguments for preserving the marriage despite its difficulties, many thoughtful people would still say it is unhealthy to try to remain in it. Many professional psychotherapists would say this: "Why help someone stay in such a painful ordeal? That's not the way to help. Look at the person who tolerates this year after year. This person has more problems than does the jealous person. Help them restore their self-confidence and sense of worthiness. Help them learn that putting up with it is unhealthy both for themselves and for their jealous partners. If they work through their masochism they probably will want out. If they do, they will be doing themselves a favor and it will probably help the jealous person to do something to solve the problem."

After one mental health professional reviewed Thelma's letter, she remained convinced that self-destructive behavior was at the root of the problem. She granted that the letter writer was articulate and persuasive but felt she was simply rationalizing away the real issues. She said many people are equally religious but divorce in similar circumstances without worrying about an eternity in hell. She believed that Thelma was so obviously intelligent that she would be able to find employment and support herself. Her children would not suffer at their age, no matter what she did. She said she doubted that everyone would disapprove of Thelma for leaving the children and the home. And anyway, she said, so what if they did? What did they really know about the situation? And she thought the fear of Rudy's retaliation was the weakest argument of all. She felt Thelma was in far more danger living with him every day than she ever would be if she had a separate residence. Even if he came after her, he would not have the power and control over her that he did while they were in the same household.

Whatever one thinks about Thelma's situation, it is certain that different people remain in such relationships for a variety of reasons. Some may be masochistic and some may not. Some may stay in jealousy-based relationships because they want the difficulty but others do not. Most people have to base their decisions on a multitude of considerations. Their rational decisions are going to be based on social, economic, and legal circumstances as well as on psychological ones.

5

Helping One's Jealous Partner

Those who are closest to jealous people can help them achieve more productive and positive lives. Understanding and support can help a jealous partner form and maintain a more stable relationship. It can eliminate some of the jealous torment as well as the suffering it imposes on others. Despite the jealousy games some couples play, and other than those individuals discussed in the last chapter who *want* their loved ones to have jealousy problems, most people do want to help liberate their companions from the hold of jealousy.

However, a lack of knowledge about what can be done often prevents them from trying. There are, in fact, some very effective activities and techniques that can be used to provide help for pathologically jealous partners, so that they are able to maintain healthier relationships and eliminate some of the suffering they impose on others. And they can help jealous people move toward more productive and positive lives. It is the objective of this chapter to spell out some of those activities and techniques.

The word "help" is now used so loosely that its meaning is becoming obscure. It means providing assistance to, cooperating with, or contributing aid to another so that a mutually desired goal is reached. Something is done *with*, rather than *to*, the recipient. Helping is not done unilaterally. If any effort to solve a jealousy problem is forced on someone, or if the provider and the recipient aren't working together on reaching the same goals, then the effort is not so much help as it is a power play.

No one can "help" a jealous person unless help is wanted. All jealous people must share their companions' wishes to minimize or eliminate their jealousy problem. If, for example, a jealous man doesn't believe he has a problem, or if he wants to remain jealous because he thinks it benefits him, he is not being helped by his wife who wants to eliminate his jealousy. The wife would be "helping" herself—which is perfectly appropriate—but not him.

If the jealous person doesn't want to change or resists the efforts of others to help, there is, frankly, little reasonable basis for optimism. Jealousy problems are difficult enough to overcome when everyone involved is highly motivated and capable of productive effort. In that case the only options are to terminate the relationship or try to instill motivation. If the partner can get the jealous person to want to work on the problem, separation may not be necessary.

If the jealous person expresses no wish to work on the problem, with or without the help of another, then arousing the motivation to do so is the essential first step. This may seem to be an insurmountable task. Jealous people have so much guilt and low self-esteem that they can't easily acknowledge that the problem exists, is serious, and that help is needed to solve it. They protect themselves from these negative thoughts and feelings, at least temporarily, through false pride and vanity.[1]

Fortunately, whether they admit it to others or not, almost all jealous people recognize that they do have problems. They sense or are aware at some level that their behavior has caused relationships to end, loved ones to suffer, anxieties to increase, and failures to occur. Many finally recognize that their "jealousy is hell." Like most people who have emotional disturbances, they are basically unhappy with themselves and want to change. The difficulty is to admit it.[2]

To encourage such admission, the partner avoids doing anything that will cause the jealous person to lose "face" or feel additional shame or guilt. To force a jealous person into admitting the problem or making promises to improve usually only results in more defensiveness and hostility. A far more effective tack is to create a secure and comfortable environment, a positive condition in which the person will not feel threatened.[3]

The jealous person is most likely to become motivated to work on the problem and to permit help from others when

- Feeling enough self-confidence to no longer fear losing the valued possession
- Feeling guilty about one's jealous actions
- Able to empathize sincerely with those who have been hurt by the jealous behavior

- Assured that one's partner is not going to become involved with a rival
- Not frightened about the immediate prospect of losing a loved one
- Recognizing that one is genuinely loved and respected
- Permitted to feel that the problem comes from the relationship rather than defects in one's character

Spouses or partners of jealous people can be very instrumental in bringing about some or all these conditions. Primarily they can help the jealous person begin to feel more self-confident and confident about the relationship. This can be accomplished especially by being attentive and interested when the jealous person speaks. Giving undivided attention, asking questions about subjects of mutual interest, and showing the desire to be in the company of the jealous person will help immensely. Paying sincere compliments to the jealous person and doing special favors or showing little attentions are also helpful. By regularly reaffirming affection for the jealous person verbally, emotionally, and physically, the nonjealous partner will contribute significantly to the development of self-esteem and -confidence.[4]

Of course, the most effective and enduring way a person develops increased self-confidence is through growing self-awareness. The jealous person will not acquire this through the efforts of the partner as much as through reading, talking with people, comparing his or her own reactions with others, and possibly becoming involved in professional psychotherapy. But the partner's efforts will make a valuable partial contribution.

It is important that the spouse or companion of a jealous person avoids provoking shame or guilt about the problem. Many people, quite understandably, have become so angry at their jealous loved ones that they want to strike back. And because they fear the consequences of direct attacks, they often rely on subtle jibes, sarcasm, and ridicule. They hope to make their jealous partners feel so much guilt that they will be too ashamed to continue the accusations and mistreatment. Unfortunately, sarcasm and ridicule will probably have just the opposite effect. The jealous person will be more inclined toward defensiveness and anger and may be even less open-minded about the need for change.[5]

When jealous people begin to empathize with others about their problems, they also become more motivated. Their partners have been made to feel considerable pain and discomfort, and when jealous people sense this and share the feeling, the incentive to change is increased. The challenge here is to facilitate empathy rather than guilt. The partner does this by showing the hurt and pain, but not attributing its cause to the jealous person. One young woman who was in this situation helped her jealous husband become more sympathetic to her plight, as illustrated in the following case:

Rosa's five-year marriage to Julio had been troubled from the beginning by his jealous accusations. She had tried everything she could to convince him of her fidelity, but nothing seemed to work. She was angry at him but showing it only fueled his anxiety and increased his insecurity, which led to even more accusations. She started developing physical symptoms— severe headaches, depression, insomnia, and nausea—that proved to be the result of her distress. She knew that these symptoms were psychologically induced, and at first she blamed Julio for making her sick. She soon realized that this was counterproductive. He denied his role in her problem and attributed it to her feeling guilty about all the things he thought she was doing behind his back.

Rosa then took a different stance. She refrained from blaming him at all. Whenever she felt ill, she quietly withdrew from contact with Julio and stayed in the bedroom. She came out to help with the household chores to the extent that she felt capable. Whenever she felt better she would ask Julio for help, for answers to why she couldn't get better. She asked him for advice on what she could do to improve her health. She never said or even implied that he was at fault. She was only asking for his ideas because she respected his intelligence and understanding. Nothing was said about his jealousy. Julio didn't admit that he played a part in this but soon began to feel some of Rosa's pain. He didn't consciously admit that his jealousy was precipitating this pain, but he was able to go for professional help with Rosa.

The jealous person should be given no objective reason to feel threatened about the loss of the loved one or other valued "possessions." Of course, the loved one helps by refraining from activities that could be viewed as suspicious. This means there should be no serious or sexually provocative involvements with others, no flirting, and no activities that appear to lead to such encounters. It means refraining from contacts, even innocent ones, with others who could be seen as potential rivals. If jealous people have reasons, whether justified or not, for feeling threatened, it will be extremely difficult for them to want to become less jealous. If their partners are unwilling to do this, even temporarily, they cannot really expect to convince their jealous partners to feel differently.

However, in the long run, no one should have to avoid everyone or refrain from activities that might seem suspicious to a very jealous person.

In fact, the eventual goal is to help the jealous person get accustomed to the partner's behaviors. Once the motivation is there and efforts are being made to improve, these self-imposed restrictions can and should gradually be lifted.

If possible, the nonjealous partner should also minimize any fears the jealous person might have that the relationship is about to end. This is usually a considerable challenge. Reassuring promises of continued loyalty are insufficient and possibly counterproductive. If unsolicited, the promises themselves seem suspect. The jealous person will wonder why such promises are being made and possibly begin to wonder if some scheme is being perpetrated. And if the promises are made only after the jealous person demands them, they aren't very reassuring.

It is more effective to make frequent references to being together in the distant future. For example, a wife could say such things to her jealous husband as, "Oh, Derek, look at that nice old couple holding hands. I hope when we get to be that age, we still take walks together and hold hands." Or a husband could say to his jealous wife, "Say, Polly, as soon as the baby graduates, let's splurge and take an ocean cruise." This is more effective and less suspicious-sounding than, "Don't worry, I'm not planning on leaving you." It reaffirms the message that the future plan is to be together.

Helping the jealous person to feel genuinely loved and respected by the partner encourages healthy confrontation of the core problem. At the heart of jealousy lies the fear of not being loved or respected. When the jealous person is told and shown that love and respect still exist despite everything, the stage is set for work on solving the problem. But this love and respect must be genuine. Any pretense would soon be revealed and would eventually result in even more distrust and less self-confidence. It is also necessary not just to have love and respect for the jealous person but also to demonstrate them. At first the jealous person may be suspicious of this show of affection, in view of the difficulty that has existed between the couple. But if it is continuous and consistent, it is more likely to be interpreted as an honest expression of feeling.[6]

It is critical that the nonjealous partner realize that the jealousy is a shared problem even though its cause may not be shared. Because the problem is shared, its solution must come from both partners. It would be tempting and maybe even valid to blame the jealous person for the entire problem, but it is ineffective to do so. Blaming the jealous person would achieve nothing but a temporary feeling of righteousness. It would lead to increased defensiveness, which would probably be followed by the jealous person's intensified attempts to blame his/her partner. Since, however, the goal is not to blame but to make progress, the partner could stress that blame is irrelevant and that both people need to work together. "It is a problem we share," says the jealous person's spouse or companion, "and we both have to work equally hard to solve it."

When jealous people decide to cooperate with their partners in working on the problem, improvement is possible. However, any improvements that can be achieved are going to be gradual and incremental. It would be an unrealistic goal to strive for basic and permanent changes in the jealous person's personality. A more realistic goal is simply to improve the relationship. This means improving patterns of communication, defusing hostility, and achieving more clear understandings.[7]

Most couples with jealousy problems have to go through several gradual stages on their way to improved relationships. Most of them must first overcome their tendency to become withdrawn or isolated from one another. Couples who have had serious jealousy conflicts often cope by trying to ignore or avoid one another. This behavior may be exhibited by either the jealous person, the partner, or both. They may act sullen and sulk or pout whenever the other is near or they each remain silent, especially in each other's presence, and often refuse to talk even when asked direct questions. This mutual withdrawal was experienced by Stacy and Louis:

Stacy was fed up. She had been accused, threatened, suspected, and abused by Louis for years. She had tried for most of that time to reason with her husband and convince him that his worries were groundless. As her efforts proved to be futile, she gradually stopped defending herself. When Louis suspiciously asked her where she had been, she gave indifferent, perfunctory answers. She avoided him whenever possible, spoke only when addressed, and refused to respond to any jealous behavior. When he accused her of anything, she shrugged with apathy and said nothing. He even slapped her and got no response. Stacy grew more aloof, and as she did she realized that she had found a more effective way of dealing with her husband and establishing some power over the situation.

Louis was puzzled. He did everything he could think of to get her to talk but to no avail. His suspiciousness and anger intensified at first but soon gave way to his own version of withdrawal. He rarely stayed in the same room with Stacy, began sleeping in another room, and ate his meals when she was out of the kitchen. The problem with jealousy seemed to be over, but it had been replaced by a relationship that might have been even worse, an "empty-shell marriage."

Such behavior has several purposes. For some it is a way of avoiding physical violence from the other. One of the partners has learned that anything said leads the other to hitting or throwing things or making serious threats. The behavior is also used to make the partner feel guilty. To disdain any communication is a form of rejection, a way of fighting back. Thus, it is a way of trying to control one's partner or to even the balance of power. Another purpose of isolational behavior is to permit the person to regain some self-control. The nonjealous person may feel so angry or threatened by the partner that violence would be the result if any response at all were permitted. So, to keep from hurting the other person or losing control of the situation, the individual closes off communication.[8]

Resuming communication is the basic goal. If this is achieved, it will certainly not solve all the problems of the relationship. In fact, it may lead the couple to assume the situation has worsened. Whereas their isolation was at least peaceful if not happy, what they are now communicating is unpleasant. But this is a step that must be taken before improvements can occur. Better communication will create an atmosphere in which the parties can begin to understand one another.

The cold aloofness that exists in isolational behavior is usually broken by the nonjealous partner. Someone has to do it, and the jealous person is usually too rigid and stubborn to initiate such actions. Initiating communication will seem difficult and risky, because it may mean giving up relative calm for more confrontations, with no guarantee that the jealousy will abate. But the nonjealous partner must eventually try. If the willingness to make this attempt is absent, it is unlikely that positive movement will ever occur.

Working toward better communications with a jealous person poses some special challenges. Many jealous people seem to speak or hear somewhat differently than do others, especially in regard to jealousy issues. The jealous person may use the same words as the partner uses, but they can have different meanings and can be interpreted differently by each. (Linguistic researchers have demonstrated that language sometimes fails to permit clear communication when the participants have different perspectives, cultural orientations, values, or personality characteristics.) An example is seen in the way Alma and Gordon discussed their jealousy concerns.

Alma remained very close to her parents even after marrying Gordon. He rarely found her at home when he returned from work, but he was sure to find her at her parents' home. Often when she was with Gordon, she would be on the phone with her parents. Already inclined toward jealousy and possessiveness, Gordon became even more so. He resented that he was being excluded and feared that Alma had no love left for him. When they entered marital therapy, their sessions were videotaped. The following is an excerpt (slightly edited) from an early session:

Gordon: You never spend any time with me anymore.

Alma: I do too. I don't do anything but spend time with you.

Gordon: Are you calling me a liar, right in front of the doctor?

Alma: No, but I'm with you almost all the time. I don't go anywhere except to Mom and Dad's.

Gordon: That's somewhere. You're there with them a lot more than you're here with me.

Alma: Well, I love them, and they need me.

Gordon: Don't you think I do too? Does that mean you don't love me?

Alma: Yes, I . . . I mean, No . . . Wait, I'm confused. What are you talking about? I think you're just jealous of my folks.

Gordon: So what? You're my wife, so why don't you act like it?

Alma: I do.

Gordon: Oh, so it's just an act, huh?

There were many other exchanges like this between Alma and Gordon. Part of the therapy was for them to review the videotapes they had made so that they could better envision how they were talking with one another at cross-purposes. In therapy it was eventually learned that Alma's overinvolvement with her parents probably occurred because she had not achieved enough autonomy and individuation by the time she married.

It was also apparent that Gordon's jealousy and rigid thinking made it difficult for clear communication and understanding to develop. Watching their interaction patterns on the videotape enabled them to see how they could speak more clearly and without so much defensiveness.

One of the special communications problems found in many jealous people is that they tend to hear and speak more rigidly than do others. They tend to see and think in "black and white" and have little comprehension of subtleties. Jealous people are more likely to take communications literally. A jealous person and a relevant other could essentially be speaking different languages without realizing it. When the partner talks about relationships and emotions that are complex and filled with shades of meaning, the talk might as well be in Latin. This leaves room for misunderstandings and miscommunications that can lead to more accusations and confrontations.[9]

The nonjealous partner must remember to match words with thoughts by communicating more precisely and without subtle meanings. If this is kept in mind, the communication will improve. It may also improve if the jealous partner realizes that the spouse or companion is making an effort to understand and be understood.

Once the jealous person's spouse or partner understands these communications problems, the next step toward ending the isolational relationship is to try to break the impasse. The spouse or partner of the jealous person starts simply by proposing a resumption of talk. The suggestion is made directly that they schedule a future time to spend fifteen to thirty minutes just talking about the good aspects of their relationship. The recommendation is to talk—not immediately but in a few days, after both have had time to think about what they plan to say.

The idea is for them to teach themselves that talking can be fun. Their recent talks have been negative and filled with problems, so both have wanted to avoid them. Once communication is pleasurable again, the couple will be less apprehensive about getting together. Later they can begin working on their problems.

Jealous people will probably be surprised by and apprehensive about such a proposal. They will want to know immediately what their partners have in mind. They may want to begin the talk right away. Otherwise they will feel anxious and fearful that some bombshells are going to be dropped, and their jealousy might increase.

Even though this response is predictable, it is best that the nonjealous partners resist the temptation to begin the discussion immediately. Instead, they provide reassurance of their love and reiterate that they only desire to return to better communication. They may need to stress that the intent is only to improve the relationship and that no separations or other changes are contemplated. The following dialogue illustrates how one wife got her husband to agree to such a talk:

Lee: Jerry, you look really good in that shirt. I like it a lot.

Jerry: [Looking up from paper] Umm? Oh, yeah, me too.

Lee: Jer', before the kids get back from practice I want to ask you something.

Jerry: What? Why? What's the matter now?

Lee: Nothing's wrong, especially. In fact, things have been pretty nice between us these last few days. I want to thank you for being so nice. I love you so much when. . . .

Jerry: C'mon, quit beating around the bush. What's up? What do you want?

Lee: [Smiling] You know me pretty well, don't you? Well, I think we should start talking again. Not about problems, just good things.

Jerry: [Sitting up and looking more serious] Why? What's wrong? What are you up to?

Lee: I'm not up to anything. I just think we ought to talk about us. It seems like the only time we talk is when we're fighting. That's not a good time to really look at ourselves. So I thought we should do it when we're getting along.

Jerry: Well, I don't like the sound of this. What's really going on? Are you going to admit that stuff about Norm? Is that what this is about? What've you got up your sleeve?

Lee: Nothing, Jer'. I don't have anything to admit about Norm, like I told you a hundred times before. I'm just trying to say that I love you and want to be with you forever, and I just think we need to talk things over now and then so we can make sure we can be happy together always.

Jerry: Oh, well, we'll see if that's true. So what do you want to talk about? Let's hear it.

Lee: Not now. Right now I just want for us to agree to talk within the next week or so.

Jerry: What's wrong with right now? You sound like you're just putting off telling me some bad news. Come on, let's talk.

Lee: No, I want to wait. The kids will be home soon, and I don't want us to be interrupted. And I haven't thought of all the things I want to say yet. And you ought to take some time to think of the things you want to say, too. Okay?

Jerry: I don't have anything to say, except that I don't like whatever it is you're doing right now. Who put you up to this?

Lee: No one. I just think we need to set aside some time without interruptions and talk about some good things between us. With none of those accusations, so we can learn to communicate better.

Jerry: Yeah, I guess. Okay, but I'm warning you, if it's bad and you're not telling me now . . . well, we'll see. When do you want to have this talk?

Lee: You pick the time, and I'll be there.

The purpose of the meeting will not be to resolve the couple's difficulties but to break the ice, to establish an environment more conducive to communication. The only goal is to make it pleasant and positive so that they will be less reluctant to talk again.

There are many things they might discuss to keep the discussion positive. They might reminisce about happy experiences they once shared. They could discuss some of the hopes they have for their future together. They could enumerate all the things they like about one another. Whatever the subject, they should try to keep it relaxed and humorous. If they find themselves starting to talk about potential problem areas, they should change the subject.

If the meeting stays positive, it will have to end before either person wants it to. Nevertheless, the exercise will be more successful if they maintain their schedule and stop on time. It is obviously better to end the talk on a pleasant note, because this will motivate them for another meeting in the future. If they continued, they would probably get into negative discussions and the meeting would conclude unhappily. They would be convinced that future talks would also become painful and go on endlessly, regardless of how much time was agreed to in the beginning. This would give them a convenient and valid excuse for avoiding any future meetings.

If they stay with their plan, they will have more chances for additional positive talks. Soon the talks could be planned on a regular, perhaps weekly, basis. After several weeks one of the partners might decide that the talks are good but that there is nothing left to say. If this happens, the couple could spend one of their talk times deciding on topics of discussion for the future, with each talk focusing on a single subject. With advance notice, both partners would have some time to prepare themselves for these meetings. These talks—during which they might exchange views on such topics as the children's future, their own goals, politics, religion, the economy, sports, current events, and so on—could include almost anything but their relationship problems.

If the jealous person's partner has difficulty finding the right time to initiate this activity, it is time for some self-assessment. He or she may believe that something always takes precedence: The partner's mood is not right, everyone is too busy, there is no privacy, dinner has to be prepared, and so on. If this continues, it is probably because the partner fears the jealous person's reaction and feels safer not talking and thus not risking more accusations and problems. Obviously, however, a time *can* be found, since the proposal should only take a few minutes to initiate, and the talk can be limited to fifteen minutes or so if necessary.

If the nonjealous partner proposes the talks and the jealous companion is too apprehensive or afraid, some additional preliminary considerations are necessary. There is a need to work harder to create a calm and pleasant atmosphere. This can be done by changing one's own isolational behavior. Becoming more vocal and expansive is in order—for example, the nonjealous partner could tell more jokes, relate more recently heard happy stories, and encourage more talk about the jealous person's interests. The partner could also look happier whenever the jealous person is nearby, sing or hum whenever possible, and laugh aloud at television programs they watch together.

The nonjealous partner may also suggest that they have some fun together. Any physically taxing activity is preferred because it can discharge some of their tensions, and cooperative physical activities are better than competitive ones. (Competition puts the jealous person at risk of losing face, which would not help make things more positive.) Cooperative physical activities include taking walks together, bicycling, doing yard work or housework together, and jogging. Less taxing activities that also emphasize cooperation include doing crossword or jigsaw puzzles; cooking a special meal, following an intricate recipe neither partner has tried before; or building a model ship or plane. These take energy, are productive and not competitive, and usually don't lead to jealousy problems.

Further to encourage an environment for positive movement, nonjealous partners must be sure to avoid any of the behaviors that have led to troubles in the past. They must be especially careful about dishonesty or deceitfulness and any behaviors that appear to ridicule the jealous partners.

Deceit is difficult to avoid because it seems so necessary to keeping the peace. All deceitful behavior—including lies, making up excuses, withholding information, telling half truths, and so on—happens so regularly that the partner almost becomes unaware of it. But deceit, in whatever form, does not help in the long run; at best it only postpones confrontations. When they do occur, the deceptiveness may become part of the controversy. The experience of Gunther, the insurance salesman, illustrates this.

Selling insurance was no job for a man with a jealous wife. Gunther learned this the hard way in the early years of his marriage to Hannah. His meetings with women, especially in the evenings, were extremely threatening to his wife. Hannah insisted on a detailed accounting of every transaction that took place between him and his female customers. She seemed to need constant reassurance of his loyalty to her. Yet his work required him to visit many potential customers, including single women, in their homes.

After a few years he learned to be less candid about his contacts with his female customers. He didn't volunteer any information about them to his wife, knowing it would upset her. Instead, he always told her he had an appointment with a man or a couple. When Hannah occasionally seemed doubtful about his whereabouts and questioned him closely, he insisted that he was not seeing any single women. He didn't realize that his wife was secretly checking his appointment book. She was well aware of the people he visited. One day she accused him of seeing other women during his sales appointments. He denied it to validate his previous claims. Her response was to tell him what she knew and to say that she could no longer trust him. She threatened to leave him unless he changed jobs. Gunther had to choose between his wife and his career. He decided to get another job but got Hannah to enter marital therapy with him. Eventually, their marriage grew stronger and both became more secure. However, Gunther never attempted to test their relationship and continues to avoid meeting other women alone.

Lies become complicated. Even if they are never acknowledged, the atmosphere and relationship still have a tone of dishonesty, and both partners will probably sense this at some conscious or unconscious level. When this is the case, the jealous person becomes more skeptical about everything and it is hard to remember what was said that caused one to avoid discussion. So, while an actual fight might be delayed, the result is more isolational behavior. Deceit causes confusion and prevents honest communication; it causes more distancing between the couple. And if the lies are discovered, as will probably happen, one will be distrusted much more in the future. The nonjealous partner who is honest will encounter some problems at first but will avoid many more serious ones in the long run.

Avoiding the temptation to ridicule is also important for the partner who wants to create a more positive environment. Sarcasm, teasing, joking about the jealous partner, and revealing the jealousy problem to others are especially counterproductive. Many who are committed to jealous partners use sarcasm and ridicule as a way of expressing their anger and frustration. Understandably, they need outlets for these feelings and use these methods to ventilate them. However, there are better ways of letting off steam. Anything done to get back at the partner—any ridicule or activity that causes the jealous person loss of face—will cause more pain than it will alleviate. Because jealous people tend to think in concrete and rigid terms, they won't find much humor in such behavior, and because their self-concepts are fragile, they feel threatened by teasing or ridicule.

If these behaviors are applied long and consistently enough, most couples will become less isolated and more communicative. Some may even overcome their basic antagonisms. Others, feeling freer to express themselves, may engage in more hostile actions than occurred during their isolational phase. Even so, this is an improvement in the relationship and represents progress toward resolving the problem. To outside observers, becoming more antagonistic and confrontative may seem anything but an improvement. Silence and cold aloofness may seem preferable to loud vocal arguments and possibly physical abuse, violence, and destructiveness. Cold silence is safer than violence, especially for those who get the worst of the encounter, but it doesn't permit any progress to be made. In the long run, much greater likelihood toward improvement exists when aloofness is ended, even if it is risky.

Antagonism represents the potential for movement because the couple has started to communicate and interact. They are connecting and have reestablished an awareness of each other's presence and behavior, even though they may not like what they see. When they face the problem rather than avoid it, they encounter more immediate unpleasantness but have more ability to resolve the problem later.

When confrontations and arguments become the norm in jealous relationships, the basic objective of the nonjealous partner is to control and minimize the intensity of disagreements. It is not realistic or productive to assume that disagreements can be avoided in jealous relationships. This would only mean that the pair has reverted to isolational behavior. Disputes need to be discussed; what is productive is to find ways to keep them from getting out of hand or severely hurtful.[10]

Many of those who live with jealous people feel they can't get anywhere because they are afraid of the consequences. They justifiably fear that if they bring up problems, they will be subjected to violence and physical abuse by their partners. Or they fear that the discussion will just keep going and the issues will be brought up repeatedly at inopportune times in the future. Yet it is necessary to discuss their problems in order for progress to be made.

They can achieve this by agreeing to talk about the problems while following certain rules for discussion. One rule is to put a time limit on their meetings and when they are over, to get away from one another for a while. Another rule is to minimize the buildup of anger that comes from give-and-take arguments. In other words, if the two people take turns talking about all their concerns, each listening to the other without interruption, it can reduce the heat. It can also permit both to express themselves fully without immediate intimidation from the other.

Meetings of this type are a good way for antagonistic couples to let off steam, express themselves, hear the other person's point of view, and limit the extent of the controversy. But they are effective only if all the rules are followed. Instruction sheets similar to the following have been used successfully by marital therapists to make sure couples understand the rules of these conferences.[11]

HOW TO SETTLE CONFLICTS FAIRLY WITH YOUR SPOUSE

Make an appointment to have a conference. The time should not be immediate. Ideally, it should occur between twenty-four- and seventy-two-hours after someone asks for it. This gives both of you equal time to think about what you're going to say. That way you'll both speak more thoughtfully.

Put a time limit on the discussion. Decide in advance how long you'll talk and stick to it, no more and no less. One hour is enough for most people. Be sure to stop when the time is up. If you don't, the boundaries are fuzzy and the discussion will spill over into areas that might be better dealt with later.

Have the discussion where there are no distractions. Distractions dilute the impact of the talk. No one beside the two of you should ever hear what has been said. So a place like a restaurant, with all its interruptions from waiters and visual distractions, is no good. The home may be the best place if no one else is around. That means there should be no chance of children or others eavesdropping or entering the room unexpectedly. There should be no radio or TV playing in the background and no reading matter to catch someone's eye. This rule about privacy is very important, because you are seeking honesty and openness with one another.

Both of you should have equal time to present your positions. If the total time you agreed to was an hour, each of you has the other's undivided attention for thirty minutes. The first speaker fills that time without interruption or even feedback. The listener says nothing at all for thirty minutes, even if the speaker wants him or her to talk. Both of you can speak on any subject. If you have no more to say, you still keep the floor, saying nothing until the time is up. Then the other one has the next half hour, with the same rules. The second speaker need not respond to what the first one has said but may do so.

When the time is up, both of you should go away from one another for at least fifteen minutes. You should avoid discussing any topics that were included in the conference for at least two hours. This defines boundaries. It keeps problems from spilling over into the rest of your lives. If you argue during the conference, you will feel better knowing that the conflict will end when the conference ends.

Agree that everything said in the conference remains confidential until you both agree to make it open. This means you can say anything without losing face with others. You can share deeper feelings than would be possible if you thought others might hear about them.

Anything that was discussed during the conference that seems to cause heated controversy should not be talked about at least until the next conference. This helps both of you feel safer about what is brought up. It can mean that the material won't be used against you at some later time.

If you have several sessions like this, take turns in setting the agenda. Decide what you want to discuss during the next session. Then let your partner pick the topics for the next, and so on. There are several advantages to this. You'll have a chance to say what's on your mind without interruption. That way your partner will finally hear your point of view and you will also hear what's on his or her mind. Neither of you will have to defend yourself or justify your actions, since you don't have to respond to the other's questions. You'll have a better chance of keeping the conflicts from getting into other areas of your life if you stop the meeting on time and step away from each other for a while.

If both partners adhere to the rules of this discussion, they can work through their antagonistic feelings without causing undue harm. They can reveal some of their negative feelings with reduced fear of problems in the future. They can call for this type of meeting whenever they feel tension is rising. It is used to keep communications going with minimum risk.

It also helps if the nonjealous partner uses timing wisely. The time to suggest having a discussion about the problem is not when a jealousy argument is in progress or even when it seems about to begin. It should be proposed when there is relative peace and there has not been a problem with jealousy for some time. This is hard to do because no one really wants to interrupt the peace for anything that might jeopardize it—and there is reasonable fear that requesting such a meeting will do just that. Nevertheless, the discussion should be proposed when the jealous person is as secure as possible and when the anxiety level is at its lowest.

Of course, the nonjealous partner can do other practical things to control mutual antagonism. Obviously, many activities that traditionally led to problems in the relationship can be avoided. For example, if the jealous person is threatened by the possibility of losing the loved one to a rival, the rival could be avoided, especially when tension seems to be increasing. If the fear is loss of control over the loved one, this can be abated by continuing to provide assurances that there is no intention of doing anything to cause pain.

Another response often used to deal effectively with hostility is to stay involved with the jealous person and avoid withdrawing, no matter how strong the temptation. In other words, the nonjealous partner remains in the same room, talks, asks and answers questions, and generally encourages verbal exchanges. When accusations are leveled, the nonjealous partner merely denies any wrongdoing, minimizes the conflict to the extent possible, and continues communicating as much as necessary. When this goal is in effect, the only time to leave the presence of the jealous person is when the threat of violence is great. In that case withdrawal is essential, but only until the situation has become less explosive. Then there is resumption of contact and continuation of communication, almost as though nothing had happened.

When activity like this is effective, the relationship will eventually evolve from isolation through antagonism into something more positive. This new phase permits the couple to reexamine what it is they want and expect from one another. When the expectations are clarified and made explicit, both partners have a better opportunity to resolve disputes. For example, a jealous husband may believe that his wife should have no independence whatsoever. He may think that wives are supposed to account for their whereabouts at all times and to get their husbands' permission for everything they want to do. He doesn't say that this is his expectation but becomes very angry whenever his wife doesn't meet it. The nonjealous wife, on the other hand, expects her husband to encourage her to be more independent. She doesn't tell him this is what she expects but is distressed whenever he doesn't meet her expectation. Both are angry with each other without really knowing why. Yet there is no hope of improvement until they redefine their mutual expectations. The necessity of doing so is seen in the experience of Brandon and Laura.

Second marriages are fertile grounds for jealousy problems, especially when the newer spouse is insecure. Laura was Brandon's second wife, and she worried obsessively about her predecessor. He was an extremely wealthy physician, and she had been his receptionist when their affair started. When it was eventually discovered, Brandon ambivalently divorced his wife, Dana, and soon thereafter married Laura.

Even though Laura took some temporary satisfaction from the feeling that she had been chosen over Dana, she couldn't stop fearing her. Dana was very beautiful and popular, a highly successful businessperson, and she did not appreciate the way her marriage had ended. Laura worried that Dana would try to take Brandon back. She dwelt on this idea almost continuously and interrogated Brandon relentlessly about Dana and his former and current relationship with her. She wanted to know how Dana made love, how she entertained, how she cooked meals, how she dressed. Laura soon found herself acting as much like Dana as possible. Everything Dana had, she wanted.

Laura was also threatened by the time Brandon continued to spend with Dana. They shared custody of their children and often met while discussing aspects of their upbringing. Laura hated these encounters and insisted that they end. Brandon explained why this was impossible. Laura's personality was volatile, and when Brandon refused her demands she threw temper tantrums. Brandon paid no attention to these outbursts even though he secretly planned to do everything possible to assure to Laura that he would remain loyal to her. He would pay her more attention, buy her anything she wanted, and make her life wonderful.

Nevertheless Laura's jealousy grew, and it compelled her to check up on Brandon. She secretly monitored his telephone calls and followed him when he said he had to go to the hospital to make his rounds. For many weeks she could find no evidence that he was seeing Dana. But finally she found the clue she had sought. It happened on the day she thought it was least likely to happen, her own birthday. She saw Dana's car parked in the back parking lot at Brandon's office. Laura immediately recognized the car, a very expensive and flashy convertible. She had often complained to Brandon that Dana had such a fine car while she was driving a junk heap. No doubt they were in the office consummating their affair, probably in the same place where she and Brandon had once cheated on Dana.

Laura was enraged. Removing the tire iron from her own car she ran to the other car and began smashing it with all her strength. She broke all its glass, dented all its metal, and ripped all the upholstery. The car was almost demolished before Laura began to feel better. She didn't care what Brandon or Dana thought by the time she had finished.

Later that night, a dejected Brandon came home. "Happy birthday, honey," he mumbled. "I have terrible news. I wanted to surprise you with a fantastic present. I bought you a new car, just like that one Dana has. I know how much you envied her that car and figured you wouldn't like any other kind as much. I picked it up during lunch hour and hid it at the office. But while it was there, some vandals came by and just destroyed it! Isn't that awful? I'd sure like to get my hands on the sick weirdo who would do such a thing."

Eventually Brandon and Laura's marriage ended in divorce. It was handicapped by the jealousy problem and by the fact that they did not have reasonable and clear expectations of one another. Laura made demands that Brandon couldn't realistically meet, and she expressed her wishes with such hostility that few would want to meet them even if they could. Brandon, on the other hand, did not specify what he wanted from his wife. He tended to do things without consulting her, which compounded her jealous fears. Had they remained together, their major challenge would have been to become more open, reasonable, and flexible about their expectations.

In clarifying and redefining expectations, both partners negotiate new rules and expectations. They clearly specify what they think is tolerable and intolerable behavior in the other person. For example, each might say how they want the other to behave around members of the opposite sex. They could agree that the same rules, whatever they are, should apply equally to both. When there is a clear understanding of the boundaries or limits of acceptable behavior, the jealous person's fears can be vastly relieved.[12]

The effort to redefine and clarify mutual expectations begins when the couple has decided to learn why their relationship is troubled. They now want to do more than merely communicate pleasantries and control their anger. When they look seriously at their relationship, they realize that much of their problem stems from each not knowing what the other expects or knowing but being unwilling or unable to meet those expectations.

People often argue about their partners' unacceptable behaviors without making it clear what they want or find acceptable. They believe the others should somehow know what is in their minds and that their failure to do so indicates a lack of love and respect. They maintain hidden agendas and feel aggrieved when their partners don't conform.

Complicating this further is the fact that the rules and ideas about what both partners want often change. Each spouse or partner in a relationship naturally has different expectations and beliefs from one day to the next about what is to be considered reasonable behavior. The expectations will change as new information and experiences are acquired. If the other has not had those same experiences or information, the expectations can't be modified accordingly unless the expectations have been spelled out. The spouse or partner may not even realize that the expectations have been changed by the other. Thus, it is important to clarify them periodically by reviewing and renewing what they are. The example of Leon and Naomi illustrates the problem of unclear expectations and efforts to redefine what they are.

Naomi, who was an elementary school teacher, also spent a considerable amount of time working in her children's Cub Scouts and Camp Fire Girls organizations. Most evenings she and the children attended or hosted meetings with other youngsters. Leon was much less sociable. He preferred quiet evenings and weekends, watching TV or working on the lawn. With such disparate life-styles, both spouses were becoming increasingly angry and frustrated with each other and were growing ever more distant.

When they first married, Naomi had tended to be somewhat possessive and jealous and felt more comfortable about Leon's preference for quiet and solitary living. Leon, in the early years of their relationship, wanted her to leave him alone. He felt crowded, as though he never had any time for himself because he was always having to attend to Naomi.

Eventually their expectations began to change. Naomi became more secure in her profession and knew she had much to contribute. She no longer felt possessive or jealous of Leon and in fact began to feel frustrated with his apathy about becoming involved in activities in the community. Leon was also becoming frustrated. He started feeling less secure about the relationship and commensurately more possessive. He wondered if she was always where she claimed to be. When other adults visited, he would later accuse Naomi of improper behavior with them. He resented the amount of time and money that was spent on his kids' organizations. He couldn't understand how he could be jealous of his own children, much less his wife who was always with them.

They began to argue with increasing frequency and violence, interspersed by periods of silent coldness. For a while he was venting his anger by screaming obscenities at Naomi and by severely punishing the children for the most minor of infractions. That only seemed to make things worse. So whenever he wasn't openly expressing anger, he was in a silent, non-communicative rage. "What's the matter?" Naomi would ask. "Nothing," was his response.

Often, when Leon would get sullen, Naomi became so frustrated that she began throwing vases and punches at Leon. Just as often he would do the same to her. Frequently they would attempt to make allies of their children. Their fights would often occur in front of the children and would be punctuated by such remarks as, "See what your mother just did? Now do you see why I have to treat her this way?"

They consented to marital therapy only after Naomi had told Leon she wanted a divorce. She said she felt they had nothing in common and that their marriage was an empty shell. He accused her of wanting to leave him because she was interested in someone else. She denied this but said she could easily become interested if she found someone who wanted to do something with his life besides vegetate. It was in therapy that they both realized how little they knew about what the other wanted. The immediate goal was to make clear what each wanted and expected from the relationship and from each other.

One method that helps to clarify expectations in jealous couples is for each person to write down what he or she thinks the other expects as well as to write down what he or she expects of the other. Partial listings of expectations that Leon and Naomi prepared in their therapist's office are as follows:

WHAT I THINK *Leon* EXPECTS OF ME

1. You seem to expect me to have no friends.
2. You don't want me to spend time in my organizations.
3. You want me to be home whenever you are there.
4. You want me to provide a witness to verify where I've been.

WHAT I THINK <u>Naomi</u> EXPECTS OF ME

1. You want me to leave you alone so you can run around on me.
2. You want me to give you all my money to spend, no questions asked.
3. You don't want me to do anything I won't let you do.
4. You want me to get out with the guys more often.

There were more than twenty additional items on Leon's and Naomi's lists. It was a revealing experience when they shared them with one another. Both said, about many items, that they had no such expectations at all. Then both asked what made the other believe these expectations existed.

The next step is for the couple to write down what they think should be reasonably expected of the other. Each person itemizes a statement that begins, "I want [Leon or Naomi] to. . . . " Neither looks at the other's list until it is completed.

When they have finished, they compare and combine. It is understood that the same rules apply to both, so eventually there will be a single list of explicit expectations. There will be many items that will be identical. The couple can make those "official" and agree to honor them. The other items should be discussed one by one. Some can be restated to make it possible to include them in the official list. Others will seem so unreasonable once they are discussed that both will agree to discard them. Some items will be discarded because one of the partners wants it to apply to the other but not to him- or herself. Some will not become official because the couple cannot reach agreement.

The final list, the official one, becomes the set of rules or guidelines to which the couple can subsequently refer. In disputes they can look at the list and determine who has violated it. They may add or subtract items from the list as time progresses, but they can continue to use it as the basis for clarifying many of their disputes.

It is important that each item on both lists is stated specifically, understandably, and realistically. That is, whatever is on the list should be within the ability of each person to achieve without extraordinary effort. Some people include such vague or grandiose items on their list that they are not worthwhile. Such statements as, "I want Naomi to win the Nobel Peace Prize so that she won't have to keep trying to prove herself to everyone"

are useless. It is also useless to write statements that are unrealistic or im-
practical. It would not help to write such statements as "My goal is to help
Leon so that he is never angry at me again. I want him to experience life
to the fullest every day and enjoy lots of people in his life." Nor would it
be useful to write, "I want Naomi to quit work so we can move to Hawaii,
where we wouldn't have any more problems."

The list that Leon and Naomi completed and agreed on was developed
after they discussed all the possible items and clarified or eliminated those
that were unclear, unachievable, or undesirable to both. The following
items were included in their list:

WHAT WE EXPECT OF EACH OTHER

1. There will be no hitting or physical intimidation of any sort, regardless of the provocation.
2. All arguments, confrontations, or accusations, will occur in private.
   The children will be sent away or the discussion will be postponed
   until no one else is able to hear it.
3. Both of us will state clearly what we want from the other. If we don't
   say, in words or in writing, what we want, then we will not be unhappy with the other for not knowing or acting on it.
4. There will be a one-hour time limit on every argument. Early in the
   argument one person will remind both of the time remaining. At the
   end of the hour, nothing is to be said about the issues raised in the
   argument for at least twenty-four hours.
5. At least one evening per week we will do something fun together.
   During this fun time no jealousy issues will be raised. Each person
   gets to choose the activity on alternate weeks and the other will participate. If for any reason this date cannot be kept, there will be a
   makeup date within two weeks, which will not replace the regularly
   scheduled fun time.
6. At least once per month, in the fun time if desired, we will socialize
   with another couple. We will not criticize one another's behavior
   with this couple during or after the meeting.
7. We will continue to work with the marital therapist until all three of
   us agree that we have reached our goals.

No two couples could or should have the same agreements. They must
be arrived at jointly and based on their unique problems and needs. When
they are clearly specified, they clarify the issues and provide more focus to

the work. They are intended to define the boundaries of the problem so that the issue does not spill over into every other area of the couple's life. As goals, they cannot always be reached but they provide a standard toward which the couple is working. Both parties agreed to the terms in advance, so the list provides some structure that would otherwise not exist, even though the terms are strictly enforceable.

One way to help couples better understand the expectations of their partners is to use the "role reversal" technique. This procedure is frequently used by couples under the guidance of marital therapists. It is hard for many couples to do it on their own, but others report considerable success with it. Basically, each partner is asked to pretend to be the other person and conduct an argument. Here is how therapists might instruct their clients to do it:

> Ask your partner to remember an incident that was upsetting to both of you. It can be a jealousy-based incident that led to a fight. Now each of you pretend you are the other person. Relive the argument from the other person's point of view. Say what your partner said. Accuse or defend just as before, only be the other person. Put feeling into it. Do what your partner did. Keep the argument going as long as you can. Now do it again. Continue playing the role of your partner. Only this time, speak and act as you think your partner *should* have behaved.
>
> After you have done this both times, discuss the feelings you had while the performance was going on. You will learn something about yourself and your partner. You will experience how it feels to be in the other person's shoes. It will help you know better how to understand and please your partner and yourself.

The activities described so far are designed to help couples in jealous relationships become more communicative, less hostile, and more clear about their expectations. These are important and worthwhile objectives, but they really aren't sufficient for controlling the jealousy problem itself. They set the stage for, but don't actually accomplish, reduction of the jealousy behavior.

The most effective, enduring way to resolve jealousy problems is to help the jealous person become desensitized to perceived threats. This can be accomplished by gradually exposing the jealous person to increasingly threatening events that do not result in the feared consequence. The goal is to help the jealous person become inured to the events that once caused such distress, and to achieve flexibility and self-understanding.[13]

The nonjealous partner can find experiences that gently expose the other to jealous situations. A suggestion that they see a movie or television show together that has a jealousy theme is one possibility. This is followed by a discussion of the show. This process is repeated with other shows and novels, and hopefully each one can be a little more intense.

At other times the spouse or partner in the relationship can gently call the jealous person's attention to the way couples are coping with jealousy experiences wherever they are seen. This must be done without any negative or guilt-provoking tone, or it loses its purpose. It is crucial to keep the jealous person feeling comfortable about these reminders.

Another activity is to bring the jealous person into greater contact with others who share the problem. Some people seek out other couples who have jealousy problems so that they can compare notes about how to handle them. The jealous person can be shown that others have different responses to situations that cause difficulties. Of course, this poses a different challenge. Because their inclination is to conceal the problem from others, many jealous people will be extremely reluctant to participate in formal or specifically designated groups of this type. Nevertheless, some spouses and partners of jealous people have been able to convince their loved ones to participate. When this happens there are usually desirable outcomes.

The next step must be taken with extreme caution and, wherever possible, under professional supervision. It should never be attempted until after all previous steps have been completed successfully. The spouse or partner gradually increases the jealousy threat, followed by even more support and positive response to the jealous person. Gradually, the jealous person becomes used to a freer and less controlled life-style. Here is a schedule used by Leon and Naomi to accomplish some of this. Each activity occurred every day for a week. In addition to the activities scheduled, some are occasionally repeated in subsequent weeks.

Week	Activity
1.	Naomi tells Leon she will be staying late at work one hour every night this week. When she comes home he is displeased but doesn't complain. Naomi is extra pleasant and attentive to him.
2.	Naomi asks Leon to accompany her every evening to a scout meeting. Leon declines. She calls him from the meeting every night and is attentive to him when she is with him.
3.	Naomi invites another couple over for dinner. She talks to

Leon every day for a week about the couple, especially the man. Leon accuses her of inappropriate interest in him. She praises Leon for being so much better with his jealousy.

4. Naomi tells Leon she is going over to spend the evening at the home of the other couple. She invites him to come. He grudgingly consents. She behaves as though she is much prouder of and more interested in her husband than in the other man.

There were many more weeks involved in the process used by Naomi and Leon, but they are not included here because they apply only to their specific situation. Each couple has to develop a schedule based on their unique goals or targets. During these times it is to be expected that the jealous person will be somewhat edgy and uncomfortable. The key is for the partner to continue the behavior while showing great support and consideration to the jealous partner. If the jealous person is not tolerating the behavior well, the nonjealous partner can revert to a less-pressured level of behavior until the jealous person seems more comfortable. After some stability is reached in the situation, the nonjealous partner can again resume the desensitizing activity.

To accomplish such goals using the techniques described here requires a great deal of patience and tolerance. Jealousy doesn't go away quickly no matter how effective the spouse or partner has been. One must understand that the process will be slow, the results may be imperceptible, and whatever progress is made will not necessarily be continuous.

For most people, it takes many weeks and months of continuous effort before they can expect to see much improvement. After all, jealousy is complex and is deeply embedded in one's personality. Most psychoanalysts who believe their method is the only way really to change a personality still require intense sessions with their patients, four or five days weekly for several years. Most people shouldn't have to wait that long to improve their jealousy-based relationships, but it will probably take longer than they would like.

Recently, when some of these techniques were described to a young woman in therapy, as a way to help her jealous husband, she seemed very enthusiastic. She said she couldn't wait to get home and start trying them. However, when she returned next week she seemed dejected. "I did what you told me to do," she said, "but it didn't work. What should I do now?"

This question is asked all too frequently, and the answer is almost always the same as the one given to the young woman: "It's good that you tried it. Now keep doing it, over and over. You have to keep doing it until you and your husband are used to it. Because of the kind of problem he has, he is going to be uncomfortable and guarded when you act so differently. You have to get used to it too, so that you'll be able to be more natural about it. You must do it so often that you can do it without thinking. Otherwise you can't really know if the technique will work or not. It might work, but if it isn't done long enough and comfortably enough, it will seem like it isn't working."

Frequently, the effort to help one's jealous partner only seems to make things worse. The jealousy may actually become more intense and problem filled or it may only appear to be so. If the effort actually leads to a worsening of the situation, it is not unusual but will probably be only temporary. This is because an important component of jealousy is the need for control as a way to hold onto the possession. As long as the partner behaves in a predictable manner, the jealous person is less likely to feel threatened. But the moment something is done differently, something that is out of character, trouble might begin. Any change seems suspicious. Even if the changes are designed to help, they are still changes and thus can be perceived as threats, so the jealous person acts worse than ever. However, if the effort continues until it becomes expected and usual to the jealous person, it is less likely to be perceived as a threat and its positive effects can begin to be experienced.

Effort that appears to have negative results might also be due to heightened expectations and disappointment. Before any concerted effort was made, the spouse or partner didn't really expect improvements. There was nothing to be disappointed about when the jealous person continued behaving that way. However, when considerable effort goes into bringing about change, there is expectation of improvement. Often there will be a temporary respite from the problem, as there is in any jealous relationship. When the jealousy resumes, there is a feeling of failure. Then it must be remembered that the situation is probably not getting worse but only appears to be doing so.

If the nonjealous partner keeps working on these activities for several more weeks, the jealous behavior and the relationship is more likely to be significantly improved. If improvement does not occur, even after these activities have been carried out for several months, it is unrealistic to expect any improvements in the future. If that is the case, the nonjealous partner has to consider whether to terminate the relationship or to remain in it. If the choice is to stay in the relationship, it will be prudent to know the strategies for self-defense in living with a jealous partner.

6

Self-Defense Strategies

Not everyone who is close to a jealous person will be able to help or resolve the problem, no matter how great the determination or effective the effort. When this happens, most objective people will eventually realize that their attempts to help are fruitless and that different approaches are necessary. If separation is not an option, the individual has one remaining alternative—it is the self-defense position.

Self-defense is the ability to minimize the jealous person's debilitating influences. It is knowing how to prevent, minimize, and terminate conflicts without becoming submissive or vengeful. It is the capacity to withstand accusations and criticisms and to do without much warm emotional support. It is the ability to maintain one's self-esteem and positive, optimistic perspectives. And most importantly, effective self-defense is the ability to keep in good health to resist the stresses and risks of this way of life.

Self-defense actions in coping with a jealous person may be very different from efforts designed to help such a person. In some cases self-defense activities may complement and support the efforts to help the jealous person, but more often than not, they won't help the jealous person at all. They can help the nonjealous partner. He or she must therefore decide at some point when the attempt to help is futile so that efforts can be turned toward more effective self-preservation.

The spouse or partner of a pathologically jealous person runs a greater risk of physical or emotional abuse when acting helplessly and without defenses. Some spouses and partners stay docile and submissive and withdraw from confrontations in the hopes of avoiding maltreatment. They reason that if they make enough concessions or don't contradict their partners, they may be able to keep the peace. At best, this may work only a short time, but the opposite is more likely to be the eventual result. The submissive and defenseless partner may avoid confrontation but in so doing usually conveys a message of weakness. The message is communicated to the jealous person that the partner is powerless and is merely to be regarded as another of the jealous person's possessions.[1]

When this happens, the jealous person comes to believe it is a basic right to treat the spouse or partner in any way desired. The jealous person's thoughts are likely to be along these lines: "I expect you to be here when I want you to do something, but away when I want solitude. I think you ought to give up any interests of your own, especially if they conflict with any of mine. I won't notice you when you do what I want because that's how it's supposed to be. I will notice you only when you don't do what I want. When you don't do what I expect, I'll be angry at you. I might have to hurt you then, so you'll remember to do better next time."

When nonjealous partners are assertive rather than submissive, they aren't taken for granted nor are they regarded as property. They will become less predictable to their jealous partners and possibly more threatening as well. Assertiveness will probably lead to more initial conflicts, the result of two equal wills and two different priorities clashing. But eventually, with the show of strength and independence, the nonjealous partner will be regarded with more respect.

On the other hand, the spouses or partners who remain submissive to jealous people are vulnerable to the syndrome known as "learned helplessness." In this state individuals respond almost automatically in a passive way to every demand or confrontation. The victims act powerless to do anything but what the others demand. They tend to become abused, and they believe they will experience less pain and suffering if they accept the abuse than if they resist. They passively accept their fate because they don't know what else to do.

People in this state often develop ideas that aren't realistic. Some believe that the partner will eventually change if they wait long enough. Some feel that they cannot live without the jealous partner, no matter how much abuse occurs. Some become vaguely convinced that a rescuer will come along to solve the problem or remove them from their plights. Ironically, in jealous relationships the perceived rescuer is often the very person who has triggered the problem—the jealous person.

The added danger of learned helplessness is that the behavior spills over into other aspects of life. For example, when people get into the habit of behaving helplessly with their jealous partners, they sometimes begin to act this way with others too. They may withdraw from potential conflicts in their jobs or with their children, relatives, and friends. They become "doormats" and are easily victimized; they become ineffective and lose the respect of others. The passive response also may take the form of isolation. Nonjealous people may passively try to avoid problems by avoiding the jealous partner as much as possible. They may also find it necessary to avoid other people or, if not avoid them, to seek solace and pity from them.

As we have seen, these responses are inevitably going to be unsuccessful. In becoming isolated to avoid conflicts, the nonjealous partner has also become isolated from valuable sources of support, losing many opportunities to get positive encouragement or informative feedback from caring associates.

It is even less effective to seek pity or rescuers. It may be fairly easy to get people to show pity or support for a while, but in the long run this does little to solve the problem. Yet many spouses or partners of jealous people don't seem much interested in learning or working toward progress. Instead, they seem to want only to complain about the jealous person and find allies. Obviously, the number of allies one acquires doesn't determine one's worth or the rightness of one's position.

One can find some sympathetic listeners and allies, but it is more difficult to keep them interested. Usually, people will withdraw if they have to hear descriptions of the same basic story over and over. So, to hold their attention, the pity seeker may have to get new data. Some people in this situation may provoke their partners into different outrages so that there will be something new and interesting to report, or they may dramatize or embellish their stories. But this can lead to serious credibility problems. It is ultimately self-defeating and is an ineffective defense.

Another passive response is to become depressed, even to the point of incapacitation. Although this can require hospitalization, chemical treatment, and intensive psychotherapy, it will more probably result in more apathy and ineffectiveness in carrying out one's normal duties. The example of a middle-aged housewife called Edith illustrates one type of passive-submissive response and its consequences.

Edith was a fifty-year-old wife and mother who entered therapy in a very depressed condition. Her gynecologist had referred her after several months of antidepressant medication proved to be nontherapeutic. She indicated to the therapist that she felt nothing but defeat and hopelessness.

She had been asked to bring her husband into treatment with her, but she came alone. "He'll never come," she said. "He thinks all psycho doctors— that's what he calls you people—are crazy."

Edith seemed close to suicidal. She had all the major symptoms of depression, including insomnia, loss of appetite, social withdrawal, low energy, feelings of inadequacy, decreased effectiveness, loss of interest in sex, tearfulness, pessimistic attitudes, and sometimes she expressed thoughts about dying or ending her life. However, she insisted she wouldn't kill herself because she lacked even the strength to do that. But she felt she was simply enduring on earth until she could be happier in heaven.

She attributed her feelings to menopause, to feelings of inadequacy, to problems managing her teenage children, and to grief about her mother, who had a chronic illness. But mostly it was her husband. She described her marriage to a troubled man but a man she still loved and wanted to help, a man she planned to stay with for life no matter what. She told the therapist:

He isn't a bad guy. He's a good man with a bad temper. He loves me and the children and would do anything for us. He had a terrible life. His dad was mean and had a bad temper too. He was awful to my husband when he was a little boy. The old man kicked him out of his own home when he was only fifteen. My husband practically lived on the streets after that. Then he went into the Army. He got kicked out of there too. They said he couldn't be controlled. He got into lots of fights with other soldiers. He said they were always picking on him. Once the Army threw him in their jail. Even after that his temper kept getting out of control. He got a dishonorable discharge when he was nineteen. Then he couldn't get any decent job with that on his record. So he just had to settle for odd jobs whenever he could get them.

He mostly worked in carnivals, the kind they set up in parking lots and shopping centers. He ran booths where they pitched pennies and stuff. That's where I met him. I was younger, then, and real impressed with him. He was real smooth—always had a flock of girls around his booth. We started going together and have been together from then on. He quit the carnival when it moved to the next town, just so he could stay where I was.

After we got married, we really had rough times. We had two kids and he couldn't hold a job. I had to work and he stayed home with the babies. He felt real bad about not supporting his kids. He showed it with his jealousy. He kept telling the kids and everybody else that I had a thing for this guy or that one. I never cheated on him. I do love him, but he never seems to be able to believe it.

He gets mad at me for everything, even when I haven't done anything wrong. I support him, because he has never held a steady job, and then I have to serve him when I get home. He knocks me around sometimes when I'm not doing something to suit him. I used to fight back a little or at least argue, but that only got me hurt. Now I don't do anything.

He won't let me have any friends. I only got friendly with one girl in the last few years. She lived next door. My husband would get real mad whenever I went over there. Then he got it in his head that I was interested in her husband instead of her. One time he went over there and accused her husband of putting moves on me. They got into a terrible fistfight. My husband is real strong, and he beat up on the guy pretty bad. Soon after that my husband decided we should move away. He said he needed a change, but I knew he was embarrassed about what happened. I was pretty embarrassed too, so I was glad to go. But it meant I had to lose my only friend and my job too. We've been on welfare and unemployment ever since.

Since then, I've been pretty much alone. My kids are growing up and they don't stay home much. I avoid people. I try to do just what my husband wants so he won't get mad and make a fool of himself again. I'm not too happy but I don't know what else to do. Maybe when the kids are on their own I'll be able to leave. I doubt it, though. I don't like living alone, and I'm too old to have another man want me. Besides, I really love him. I keep thinking he'll mellow as he gets older. I sure hope so.

Edith's submissive behavior did not help anyone. It didn't help her husband with his jealousy problem, and it didn't help to make her own life better. Nor did it make the relationship any easier or lead to the harmony she was presumably seeking. All it really did was contribute to her becoming more depressed and less effective.

Unlike many people in her circumstance, however, she was able to overcome many of these problems. She was placed in a group psychotherapy program for women in similar circumstances. It provided her with a healthy outlet, an opportunity to ventilate her feelings and relate to others. She was empathetic and understanding, and her fellow group members soon recognized her perceptiveness and wisdom. Her self-esteem returned. She began to care about her appearance. She started applying the advice she gave to others in the group to herself. She had told other members to stand up for themselves when they had encounters with their husbands. She became more effective in dealing with her husband when she stopped being submissive. After a period of more intense fighting, he got used to her assertiveness and began to give her far more respect than he ever had before. Their marriage, while still troubled, is far healthier.

Depression, learned helplessness, ineffectiveness, lowered self-esteem, and other mental and physical disorders can be avoided by most people, even though they remain in unresolvable jealous relationships. To do this, it is necessary to plan effective self-defense strategies. One might take many possible actions for self-protection in dealing with a jealous person, but not all of them are effective; in fact, some are counterproductive.

Strategies that will predictably be ineffective include those that try to hurt the jealous person. Activities that occur merely because of anger or the need for revenge can only lead to a cycle of increasingly unhealthy confrontations. Self-defense tactics meant only to make the jealous person feel guilty or humiliated are also going to fail. When humiliated or guilty, the jealous person isn't likely to become contrite or seek to improve but rather to get angry and seek more control over the partner.

Threatening to leave without actually doing so is the worst of the ineffective self-defense tactics. Ironically, it also seems to be the most frequently attempted activity by partners of jealous people. The nonjealous partner typically says something like, "If you don't stop accusing me and checking up on me, I'm going to move into an apartment and stay there." Making such a threat, however, is counterproductive unless there is willingness and ability to actually carry it out. One must be prepared to make the move fairly promptly and permanently for it to have any of the desired effect on the jealous person.

Although the intent of such threats is supposedly to frighten the jealous person into more reasonable behavior, they usually have the opposite effect. Jealous people act badly largely because they are already frightened about the possibility of losing their loved ones. If such threats seem serious, they will indeed cause further worry. However, the probable consequences will not be improved behavior but rather an exacerbation of the behavior that was already found unacceptable.

The nonjealous partner or spouse who makes a threat and is unable or unwilling to carry it out is placed in a weakened position. The jealous person will be more anxious and fearful about the threat but will also see very soon that the threat won't be carried out. This will expose the partner's powerlessness, allowing the jealous person to take greater advantage of the situation than before. Because fear of losing the partner underlies the irrational behavior, the threat only intensifies the jealousy. Thus, making threats without carrying them out is as effective as trying to put out a fire by drenching it with kerosene. It might momentarily smother some jealousy but it returns more intensely than ever.

Another common mistake often made in trying to cope with these situations occurs when the nonjealous partner starts accusing the jealous partner of wrongdoing. For example, if a jealous man accuses his wife of being interested in Mr. Gordon next door, she starts accusing him of being interested in Mrs. Gordon. If he interrogates his wife in an attempt to determine some evidence of wrongdoing, she starts interrogating him about his recent whereabouts.

The nonjealous spouse or partner doesn't usually initiate new accusations. These charges are made only as a reaction to the jealous person's unacceptable behavior. Eventually, however, many partners or spouses of jealous people start initiating accusations even without immediate provocation. It happens when the spouse or partner becomes so angry or frustrated that he or she gets into the habit of leveling charges. Soon the pattern of accusing the accuser becomes a norm for both people.

The purpose of this strategy is to relieve some angry feelings, get a break from being suspected, and turn the pressure onto the jealous person. The spouse or partner goes on the offensive and tries to get the jealous person to feel the same discomfort that has been imposed. It is a form of vengeance.

In the long run, this strategy is almost always ineffective. It makes both partners more anxious and warier of one another, and it creates or adds to a tense and confrontative atmosphere. Thus, it precludes many opportunities for positive communication and understanding. Furthermore, the nonjealous partner probably won't be as good at leveling accusations. The jealous person is more experienced at it and, unlike the nonjealous partner, will believe the accusations are true. The nonjealous partner will therefore probably lose most encounters in which accusations are thrown back and forth and, in losing them, will have an even weaker, further subordinated position.

Another reason this activity ultimately fails is that it conveys a message to the jealous person that is harmful for all concerned. It says the partner condones this kind of activity. When both people participate in the accusatory behavior, it obviously becomes even more difficult to restore a relationship based on trust and mutual support.

Tattling on the jealous person is another ineffective defense. In this case the nonjealous person tries to cause trouble for the jealous person with employers or other important associates. For example, a wife is sick of her husband's abusiveness and accusations but feels powerless to stop it, so she calls his boss. She tells the boss that her husband mistreats her and is emotionally unstable. Or a husband calls his wife's parents and reports that she gets angry at him for spending more time with the children than with her. These are forms of tattling—the same behavior that is seen among jealous and envious siblings who are competing for preeminence with the parents. It is no more effective for adults in jealous relationships than for children. Tattling on the jealous person cannot possibly result in a diminution of the jealous behavior, but it can easily result in its escalation.

The ostensible purpose of tattling is to gain allies who can help control the jealous person and enhance the partner's relative power. The premise is that if others who have influence with the jealous person realize how many problems exist, they will force a change. The person who has been called will supposedly be able to do what the nonjealous partner has not been able to. The tattler also expects to get more pity, sympathy, or some form of respect.[2]

This strategy is ineffective in the long and usually even in the short term because none of the partner's goals are reached. Other people cannot change the jealous person's personality or cure the affliction even if they want to, and they would hardly gain respect for the tattler. They may not even believe what they are told. Most of those who are notified about inappropriate behaviors know the jealous person better than they know the caller. They probably haven't seen any behaviors like the ones now being reported, so the caller's truthfulness is suspect. Before long the boss or parents begin to think the caller is interfering and disloyal. They feel more sympathy for the jealous person than for the partner.

Then, when the jealous person hears what has been done, there are more conflicts at home. At best the jealous person may react by also look-ing for allies; this would mean that the couple has started playing the "courtroom" game. At worst the jealous person may be so angry about the disclosures as to cause serious harm to the nonjealous partner. In either event the partner or spouse has solved nothing, has not been successful in self-defense, and ultimately feels guiltier and more ineffective.

Much more drastic means to cope with jealous people involve affairs or promiscuous activities engaged in by the nonjealous partners. Nonjealous spouses, especially, might engage in sexual activities with one other person or with many, as a way to get even. They might not have sexual rela-tionships but develop flirtations or celibate love involvements. Some people in this position might simply develop infatuations.

Whatever the form, the intent is to cope with the jealous partner's suspiciousness and jealous accusations by implementing a self-fulfilling prophecy. "Well, if I'm going to be accused of it all the time," the spouse might say, "I might as well do it." People use many justifications for extramarital involvements. Perhaps the most common is that they long for affection, respect, and love and that these needs are not met in relationships with jealous partners. Another reason is that they are angry at the jealous persons' abuse and insensitivity and want revenge. Others become involved or promiscuous in order to rebuild their own self-esteem and sense of sexual attractiveness. Two excellent books that discuss the psychological and sociological reasons for such behavior are Herbert Strean's *The Extramarital Affair* and Laurel Richardson's *The New Other Woman*.[3]

However one justifies them, promiscuity or involvements with others are not effective self-defense strategies in living with a jealous person. They may meet some other needs, but they certainly won't reduce the problems that come from the jealous partner. They won't stop the accusations, even if the jealous person is unaware of what is going on. The suspicions are there anyway, and the inevitable vigilance and interrogations will put even more pressure on the spouse or partner. And the nonjealous partner will probably act more guilty or suspicious, fueling more accusations. If the affair is admitted, the relationship will deteriorate further. Any short-term gratifications have to come at the cost of more severe long-term problems.[4]

Some spouses or partners of jealous people cope not by having affairs but by giving the impression of doing so. They induce jealousy and provoke insecurity in the jealous person and then prove that the suspicions were unfounded. For example, a spouse or partner leaves "evidence" around that suggests infidelity. The evidence might be a name and phone number on the back of an envelope, lipstick on a collar, being unaccountably gone for several hours, being seen in the presence of a potential rival, and so on. When accusations are made, the partner denies the charges, proclaims innocence, and triumphantly offers proof of no wrongdoing.[5]

The nonjealous partners' statements might be something like this: "Go ahead, Lisa. Call the number on that envelope. Ask for Debbie Norman. That'll help you remember she's the one who sold us this house before she died a few years ago." "Of course, there's lipstick on my collar! It's where you kissed me this morning. See, it's your color. No one else would wear anything like that." "All right, Dan, if you insist I'll tell you where I was all afternoon; I'll tell you. I was with your mother and we were planning your surprise birthday party." Or, "I know your sister saw me and Mister McMurtry at the restaurant today, Clarke. She didn't notice me until I waved at her. Did she know we were with everyone else in my office, too? Why don't you call my boss and ask?"

Several purposes are implicit in such self-defense strategies. They are used to confuse the jealous person and cause doubt about the suspicions. Presumably, if one is continually shown to be wrong in making accusations, there will be reluctance, eventually, to feel or express them. Another objective is to make the jealous person overcome the suspiciousness. If the partner keeps producing perfect alibis, then presumably the jealous person will come to realize that there is no basis for doubting the partner's word. The objective is also to give vent to the partner's angry feelings and to assert some sense of power in the relationship by making the jealous partner feel foolish in the accusation and in winning the dispute with the jealous person.

The strategies may provide immediate satisfaction for the partner but will not result in effective self-defense. The jealous person will not stop suspecting or making accusations when feeling less self-confident or less powerful in the relationship. Accusations and suspiciousness will probably get worse as the jealous person's self-esteem is further eroded. Becoming angry at being made to feel foolish will probably result in more serious abuse and increased efforts to find incriminating evidence.

Ridiculing the accusation and the accuser is another strategy that ultimately proves ineffective. When people get angry and frustrated with their jealous partners, they often cope by laughing at the jealous behavior and sometimes trying to get others to do the same. For example, the nonjealous partner calls attention to every idiosyncrasy and mistake made by the jealous person, including those unrelated to jealousy: "Say, Lou, your glasses are dirty. Better clean them so you won't miss any clues of me flirting with Mac." "Vicki, you're slipping. You only gave me one dirty look for talking to the waitress." "Hey, do you guys see how my wife is getting mad at me right now? It's because I'm talking to you instead of her. Poor Helen. Why don't you go pout, dear?" Ridicule might permit the partner a momentary release of anger, but it causes long-term damage. It tries to degrade the jealous person and diminish his or her sense of adequacy.

Actively competing with and defeating the jealous partner at something is another ineffective self-defense strategy. A wife, for example, keeps inviting her husband to play cards or board games, knowing that she will probably win. Or a husband who is a better cook than his wife or has more rapport with the children or is more knowledgeable about world events keeps comparing his talents in these areas to hers. One form of this competitiveness is commonly seen among couples who are not evenly matched in their respective verbal skills. If the jealous person is not very articulate and the partner is, the partner may start arguments that will end in a sense of conquest. The partner may not be right but, because of being more capable of verbal expression, gains the appearance of clear-cut victory, at least for the time being. The jealous person who is not as articulate is likely to resort to withdrawal, physical violence, yelling, or hysterical emotions.

Some partners of jealous people compete by doing well in their professions, earning higher salaries than their partners, and implying that this means they have more value as human beings. Some compete by dressing well or developing some talent or skill or accomplishing something of note. Because of these activities they draw attention away from their jealous partners when they are in the company of others. They gain recognition from others in such a way that the jealous person is ignored.

This does not mean that such activities are ineffective if attempted for more valid reasons than conquering the jealous person. If the partner is working to achieve these objectives for the sake of accomplishment, social or material reward, or self-improvement, then the activities are important and worthwhile. But if they are done only to make the jealous person feel inferior, then the goals are misguided.

This strategy is ineffective because it further erodes the jealous person's self-esteem, thus intensifying the jealous behaviors and resulting in more tension and conflict between the partners. Moreover, bringing down the jealous person to a point beneath the partner doesn't enhance the partner's overall feeling of worth. The immediate satisfaction it may provide is followed by eventual discomfort, guilt, and dissatisfaction.

Probably the most damaging of the ineffective self-defense strategies is for the nonjealous partner to terminate the relationship without thorough preparation. Often the spouse in this position will find conditions so intolerable that immediate escape seems to be the only answer. Running away seems the only defense. But if this important step is taken without effective planning, the results can be disastrous.

People who have done this often find they cannot stay away. Perhaps they have no money or job skills or suitable places to live. Maybe they have left their children or friends or church or other sources of emotional support in order to get away from the pressures of life with the jealous person and find they cannot do without them. Possibly they even find they miss the jealous partner or find that they have not yet worked through the separation process and need more time to do so.[6]

Ending the relationship may be a valid response, but implementing this decision will not be so effective as when it follows careful planning and preparation. Those who have left prematurely and precipitously often find it necessary to return, and when this happens their position and self-respect are damaged considerably.

With so many activities considered ineffective, it might be surmised that there is nothing left to do that is effective. Actually, many devices and techniques that have proved useful are available to the spouse or partner of the jealous person. Before discussing them specifically, it must be remembered that not all the techniques are effective for all situations or people. And it must be remembered that these techniques are not designed as "cures" for the problem but only as devices to aid in better surviving the unpleasant circumstances.

The most important of the self-defenses, by far, is for the spouse or partner to keep in good physical and emotional health. If one becomes incapacitated because of illness or infirmity, the other effective strategies won't be worthwhile. Many people in this position, because they lose some sense of self-worth, tend to let themselves go. They don't get enough exercise or proper nutrition. They don't permit themselves time off for recreation or vacations. They don't permit themselves any respite from the incessant stress. They come to feel they don't deserve any better. They become so immersed in their problems that they are hardly aware that their health is declining.[7]

Spouses or partners of jealous people must make a conscious effort to follow a program of health maintenance. This includes an annual checkup with the family physician. It may include some form of exercise taken regularly. Even a twenty-minute daily walk in the neighborhood can be remarkably restorative for problems of this type. It includes a proper diet. Those who live under these conditions may never feel hungry and sometimes have to force themselves to eat in order to maintain the proper nutritional balance.

Preserving a healthy emotional and mental state is also important. To achieve this an individual especially needs to avoid isolation and social withdrawal. The spouse or partner of a jealous person is often tempted to stay away from people to minimize conflict. But avoidance can lead to more emotional disturbance. In keeping mentally healthy, the nonjealous partner must maintain some social contacts even if it means conflict at home. One also must find opportunities to grow and learn, to develop interests and participate actively in them. Everyone needs an occasional respite from stress. If one is in no position to take vacations, at least it is possible to be in "safe" places for limited periods of time. For example, it is relatively easy to make frequent visits to relatives, go to church, accompany the children to a movie, and so forth.[8]

People in this position can also read and learn about their own state of mind. It is reassuring to read that others share these circumstances and feelings. The bookstores are filled with good self-help books that serve this purpose. Some people who live with jealous partners say the ones most helpful to them have been Carl Rogers' *Becoming Partners*, Bach and Deutch's *Pairing*, and Virginia Satir's *Peoplemaking*. They are all easy to read and yet thoughtful and psychologically sophisticated books dealing with many of the issues in maintaining relationships and intimacy.[9]

It is also crucial that special precautions be taken to defend against depression. As we have seen, this is such a common response to living with a jealous person that everyone in this situation must be alert to it. Depression tends to enter one's life so gradually and unobtrusively that it is often noticed by others before the victim realizes consciously that it exists.[10]

To defend against it, a good first step is to watch for its symptoms and to get others to help by watching for them too. The person in this position might ask for help from a few close relatives or friends: "Please tell me if you ever notice me starting to show signs of depression. If I start to look sadder than usual, or don't seem as energetic, or don't ever want to eat or sleep, or look tired all the time, let me know." If the signs are noted, a visit to the family doctor is important. This is needed to rule out the physiological causes of depression, which can be treated with medication.

Many depressed individuals do, in fact, seek treatment primarily through medication. This can be useful if the depression is related to chemical or physiological imbalances. Some find relief from the serious "cyclothymic" and "bipolar" forms of depression in the closely monitored and systematic use of lithium salts. For others the use of such antidepressant medications as Asendin, Desyrel, Elavil, Sinequan, or Surmontil has been helpful. However, medications can't and don't claim to solve the situational problems that contribute to depression. In this sense they are as effective as aspirin would be in treating a broken leg.[11]

In dealing with jealous relationships, it is ultimately more effective for the partner or spouse to express feelings openly. Some forms of depression are minimized when healthy releases for anger are found. If the ability to defend one's position—not to play the "doormat" or helpless partner—is developed, the self-defense efforts are more effective.[12]

One doesn't always have to express anger at a partner in order to release it. Some of it can be dissipated through various healthy outlets. Active, productive physical exercise is important. Participation in sports that do not involve competition with the jealous partner are also helpful. Talking with people, especially about controversial subjects such as politics, can be a good release. These provide effective emotional outlets without the problems that accompany expressions of anger directed at the partner.

Suppressed anger and its corresponding depression can also be avoided by developing some positive experiences with the jealous person, even during the difficult times. It may seem and feel incongruous to be subjected to accusations and verbal abuse and then immediately suggest going out to a movie or bowling together. But if this can be done it is helpful. One way people make such abrupt switches is by understanding their jealous partners' insecurities. They know the accusations are not because of their own shortcomings but because of their partners' emotional disturbances. In other words, they don't take it personally.

A more assertive stance will not necessarily prevent violence, but overall, the submissive approach is more likely to permit it. The partner of the jealous person may become involved in more arguments in the beginning but is more likely to keep them from continuing endlessly and escalating out of control by maintaining a strong stance.

Many people who are confronted with accusations or deprecating remarks have the natural inclination to try to convince their accusers that they are wrong. They might deny the accusation and then offer proof of no wrongdoing. But then the jealous person continues to insist that the partner is guilty and the resulting debate becomes a "Yes, you did," "No, I didn't" dialogue.

Obviously neither is going to change the other's mind during such exchanges. The conflict may only become a competition to see who can win. Both parties have their egos at stake. Their goal is no longer—if it ever was—to exchange information but to defeat the other. If the nonjealous person tries to even the score by countering with new accusations, the result is an escalation of charges and countercharges. Outtalking the jealous person only causes a further loss of face, which results in more jealousy reactions later. However, if the nonjealous partner submits, there is a feeling of hopelessness and helplessness. It is a no-win situation for both.

The best recourse is to avoid being put in this position. The nonjealous partner does this by refusing to dwell on the accusations, changing the subject or not talking until the partner begins discussing something else.

The nonjealous partner stays in the same room and talks about whatever is of interest instead of trying to defend against the unfounded accusations. A simple explanation made once may be appropriate, but after that it does no good to repeat it. If necessary, when the jealous partner demands further details, one can remain absolutely silent after the first explanation. This will probably infuriate the jealous partner the first few times, but eventually it shows that the power is not all on one side. Here is how such an encounter might sound:

Dale: How come you were gone so long? I was expecting you home an hour ago.

Bonnie: I got held up at the meeting. We got into a discussion, and I lost track of the time.

Dale: Well, come on. Get with it. You know how I feel about that. It makes me uptight.

Bonnie: Yes, I know. I should have called, but I got carried away. I apologize. Why don't we forget it now and get started on dinner?

Dale: I couldn't eat now. I want to know what you were doing. Who was there with you?

Bonnie: Oh, just the usual group. No one new. No one you need to worry about, if that's what you're getting at. I'm sorry you aren't hungry. Boy, I am. I think I'll start dinner. I wish you'd join me.

Dale: What do you mean, the usual crowd? Who's usual? How do I know you weren't doing something you shouldn't have been doing?

Bonnie: You don't. You have to trust me. I love you and I don't intend to hurt our relationship. But I've done nothing wrong and I don't need to be interrogated about everything I do. I'm not going to answer any more questions about it. I'd like to talk with you about lots of other interesting subjects and if you'd like to talk, great. If you want to just dwell on this, then there's nothing more I have to say.

Dale: Aha! You sound like you're trying to change the subject. You sound like you have something to hide. I'm going to get to the bottom of this. Who were you with and what were you doing?

Bonnie: Let's see. I wonder if we should have hamburger or spaghetti for dinner. I think spaghetti. Is that okay with you?

Dale: I asked you a question, dammit!

Bonnie: I told you what I was going to tell you. Do you want garlic bread with your spaghetti?

Dale: Now I'm really getting mad. Will you answer me?

Bonnie: Who won the ball game?

Dale: I'm going to call up those people and find out if you were with them.

Bonnie: I guess I'll turn on the radio to hear who won. Let me tell you about old Mrs. Jones at the office. It's really interesting.

Dale: Why were you late? Who were you with? What were you doing? I've had people tell me you were seen in Riley's Bar today. What was going on in there?

Bonnie: Gee, I like that sweater you're wearing. You should wear it more often. It's very becoming.

Dale: Listen, dammit, will you stick to the subject? Now what's going on? You better tell me if you know what's good for you.

Bonnie: Did you get the sweater at the mall? I wonder if they'd have one for me. I think we'd look good in matching sweaters, don't you?

Dale: That's really cute. You're just trying to change the subject. But it won't work. Start telling me what's going on.

Bonnie: Mmm, that spaghetti sauce is smelling good. I hope you'll have some.

Dale: Okay, a little. But I told you I'm not hungry. We'll talk about what you were up to when we eat.

Bonnie: Let me tell you about Mrs. Jones instead.

Dale: Why, what happened to her?

This dialogue illustrates one of the many ways to deal with confrontations. Obviously, each encounter is unique, but the common element is to stay out of the defensive trap. The nonjealous spouse or partner states the position once and then stops discussing it. When there is no other information to present, nothing is accomplished by repeating what has already been said. The jealous partner will be very frustrated with this and may try intimidation. If the partner is not intimidated, the conflict has nowhere to go.

During these confrontations the partner does not accomplish anything by trying to educate the jealous person about the nature of jealousy. It *is* important to attempt to educate the jealous individual, but not at that time. There would be little listening or comprehending anyway, and neither partner can speak as rationally and articulately then as when calmness prevails. The jealous person's mind would be closed to any information about jealousy. During arguments it is best to say as little as possible about jealousy. The primary goal during these confrontations should rather be to demonstrate some independence of thought and to control the conflict.

Honesty is another important ingredient for effective self-defense. The spouse or partner is in a much stronger position if always truthful with the jealous person. Occasionally, one is tempted to lie or distort things a little to keep the peace. Some people may know that they have done nothing to be ashamed of but also realize that their jealous partners would make an issue out of something if they had full knowledge. So, rather than face a conflict, they give misleading answers.

Deceptive behavior can only result in temporary gain that soon gives way to greater problems. The jealous partner will sense that something is wrong and note any discrepancies. To avoid being trapped in falsehoods, the nonjealous partner has to keep track of everything said. If any deceptions are finally revealed, the jealous person will be likely to use that fact to justify even greater distrust and heightened vigilance. This can't happen when the nonjealous partner is truthful.

This does not mean, however, that one must disclose everything about relationships that existed before the marriage or present commitment. The jealous partner might be inclined to grill the partner about involvements with others before their relationship began, and, indeed, a common pattern in jealous people is their tendency to dwell on their partners' previous relationships. It might be tempting to disclose every detail about such relationships in the hope that the matter will henceforth be dropped. But this rarely happens. More often than not, the jealous person feels even more threatened and the interrogations get more frequent and intense. For most people involved with jealous partners, it is more effective to declare that all encounters prior to the present relationship are off limits for discussion.[13]

Many spouses or partners might prefer dishonesty if they are involved in some wrongdoing. If, for example, a wife is having an affair, she will probably want to conceal the fact from her jealous husband. Ultimately, however, this serves no worthwhile purpose if her husband is pathologically jealous. He is suspicious anyway, and she cannot be sure if his suspicions are the result of his jealousy or because he has found some incriminating evidence. If she feels the need to maintain the involvement and the deception, she needs to reexamine why she remains in the relationship at all.

One of the most effective defenses of all is the support group. This consists of several spouses or partners of jealous people meeting regularly to exchange ideas about effective coping. The purpose of the group is not to provide pity but to encourage understanding. It helps keep up the members' spirits and gives them a chance to talk with others, gain perspectives, and better understand themselves and their situations.[14]

By comparing notes, support group members come to realize that they are not nearly as alone as they once believed. They give and get new ideas about dealing effectively with their partners. They see themselves as they are seen by others and begin to understand what they might be doing to contribute to the problem. In helping others they realize their own worth and know that their ideas have merit. They discharge some of the anger that has built up in the relationship so it doesn't need to be expressed to the jealous person or to innocent bystanders.

Finding groups of this type can be challenging. They are not available in every community, and many support groups are not oriented to dealing with jealousy issues. Information on support groups of this type is available from the Women's Action Alliance. They produce an annual directory of services and support groups around the nation.[15]

The other challenge for the partners of jealous people is in attending such a group. Jealous people will probably be threatened if they are aware of the purpose of the group and the issues discussed there. On the other hand, if they are not told about the group, their suspicions will intensify and they are likely to put added pressure and stress on their partners. Non-jealous partners must be determined to meet this challenge and participate in the support group despite these pressures.

The ideal support system would be a small group of perhaps five to seven people of the same sex who are willing to meet regularly and share their ideas, values, problems, and solutions. The group would meet at a predetermined time no less than once monthly and preferably twice monthly. The members would take turns discussing themselves and their common problems, agreeing to keep information honest and confidential. If someone is in need of help where no such group exists, it may be necessary to start one.

It is difficult to start support groups, especially if their purpose is to deal with jealousy issues. Because jealousy is a problem that is not discussed with the same kind of candor as are alcoholism, spouse abuse, legal matters, physical dysfunctions, and drug abuse among children, it is hard to find others in the same position. And it seems harder for men to start and maintain these groups than for women.

However, with a little perseverance anyone can start a support group. The individual who wants one can attend some of the other self-help groups and there meet others with similar problems or interests. In these groups there are sure to be some members who have additional problems with jealousy. These people can be invited to meet regularly for this purpose. People in this position can also consult their clergymen, who may well be counseling several other people with similar problems. Cautiously talking about these problems and asking around for others in a similar situation can also be helpful. The people will turn up. They are bound to because there are so many of them.

One major obstacle in organizing a support group will be in resisting the objections of the jealous partner. Jealous people will be apprehensive, threatened, and fearful about the loss of control represented by this group. They will probably try to discourage and sabotage attendance. To avert this possibility, the partner may be tempted to conceal the group's existence. This is probably not a good idea. The group will take a great deal of time and require the partner's presence out of the home at conspicuous times. Trying to keep it a secret will lead to greater suspiciousness and closer scrutiny until the group's existence is finally revealed. If, on the other hand, the partner is open about the group from the beginning, the suspicion is minimized. The jealous person will be threatened, as by anything new. However, as soon as the idea becomes familiar, the jealous person may come to believe that it is intended as a positive experience for the relationship.

Support groups seem to do better when all the members are of the same sex, are fairly compatible in intellectual level of functioning, have a willingness to meet, and have similar problems. The following ground rules are useful to people who are starting support groups.

GUIDELINES FOR A JEALOUSY SUPPORT GROUP

1. *Meet regularly.* Set the time for once a month (or week or every other week) and stay with the schedule. Momentum and consistency are extremely important. Members count on one another, and regularity makes this possible. It also helps members stick to business and not get too casual.

2. *Set a time limit for each meeting.* Ninety minutes seems optimal, if the

group consists of six people. If no set time exists, groups tend to meander aimlessly rather than get into the subject. Also, without a definite ending, members find it difficult to plan their schedule. With possessive and jealous partners waiting at home, this becomes an important factor. The group is a unit, so all members should stop at the same time. All members should agree on the time when they agree to the meeting.

3. *Designate a group coordinator.* This person is in charge for a specified period of time (two or three months seems optimal). After that another person is designated. The coordinator has simple but important duties. He or she starts and closes the meeting on time, makes sure there is a suitable location for future meetings, and that everyone knows where they will be held.

4. *Select suitable sites.* The location for the meeting can change each time or remain in one place. One setting is preferable, but practical considerations may preclude this. Most groups tend to rotate the location through the homes of various members. Others choose a neutral setting, such as a room in a church or a public library. The location of the room is not as important as its conditions, the most important of which is privacy. It should be free of the risk of interruptions or eavesdropping.

5. *Keep stable membership size.* The optimal size is six, but two more or less are also manageable. Once the group has started, its size should remain constant. This might be difficult. If the group works well, others will want to join it. Members, feeling compassion for others who have shared their experiences, will be tempted to admit them. But permitting this would soon cause the group to become ineffectively large. No one should be permitted to join until someone else is ready to "graduate."

6. *Keep the group focused.* Members agree to make sure the group doesn't become a Kaffeeklatsch. Members will grow to like one another and will be tempted to socialize. But their common purpose is coping with jealous relationships and related topics. Any deviations detract from the purpose. Unlike members of formal group psychotherapy sessions, members of these groups may socialize at times other than the designated meetings.

7. *Maintain confidentiality and honesty.* When members join the group they promise to refrain from disclosures to people outside the group and to tell one another only the truth. They promise they will not reveal anything to nonmembers about what has been said in the meetings. This makes them feel free to express themselves. They also agree that whatever they say in the group will be the truth as they know it. This doesn't mean individual members have to reveal everything about themselves if they don't want to. It only means that whatever they choose to say should not be intentionally misleading. Otherwise the advice they will be given will be based on untruths and might be very confusing and ill conceived.

8. *Develop a hot line.* This means each member keeps the phone numbers of all the others and is permitted to call any one of them during times of acute stress at home. Whatever is said during the hot line calls is reported to the whole group, limiting the formation of subgroup cliques. The hot line provides each member with a source of immediate feedback, encouragement, and support. It also helps the individual get away from the stressful situation for a while.

Groups of this type can be invaluable for nonjealous spouses and partners, particularly if all members stick with the rules. Some groups have invited their jealous spouses to accompany them to meetings on occasion. The jealous people have felt supported and were able to learn from the experience too.

The keys to defending oneself against the hazards of life with a jealous person are clear. The individual must take care to maintain physical and emotional health, act assertively and avoid the "doormat" role with the jealous partner, be self-confident in conflicts, and keep in close contact with others for support.

7

Protecting Children from Jealous Parents

Parents are usually quite familiar with their children's verbal expressions of jealousy: "Mommy, do you like Kenny or me best?" "Why do I have to go to bed when Tommy gets to stay up?" "Daddy, don't let Mommy sit on your lap anymore because that's going to be my place from now on." The more perceptive parents also recognize expressions of jealousy when their children act out their hidden emotions. For example, a child sometimes has an "accident" that hurts his little brother who was given some exclusive privilege. A girl who believes she has fewer toys than her brother might "unintentionally" lose or break his toy car. An older boy might see his little sister, whom everyone adores, and hug her so hard that she cries. A young child attempts to squeeze between parents who are hugging one another. A youngster declares an intent to replace one parent and marry the other on reaching maturity.

These are usually common and normal indicators of the jealousy derived from sibling rivalry and envy of the parental relationship. While these expressions can sometimes irritate parents who might feel a need to arbitrate or control their children, they are generally no cause for alarm. In fact, they can usually be reassuring to caring parents. They demonstrate that their children are comfortable and secure enough to be open about their conflicts. These expressions permit children the opportunity to work through jealous feelings, learn from them, and use them in healthy ways as significant parts of their developmental processes.[1]

Nevertheless, while most children who indicate jealousy feelings are not necessarily on the path toward adult jealousy problems, there are certain children who are highly vulnerable to future difficulties with jealousy. They are the offspring of jealous parents. Every child who has a seriously jealous parent faces many hardships. It is important that conscientious parents, especially those who have jealous spouses, know about the special hardships experienced by these children and what can be done to minimize these difficulties.

Many children who are raised by jealous parents grow up in unhealthy environments. They constantly face uncertainty, inconsistency, and danger. Their developing personalities are formed with self-doubt and worry. They are likely to carry with them into adulthood and old age the emotional traumas they encountered as youngsters. They are especially vulnerable to serious and chronic emotional problems.[2]

Many types of family interaction patterns based on jealousy problems create unhealthy environments for children. Some examples follow.

A mother is jealous of her four-year-old daughter. The child flirts with her father, and he responds with joy and affection. The mother senses that she is no match for her daughter in competing for the father's attention. Without realizing it, the mother soon finds herself keeping the two of them apart as much as possible.[3]

A jealous father encourages his children to spy on their mother and report any suspicious activities to him. He rewards them when they do the job well and disapproves when they can find no evidence of wrongdoing.

The children are nearby when their parents suddenly start a jealousy-based argument. One parent accuses and the other denies. Their exchange continues and escalates until they turn to the children and ask their opinions about who is right.

A young girl feels she is given less attention than her older sister. She discovers that her parents reward her with more attention and privileges when she reports to them any of her sister's unacceptable behavior.

A woman who suffered sexual problems was repulsed by her husband's sexual overtures. She found excuses to have their young child sleep with them, thus protecting her from her husband's advances. The child was used virtually as a "chastity belt." The father began to resent and feel jealous of the child's relationship with the mother.[4]

A young father is proud when his wife delivers their first child. Soon, however, he notices that his wife is so preoccupied with the baby that she has little time for or interest in him. The father is particularly upset when observing his wife breast-feed the baby. He begins to feel resentment toward the baby, and his hostility persists and intensifies throughout the child's formative years.[5]

Obviously, parenting of this type has negative influences on children. Children of all ages will sense when their parents are jealously threatened by them. And they will naturally emulate many of their parents' unhealthy as well as healthy traits. They learn to see and understand the world much as their parents see and understand it. If the parents have distorted views, the chances are greater that the children will acquire these misperceptions. Moreover, children naturally behave in ways that seem to result in rewards. If their parents reward them for behaving in jealously unhealthy ways, the children continue until the behavior becomes deeply ingrained.[6]

Compared to children who grow up in healthy homes, the children of jealous parents are much more vulnerable to a variety of serious problems: They are more likely to develop feelings of inadequacy and insecurity, to be less decisive, and to be more reluctant to make even simple decisions. They are vulnerable to imitating their jealous parents' behavior. They are more likely to become overly possessive and concomitantly less willing to share with others. These children are also more liable to be distrustful and suspicious of others and intolerant of unfamiliar ideas and behaviors. They often become narcissistically devoted to attention-getting behaviors. They are less able to form healthy relationships, especially with members of the opposite sex, and they have poor prospects for successful marriages or relationships. The children of pathologically jealous parents are much more likely to become pathologically jealous themselves. Finally, these children are more likely to be abused as children and to be abusers of their own children later in life.[7]

Child abuse is now being recognized as a national epidemic, and parents with jealousy problems are among the major perpetrators. Many of the studies of spouse abuse and family violence reveal that children are victimized at least as often and at least as severely as are spouses. Parents who have serious jealousy problems often vent their anger and frustrations on their children, who provide a convenient and less conspicuous target. The case of the "Norman" family illustrates one situation of this type.[8]

Mr. Norman had an extremely violent nature. He had been arrested on several occasions for fighting and for assault. Once, for a short time, he had been confined to a psychiatric hospital with a diagnosis of having a "paranoid character disorder." Of course, most of his violence was directed at his wife and two children. He frequently accused his wife of cheating on him and his children of being accomplices in her affairs. When they denied any wrongdoing or complicity, he often became enraged and struck at them.

For many years Mrs. Norman endured such treatment and acted as though she was helpless to do anything about it. However, even she had her limits. After one severe beating resulted in her hospitalization, she was later referred to an abuse shelter and professional counseling. With this support she began to make some positive changes. Sometimes she fought back. Sometimes she took the children out of the home and lived in the shelter for a few days until her husband indicated an intent to mend his ways. And, most effectively, she often got the police and legal authorities to arrest him.

Mr. Norman faced judges, probation officers, and jail guards with increasing certainty whenever his jealous violence resulted in abuse to his family. He soon learned that he had to control his temper in the presence of his wife. But this didn't change his personality or correct his problem. In fact, the jealousy problem worsened as he became more fearful of losing the control he thought he had over his wife.

With the problem worsening and his former outlet essentially eliminated, Mr. Norman found a convenient target for his anger and frustrations: his children. He usually chose times when Mrs. Norman was not present and when one of the children had violated some expectation made or implied by their father. He was more likely to punish them when he was upset or particularly jealous than when they violated some rule.

They became his safety valve, and his punishments would be far in excess of anything warranted. Accordingly, he would find an excuse to punish them for almost any possible behavior, for such infractions as making too much noise, watching too much television, and not getting perfect report cards from school. He would even spank them for failing to disclose where Mrs. Norman really was during an alleged shopping trip. Usually the discipline was quite severe and prolonged. He beat the children with his hands, with his belts, and with sticks, on all parts of their bodies. He threatened them with even worse punishment if they revealed these practices to their mother or anyone else.

The children naturally became very fearful and angry. They starting fighting and blaming one another for all violations of the family rules. Both became insecure and lost considerable self-esteem. They still bear many of the mental as well as physical scars of this treatment. Finally it ended when Mrs. Norman, with the help of the school authorities and the staff at the shelter, brought charges against her husband. Mr. Norman was imprisoned for several months and then placed on very closely scrutinized probation. During his absence Mrs. Norman got a divorce and removed herself and the children from further contact with him. Only later were they able to restore themselves and achieve a degree of contentment. Even so, they may carry the emotional as well as physical scars of the abuse throughout their lives.

The effects of abuse may be even more damaging to children than to spouses. Children have fewer options for avoiding such treatment and are more prone to incorporate these experiences into their developing personalities. Some researchers conclude that many abused children believe they can do nothing but accept their fates, and they may grow up feeling helpless and dependent.[9]

Other abused children develop the idea that parents are supposed to treat their children this way, so they, too, are likely to become abusive parents. When their abusive parent has also been a jealous parent, the likelihood that they will grow up with similar problems is greatly increased.[10]

Child abuse is only one of the unhealthy family patterns that contribute to feelings of insecurity and inadequacy or worthlessness in children. Child abuse is the product of the parent's emotional disturbances, not the child's bad behavior. However, most children have no way of knowing for certain that they aren't to blame. If they are punished so severely, they come to believe it must be because they are so bad. As a result they feel they cannot count on themselves and must depend upon others. However, in their limited experiences, they have learned they can't count on others either. They are helpless and at the mercy of conditions over which they have no control. Obviously, when they eventually find that they *can* control or possess something, they will be inclined to hold onto it with unyielding intensity.[11]

Childhood insecurity is often fostered by parental insecurity, and a parent with a jealousy problem is bound to be insecure. Such parents are inclined to upset their children by describing their own worst fears as though they were facts. For example, many jealous parents impulsively tell their children that the other parent is planning to abandon them to run off with someone else. The child has no way of knowing these are merely the jealous suspicions of the disturbed parent and becomes fearful of losing the other parent. This child might well become as possessive of and vigilant over the other parent as is one who made the accusation.

The jealous parent who has little self-confidence, as is usually the case, is unable to present a child with a picture of stable authoritativeness. Such a parent will often keep changing the rules that apply to the child's behavior. The severity of punishments or magnitude of rewards may be less related to the child's behavior than to the mood of the parent. When the jealous parent feels particularly threatened, the child is more likely to be punished, regardless of what he or she has done.

Other parents with jealousy problems, largely because of their own low self-esteem, resist authoritativeness with their children. They are uncomfortable imposing and enforcing rules. For example, they might ask their child's "permission" when they state a rule: "Kenny, I want you to eat all your peas, okay?" If the child doesn't grant this permission, they might change the rule: "All right, since you won't eat your peas you'll get no dessert." The message the parent conveys is that rules are negotiable and that little is stable or consistent.

The child of jealous parents is vulnerable to becoming more nervous or anxious because of the continual stresses in the environment. A child who is in constant danger of punishment, rejection, and contradictory expectations, cannot easily avoid this. One of the major sources of stress they face in jealous homes is in being forced to choose between the parents. Jealous people are predisposed to seek others to confirm their suspicions. Their children are the most convenient source for this confirmation.

The jealous parent might accuse the other and then ask the children for support. A child's answer can be interpreted as supportive even when no confirmation was intended: "So, you were on the phone with that office floozy while I was at the store, weren't you, Tom? Wasn't he on the phone while I was gone, Beth?" The child may be seen as having taken sides or even as confirming that the action took place, even though no one else but the jealous person interprets the action as being wrong.

The child is manipulated or intimidated into apparently taking sides with the jealous parent. This can't help but make the youngster feel guilty and disloyal to the other parent. On the other hand, if the child takes the nonjealous parent's side, it is likely that the jealous parent will be abusive.

Another of the risks confronting children who grow up in jealous homes is that they are less likely to become able to form healthy relationships of their own. Most such children will find it difficult to form friendships, even as adults. This will be especially true in forming relationships with members of the opposite sex. They will probably have more difficulty finding suitable mates. Those who do marry run greater risks of having unhappy marriages and have higher probabilities of divorce.

The ability to form meaningful relationships built on mutual respect, love, and trust is developed in childhood. It takes place when children witness how adults relate to one another and show affection and respect. It is fostered when the parents enjoy the company of the children and encourage them to participate in family activities. It occurs as youngsters are stimulated to form childhood friendships. In childhood play there are opportunities to learn cooperation, sharing, and the joy of companionship.

When the child's role model is a jealous person, many of these avenues are closed. The child sees little cooperation or pleasure in giving and sharing. The jealous parent isn't likely to have successful friendships. The home does not tolerate relationships with too many others, especially with members of the opposite sex or with people who behave in ways the jealous parent finds unacceptable. These youngsters become more inclined to stay alone or to be distrustful of other children. If these children have siblings, there is likelihood of more serious conflicts but little cooperation or companionship among them. As these children reach adolescence and adulthood, they have probably had little experience in successful relationships. Without having developed such skills, they find that they can't easily maintain happy relationships except through control, suspiciousness, or intimidation.

If these children are not helped or protected from these risks, they tend to react in unhealthy ways. Typically, they engage in manipulative and disruptive behavior, attention-getting activities, acting out, self-destructive behavior, and collusion with the jealous parent.

The self-destructive behavior may take many forms. The child may react to the stresses of the jealous home by doing poorly in school and being an underachiever in various pursuits. Some children's self-destructiveness occurs through deliberate provocation of the jealous parent, knowing that the infraction will lead to punishment. Some children become accident-prone as they unconsciously attempt to punish themselves for their imagined "badness" or feelings of inadequacy. Many psychoanalysts and personality theorists believe that masochism originates or is perpetuated in these childhood experiences.[12]

Acting passively and helplessly is another coping mechanism used by many children in such circumstances. When these children become convinced that whatever they do or don't do will result in the same disapproval from their jealous parents, helplessness may be perceived as the only recourse. This is even more likely to happen if their parents act passively. They may emulate the learned helplessness of their parents.

Others try to cope by openly siding with one parent. Unconsciously and sometimes consciously, they might collude with their jealous parents.

They get some reward or gratification out of having some power to manipulate the situation. For example, a child might deliberately report any "suspicious" activity to the parent even when the information is not solicited: "Mom, I heard Daddy talking to someone he called 'honey' while you were gone." Or the child might be more subtle and simply say or imply things that are known to lead to confrontation: "Hey, Mom, why does Dad always like to spend so much time with that teacher of mine, Miss Ellswick?"

A child may attempt to achieve the same objective by trying to win a favored position with a parent over one of the siblings. This is typically done through tattling and then conveying to the parent that he or she would not do such a bad thing: "Mother, Kenny made a mess with the peanut butter again, but I cleaned it up."

The coping mechanism used most frequently by children of jealous parents is known as "acting out." The acting-out child does not, and may not be able to, verbalize any unhappy feelings but expresses them through actions. The child may not say, "I feel angry because of the way I am being treated" but expresses the feeling through some destructive action. The child might "accidentally" break a treasured family heirloom or provoke arguments between two other siblings and then walk away from their battle. Attention-getting behaviors are the most common form of acting out. Such behaviors are impossible to ignore, leading children into frequent trouble with school or law enforcement authorities.[13]

The Johnstone family and their eleven-year-old son, Tommy, provide an example of how acting-out behavior is seen in jealous households. The Johnstones entered family therapy at the insistence of Tommy's school. The child was a fifth-grader at the school but spent nearly as much time in the principal's office as in his classroom. Tommy was a hyperkinetic child who had been treated with the drug Ritalin for several years. Even with this medication, he frequently disrupted his class by making faces at other children, shouting obscenities when the teacher wasn't looking, dropping books and papers, hitting, stealing things from classmates, and so on. He sought the attention of his classmates and found he could get it through annoying behavior. His actions were designed to get other children to laugh and follow his disruptive lead.

The school counselor who referred Tommy for treatment believed his problem was related to family conflict. She had reason to believe that the father was abusive and that the whole family had problems. Mr. Johnstone was a lawyer, and Mrs. Johnstone worked in the personnel department of a large company. They were devoted to their jobs, and the children were usually left in nursery schools and with baby-sitters. Tommy's siblings were eight-year-old Elizabeth and five-year-old Kenny.

The parents wanted help for Tommy but were discomforted by the suggestion to involve the whole family in therapy. They consented only with great apprehension. The first interview was videotaped, and the transcript from early in the session was as follows:

Mr. J: I admit we haven't spent enough time with the kids. Tommy gets out of line a lot. When we spend more time with him he seems to get better.

Mrs. J: True, I guess. But don't forget, you know, he's on medicine. It's not just us . . . we're not really the cause of . . . it's just that . . . well, you know, he's hyper . . . he has this physical problem . . . don't you, Tommy?

Tommy: I dunno . . . I want . . . [Pause]

Mrs. J: What Tommy wants to say is that he tries to be a good boy but he has these urges to make trouble sometimes. Isn't that right, Tommy?

Tommy: I dunno. [Long pause]

Mrs. J: He usually talks a lot more than this. What's the matter, Tommy? You must tell the doctor. He's trying to help you with your problem. Aren't you, Doctor?

Therapist: It's pretty hard to talk to someone you don't know. But let's not force anyone here to say anything if they don't want to. That's okay. You kids haven't had a chance to talk. What's your name?

Mrs. J: Her name is Elizabeth. She's shy. It's hard to get her to talk. We call her Beth.

Mr. J: And this one is Kenny. He's the runt of the litter.

Therapist: Elizabeth, do you know what 'runt of the litter' means?

Elizabeth: Yep. It means he's the baby.

Kenny: I ain't no baby! You're a baby!

Mr. J: Take it easy, Kenny. She was just answering the doctor's question. Right, Liz?

Elizabeth: He *is* a baby, sometimes.

Therapist: Elizabeth, your Mom called you Beth and your Dad called you Liz. What do *you* like to be called?

Tommy:	She likes to be called turd breath. [Laughs loudly]
Elizabeth:	I do not! Shut up, Tommy! My name is Elizabeth, but I don't care if you call me Beth or Liz. Just not anything that Tommy says.
Therapist:	Do you kids call each other names a lot?
Mrs. J:	Oh, you should hear them. Sometimes they . . .
Therapist:	I was wondering what you *kids* called each other. Elizabeth, what do you call Tommy and Kenny?
Elizabeth:	I just call them their names. Except when they call me names first. Tommy is always calling people names. That's why nobody likes him.
Tommy:	You call people names too! You're the one who starts it. You're a tattletale too!
Therapist:	Tommy, she said nobody likes you. Where does she get an idea like that?
Mrs. J:	Beth, you shouldn't say things like that.
Mr. J:	Let them talk, Judalyn.
Mrs. J:	I *was* letting them talk. I was *trying* to get them to talk. Why don't you ever try to get them to cooperate?
Mr. J:	I only meant that—
Mrs. J:	Well, anyway, let's not have a fight about it. Tommy, the doctor asked you a question. Why don't you answer him?
Tommy:	I dunno.
Therapist:	Tommy, Elizabeth said that nobody likes you. Where does she get an idea like that?
Tommy:	Everybody likes me just fine. Except for Miss Ellswick. She don't like me. But everyone—
Mrs. J:	That's Tommy's teacher. I think he's right about her. She's a little biased against him. That's part of the school problem, I'm sure.
Mr. J:	You interrupted Tommy, again, Judalyn.
Mrs. J:	Will you *please* let me finish. *You* keep interrupting *me*. I think what he's doing is called 'projection,' isn't it, doctor?
Mr. J:	See, now you got the subject away from Tommy again.
Mrs. J:	Tom, I'm simply trying to tell the doctor who Tommy's teacher is. I don't see what you've got to say about it anyway. I'd rather not say this in front of the children, but it is obvious that we've

got problems too, and that's why Tommy has some of his problems.

Therapist: Tommy, you were saying something about Miss Ellswick. What about her?

Tommy: I dunno. [Long silence]

Therapist: Okay, I said nobody had to talk if they didn't want to. Judalyn, what kind of problems do you think you and your husband have that cause trouble for Tommy?

Mrs. J: Could the kids wait in the waiting room? I don't like to air my dirty linen in front of them.

Therapist: Maybe sometime we can talk privately, but for now I think it'd be better for us all to stay together. Let's talk about it openly. You're a family. I'll bet the kids have heard about these things before anyway.

Mr. J: *I'll* say they've heard it before. We're always fighting in front of them.

Therapist: Both of you, what kinds of things do you fight about?

Mr. J: Well, the worst is she's always telling the kids I've got a girl-friend.

Mrs. J: Well, you *do*—listen, do we have to bring this up now?

Mr. J: Why not? You always bring it up at home. I don't have a girl-friend, but she thinks I do. And she gets the kids to check up on me. I work hard, and sometimes I come home late, and when I do, the kids are glaring at me, just like their mother is. She's got them convinced I'm going to run off and desert them.

Mrs. J: That's not . . .

Mr. J: I'm not finished. How about the time you got the kids in the car and drove to my office to see if I was really there? And what about when you sent Tommy into the restaurant to see if I was really at a company dinner? And remember when you told Tommy to keep checking the mileage on my car to see if I was being honest with you? Don't you think that has an effect on him?

As was evident in this session, the Johnstone family was troubled. Mrs. Johnstone tried to control by interrupting the others and interpreting their words. Mr. Johnstone tried to control by remaining detached. Each child did so by disruptions and by criticizing one another. Though Tommy was the focus, it was soon apparent that all members of the family lived in a highly charged, tense atmosphere. Their anger made it hard for them to control their feelings and those of the others. Tommy acted out his at school through his attention-getting behavior. He was rather ignored and suppressed at home, but at school it was hard to ignore him. The conflict between the parents was obvious to the children. What wasn't clear was why it existed and continued.

One reason was Mrs. Johnstone's jealousy. She was painfully insecure and lived in constant dread that she would be rejected or abandoned. Her defense was to limit her husband's opportunities to find her replacement. She also coped by trying to enhance her position with the children. She tried to control their thoughts, gain their sympathy, and alienate them from their father. She was convinced and tried to convince everyone else that her husband was unfaithful. She had told the school authorities that her husband was abusive and had a drinking problem even though she eventually admitted that this wasn't the case.

Misguided though they were, her efforts were effective. The children vaguely believed that their father had a girlfriend. They picked up their mother's fear that he didn't love them and would soon abandon them. Their erroneous ideas drew them closer to their mother. They sought her support and comfort and gave support and comfort in return. This alliance encouraged Mrs. Johnstone to continue with her irrational assertions.

Another source of stress was Mr. Johnstone's avoidance. He admitted that he stayed away from the home partly to prevent so much tension. He worked long hours and showed too little interest in the family when he was home. He didn't feel close to the children or to his wife, which, of course, intensified their fears. All the children, but most noticeably Tommy, dealt with their fears by attention-getting and disruptive behaviors. Tommy's hyperactivity was exacerbated by the household tension to which he was exposed every day.

Mr. Johnstone faced a dilemma. It is one experienced by many parents who have seriously jealous spouses. He felt he had only three choices in dealing with his wife if he wanted to minimize problems for the children. When accused, he could deny the charges. But this usually led to explosive arguments that resolved nothing but magnified the family tension. Or he could say nothing when the charges were made, leading the children as well as his wife to believe the accusations. Or he could absent himself as much as possible and thus minimize the opportunity for conflict. Mr. Johnstone basically chose the last.

How else can parents spare their children the consequences of growing up in jealous homes? This worthy goal is challenging in the best of circumstances, but it becomes nearly overwhelming when one parent undermines the efforts of the other to achieve it. Unfortunately, it is usually the nonjealous parent who tries to protect the children while the jealous parent is trying to subvert the effort. Jealous parents usually don't do this intentionally. They usually believe they are helping their children, too, by alerting them to the dangers that are imagined. They seek alliances with their children only to have more authority to assert over the other parent, supposedly to preserve the integrity of the family.

There are many effective ways the nonjealous parent can protect the children from the unhealthy influences of the other parent. Of course, the most effective way is to help the jealous parent overcome the jealousy. Another way that is troublesome but often helpful to the children is to separate from the jealous parent. However, these are the most drastic and difficult possibilities. If it is not possible to separate or change the jealous person, the best thing one can do is provide an environment that minimizes the problems children face.

One way to do this is to avoid having jealousy-based arguments in front of the children. If the parents can agree to keep their confrontations away from the children, they will spare them considerable turmoil. Children who have to witness parental debates about possible infidelity and abandonment can only become more insecure and confused. However, it is not always easy for parents to regulate when and where their confrontations are to be held. Thus, it is necessary to find a way to get the other parent to cooperate and to maintain a stance that enforces their agreement.

The most satisfactory way to do this starts when the nonjealous parent finds an appropriate time to discuss a proposed agreement. This time should only be when there is relative tranquility between the spouses. In other words, it is ineffective to try to establish an agreement while in the middle of an argument. During the quiet period one parent proposes that both agree to move any future arguments away from the children. It can be explained that the children are needlessly harmed by these conflicts. Any accusations can be made just as well in private as in the presence of the children.

Reaching an agreement is only the start. The nonjealous parent must still find a way to enforce it. This is because it is easily forgotten or considered unimportant in the heat of the next confrontation. If the parent is certain that an argument is unavoidable, the children should be told to leave the room until they are asked to return. When they have gone, the nonjealous parent expresses appreciation to the spouse for fulfilling the agreement. If the spouse ignores the agreement and insists on arguing in the children's presence, the nonjealous parent can firmly refuse to respond in any way to the accusations.

To respond, even with denials or corrections, is to negate the agreement and open the door to further controversy. If it is agreed that something won't be discussed then it shouldn't be, no matter how outrageous the accusations. This behavior may not seem effective at first, but it can gradually demonstrate to the jealous person that the rule is going to be maintained.

Even so, the children will be aware of conflicts between their parents. Some children who are sent away from these arguments might become even more anxious because they imagine the worst. To protect these children from controversy might seem to be a cure worse than the disease. This may be a valid concern in most domestic conflicts, but where jealousy issues are the focus, the situation is too volatile to permit the children to stay. Instead, they should be told that the parents are having a disagreement in which unpleasant words might be spoken. Then the children should be told that they are loved and will continue to be protected. They should later be given adequate opportunity to ask whatever questions they have. Answers should be given, but they shouldn't deprecate the other parent.

Tom and Judalyn Johnstone provide an example of how to respond to concerned questions from their children. After a few sessions of family therapy, they agreed to keep their conflicts away from the children. They also agreed to reduce the children's anxiety by explaining things to them more rationally:

Tommy: Mom told us you had a girlfriend. Don't you love us anymore?

Mr. J: Yes, Tommy, I love you all very much. I know you have all thought I wanted someone else instead of you. You all believed that because I was gone so often. I was working a lot, as you know, and that made your Mom lonesome. I should have been around her and you kids more. From now on I'm going to try harder to be.

Mrs. J: Tommy, I'm not sure about the girlfriend business. It's just that I love your Dad so much. I have the fear that I'm going to lose him. But I know he loves us all and doesn't want to leave us. So let's all forget about girlfriends. I'll try not to bring it up again.

Tommy: I sure hope so.

The Johnstones started making progress when they openly expressed their fears but stopped making accusations in front of the children. They found they could create an atmosphere in which they could ventilate their feelings with each other, but in a more positive direction than they had previously known.

Another way to help protect children from the risks of living in a jealous home is to avoid forcing them to choose sides. Having to choose sides forces children into an impossibly difficult position. To choose one is to displease the other. Siding with the jealous parent means they will eventually be more inclined to emulate that person's emotional problems. Siding with the nonjealous parent will cause the jealous parent to feel rejected and will probably lead the jealous parent to persist in efforts to gain their support by formulating ever-more-convincing accusations. Another conflict and another need for choosing sides is bound to occur. No one wins. But the children always lose.

Jealous parents tend to work harder at winning their children's favor. This is the result of their need for love and respect and to have their suspicions confirmed. This poses a serious dilemma for the nonjealous spouse. Fighting back, denying accusations, and competing for the children would only result in escalating the conflict. Ultimately, that would be destructive for the children. If, on the other hand, they don't defend themselves and their own position, they fear the children will assume the accusations are valid.

Nonjealous parents should resist the temptation to defend themselves, no matter how outrageous the charges. Most children won't be inclined to reject their parents simply because they refuse to comment on the charges. The children don't want to believe such bad things about their parent anyway, so denials would not be that effective. On the other hand, denials made in front of the children would probably have two undesirable outcomes. They would put more pressure on the children to choose sides— the children would have to believe the charge or believe the denial. And denials would cause the accusing parent to try harder to convince the children of the accuracy of the charges.

Thus, the most practical way of keeping the children from having to choose sides, or actually the "least bad" of several bad alternatives, is to play down the controversy and try even harder to move it away from the children. This is not to imply that the accused spouse should be passive or weak. It only means that this parent chooses a more suitable battleground.

Another way to help children cope in jealous families is to use sibling rivalry effectively. The first jealousy that most people encounter in their lives is in conflicts with their brothers and sisters. Sibling rivalry is normal and potentially healthy if the parents use it effectively. It is an opportunity for children to learn about dispute solving, negotiation, and sharing. So it is an opportunity as well as a risk.[14]

It is healthy for children to learn that they cannot and need not have a parent's exclusive attention. Perhaps the single most crucial element in the development of a healthy personality is the child's growing ability to forgo exclusive ownership of a parent. If they don't develop this capacity, if they devoted themselves only to getting others to meet their needs without regard to the needs of others, they become more vulnerable to jealousy problems. If handled properly by parents, siblings have a way of keeping one another from thinking this way.

An important influence on the way brothers and sisters compete and overcome jealousy problems together is the sibling position, or "birth order factor." Obviously, the jealousy experiences of an only child are going to be different from those of a child who has several older or younger brothers or sisters. Most parents are aware of the unhappy reactions that young children often display when new siblings enter the family.[15]

Social psychologists, in studying the birth order factor, have arrived at several conclusions regarding jealousy and sibling position. They conclude that, all other things being equal, only children are less inclined to develop jealousy problems because their unique position in the family is not threatened. However, when an only child becomes a firstborn, the child is more likely to be jealous of the siblings than vice versa. Middle children tend to become better negotiators and compromisers and have fewer problems with jealousy in themselves. Youngest children are more inclined toward possessiveness and less toward sharing and thus are somewhat more prone to having jealousy problems.[16]

Parents use sibling rivalries more effectively when they recognize the nature of sibling jealousy. Two children might have a dispute over a toy or a privilege. In jealousy, as we have seen, it is not the object itself but what it symbolizes that is at issue. The implied question is: "Am I as loved and important as my brother or sister?" If the parent's decision is to let sister have the toy, the message is far more ominous than simply being deprived of the toy.[17]

Rather than trying to repress normal rivalry among siblings, the wise parent will help them express any unhealthy feelings in a direct and positive way. The parent can then help the children develop skills in cooperation and compromise. This happens by recognizing each child's individual and unique needs and helping transform the rivalry into a healthy and adaptive aspect of life.[18]

When parents regularly reaffirm their love for their children and demonstrate that there is enough for each, regardless of the child's competitive efforts, they will minimize these difficulties. Rivalry problems are thus more commonly seen in homes where the parents are essentially not very loving or demonstrative of affection. The children feel they have to fight for it by getting the parent to favor them at the expense of others.

Children commonly do this by trying to get their parents to arbitrate their disputes. If the parent offers a verdict proclaiming that one child is right and the other is wrong, the parent is only inviting a recurrence of the dispute. The child who was supported is rewarded and will be inclined to do it again. The child who was not supported will attempt to develop better arguments or find new evidence or try to catch the other child in something that can lead to another decision. Unless one of the children has grossly violated a family rule, however, or is likely to be physically hurt, it is best to encourage children of jealous homes to settle their disputes themselves.

One way this might be done effectively is by diverting their attention from the conflict and onto something else of equal or greater interest. For example:

Tommy: Hey, Dad, Kenny lost my model airplane. Make him find it.

Kenny: I didn't either lose it. I never touched it. Make him quit lying about me, Daddy.

Father: [Ignoring argument] Say, I have to go to the gas station in a little while. Would you boys like to go with me? Then when I get back we can all look for the model together.

This greatly reduces the chances of jealousy between the siblings and usually doesn't put the younger children at too much of a disadvantage.

There will be times when the parents can't avoid having to arbitrate disputes. When this happens, they should refer to the family rules about how disputes are settled. After the ruling, the parent makes it clear that there is equal love for the child whose position was not endorsed.

Conscientious parents do not show favoritism. This would, of course, generate even more jealousy problems in the children, including the one who is "favored." The child who is not favored would manipulate for attention through disruptive or attention-getting behavior. The favored child will not be sure it is possible to maintain the favored position. Both children will be inclined to tattle on each other and behave in an ingratiating manner with the nearest parent.

Tattling can be symptomatic of problems for some children, especially those who feel less favored. It is their way of restoring the balance. Parents who permit or even encourage tattling are doing their children a disservice. They will be more effective if they ignore the information and meet the children's need for affection. However, many parents encourage it unwittingly. Parents may continually tell their children not to tattle and then listen intently when the child provides incriminating information about a sibling. If the parents then take some action against the sibling, the tattling child has been encouraged to continue this regardless of any verbal admonitions against it.

Children shouldn't be compared with their siblings or other children. Comments like "Why can't you be more like your brother?" are sure to lead to more jealousy problems than any good that could ever come from such questions. If each child is treated as a very unique person who is unlike the siblings, this will be less likely. Each child deserves some time alone with the parent. If all the attention given to the children must be shared by siblings, there is some further risk of jealousy problems. The amount of individual attention should be relatively equal.

Consistency about family rules is another factor that can help children cope in jealous households. Family disputes sometimes get out of hand because there is no automatic mechanism for settling them. In these circumstances, anyone whose viewpoint is rejected might feel personally wronged. The child thinks, "Kenny got the toy because Mom likes him best." They fight more intensely because the family doesn't seem to base decisions on objective rules but on more personal criteria or moods of the moment.[19]

In all homes, but especially in jealous ones, it is important to establish clear and consistent rules. These rules can then be referred to in resolving any disputes. This gives the child the sense that he or she hasn't been personally rejected by a parent. It was the rule, not the parent, that determined the decision. The rules should be the result of a family discussion. Such a discussion shouldn't be about any specific dispute, because that would only lead to more controversy. All family members agree together on each rule and its enforcement. Even very young children should have a voice in the development of such rules.

Rules that some families have established include the following:

- Don't use physical harm on one another.
- Don't tattle.
- If someone is doing something you don't like, ask them in a nice way not to do it.
- If they keep doing it, just go away from them.
- Always ask permission to borrow something that belongs to someone else.
- If someone takes something of yours without permission, remind them they haven't asked permission.
- If they refuse to give it back when you didn't give permission, walk away for fifteen minutes. Then ask for it again.
- If they refuse to return it after fifteen minutes, then take something of equal value or importance that belongs to the other person. This may be kept until the original object is returned.
- If a borrowed object is returned damaged, the lender may keep something of equal value that belongs to the borrower until it has been restored, replaced, or the lender says it is not necessary.
- When a person shares possessions with the others, he or she is special and is to be given praise and credit by everyone in the family.

It is a rare family, particularly if it has jealousy problems, that could consistently adhere to rules of this type. They are more like goals than absolute standards. Their intent is not to suppress people but to provide a means of settling issues so that no one has to feel personally rejected. Any family rules are more effective if written down and expressed in terms that are clear to all. This makes them accessible for consultation by anyone in the family.

Being a good role model is of crucial importance in helping to minimize the problems faced by children in jealous families. Because children acquire their values and personalities largely through imitating their parents, it is important that the parents present themselves as positive and happy people. Children typically pattern themselves after their parents and use them as the frames of reference in their own developing identities.[20]

However, in the jealous home this is complicated by the fact that the children could well model themselves after the jealous parent. The non-jealous parent can combat this by becoming more influential with the children than the jealous parent. This is a reasonable objective, because the children will tend to emulate the parent who is more attractive and closer to them. And they tend to behave in ways that are rewarded and avoid behaviors that have unhappy outcomes.

If the nonjealous parent seems depressed, withdrawn, beaten down, and apathetic because of all the pressures caused by living with the jealous spouse, the children won't want to be close to this parent. They won't try to imitate this person either, even if the parent is good, blameless, and filled with justifiable grievances. If, on the other hand, the jealous parent is more domineering, controlling, and expressive, the children might tend to imitate that behavior, especially if it is encouraged in them. This parent may seem more exciting, understandable, and alive to the children, whatever his or her other deficiencies.

One aspect of role modeling that should be emphasized is to encourage children to emulate their parents' tendencies to give and share. Parents can help their children reduce jealousy problems in large part by fostering this trait. They can do this by demonstrating how one ultimately derives more when they share than when they don't.

For example, at dinner one evening one parent suggests that all the family members bake brownies and take some over to a neighbor who lives alone. While making the brownies the family decides who has the privilege of delivering them. The children could draw straws or decide who is the most deserving of this opportunity that day. If all the children are shy or otherwise reluctant to carry the brownies, one parent gets the honor. After the delivery is made, the family members can happily discuss how pleased the neighbor was, and the event can be remembered in subsequent days. If the neighbor reciprocates in any way, the children have another lesson. They see the happiness it brought to everyone, and they will be more inclined to duplicate it in the future.

It is even more effective to educate children in giving and sharing with their parents. When a child does something for or gives something to the parent, the response is important. If the parent is very casual about the gift or assumes it is the child's obligation, a negative message is conveyed. This parent is claiming to deserve it or that the child owed it anyway so it wasn't really seen as a gift. When children give, they should feel their parent's happiness. The parent should be sincerely delighted. At the risk of boring others, everyone should be told about the kindness in front of the child.

Avoiding tendencies to reward children for jealous behavior is another crucial task of the concerned parent. People who develop jealousy problems do so largely because their jealous behaviors were rewarded when they were children. Because such rewards are more often than not given inadvertently, parents who wish to spare their children this fate should be wary of their tendency to provide them without even knowing it.

The behaviors that are most likely to precipitate jealousy problems in children include such things as the inability to share, selfishness, suspiciousness, tattling, being intolerant of different ideas, and the other traits discussed in previous chapters. The concerned parent should never encourage such behavior and should actively discourage it. For example:

Kenny: Tommy always hogs the TV set when you're gone. Make him share.

Tommy: I get to choose what to watch 'cause I'm the oldest.

Mother: Well, I think we're going to get another set, so you won't have to worry about this.

It would be more effective to reward not for jealous behavior but for its opposite. For example:

Kenny: Tommy always hogs.

Mother: No tattling, Kenny. What have you boys been up to?

Kenny: I wanted to watch cartoons but Tommy—

Mother: I see Tommy's favorite show is on. It's really nice of you to share like that, Kenny. And I know Tommy wants to share too, because he's also a good boy. Right, Tommy?

Another activity that will help children avoid jealousy situations is to expose them to people's individual differences. One of the most serious symptoms of jealousy problems is intolerance for others who do things differently. The intolerant person comes to believe that there is only one way things are to be done, one standard of conduct. The pathologically jealous person becomes inflexible and rigidly demands conformity to these ways. As this trait becomes solidified, it makes it that much more difficult for the jealousy problem to be overcome. The way to limit its childhood development is through exposure to and acceptance of others.

There are many ways of doing this. Parents might encourage their children's involvement with many kinds of people. It is helpful when children become active in organizations, church groups, and civic activities in which they are in contact with other people. Encouraging their participation in exchange programs, pen-pal relationships, and friendships with other families is also effective. Families that remain relatively isolated or families that confine their relationships to those who mirror their behaviors and values are more likely to risk jealousy problems in their children.

The last and most important activity for parents who want to minimize jealousy problems in their children is to let them know that there is plenty of love to go around. Much jealousy originates in the fear that there is only a finite supply of what one needs and that when some of this supply goes to another, there will not be enough left for oneself. Loving parents convey that there is a more than adequate supply of love and protection for all their children, and thus, no one child need be afraid of some future deprivation. Consequently the child will not need to resort to desperate tactics to acquire some of the limited supply of love.[21]

When one parent—and preferably both—is able to fulfill some of these objectives, the risks of problems faced by the children are greatly reduced. Even so, children who have parents who are pathologically jealous will always be at a disadvantage. They will always be more inclined toward jealousy themselves simply because of constant exposure to it. But they will be less likely to suffer from its long-term ill effects if they have a solid foundation in the love and respect that the nonjealous parent can provide. Everything done to enhance the child's self-esteem and sense of self-worth will help minimize the jealousy problems that will be encountered as an adult.

8

Ending Jealous Relationships

Ending a relationship that was once based on love is never easy. Yet it is far more difficult when that relationship has been with a jealous person. Most separations have predictable sequences—there is the growing anger, then threats and accusations, doubts and second thoughts, controversy over division of property and custody, and finally a recognition that it is really over. Eventually, most separating couples overcome their anger and sensibly devote themselves to getting on with their respective lives.[1]

However, the end of a jealousy-based relationship is less predictable. The bitterness tends to be more intense, and the anger lasts longer. There is less compromise, less willingness to forgive, and less flexibility in easing out of the commitment. Even after the separation has taken place, most jealous people will seek to return and strive to maintain the relationship. For many, separating does not really mean freedom from the jealous person but does mean even more insecurity and uncertainty. Because jealousy's essence is to hold on to one's "possessions," it is extremely difficult to break the tie.

Nevertheless, separating is an action that must be seriously contemplated and implemented by many people who are married to or involved with very jealous persons. What should be considered in deciding to separate and in its planning and implementation? How can the separation process be undertaken in a rational way so that it causes as little harm as possible? Why do people find it so difficult to escape these situations?

There is no single reason why people stay in unhappy jealousy-based relationships. Some people stay because they hope and expect future improvements. Some stay because they still love their partners and find that the negative jealousy is offset by many more positive qualities. Others remain in the relationships because they are afraid of the consequences and feel they have no way to survive independently. Some are so depressed or feel so helpless that they no longer have the drive to carry out the plan. Many people remain because they feel marriage is a sacred blessing that can never be broken without committing a horrible sin. Others think they should retain their marriages in order to provide a familiar home for their children. A few stay with jealous partners because they basically want to be mistreated or abused. Most people stay not for a single reason but because of a combination of these and other factors.[2]

Practical and rational reasons keep many jealous marriages together. Some people carefully weigh the alternatives available to them and choose the course that presents fewest problems. They might reason that they or their children will be worse off outside the marriage, no matter how bad it is within.

Many people simply feel it will be too difficult to end the relationship. They fear they will lose their families, their homes, and everything for which they have worked so long and hard. Or they recognize their need to be affiliated with someone and are sensitive to rejection. They doubt that a separation would free them. They have already endured their partners' stubborn possessiveness and determination never to let go. They feel they have no way of improving the relationship or solving the problem, no more hopes or plans for the future. They begin to rationalize that maybe it's not really so bad, that they aren't that unhappy, or that no one is happy nowadays anyway. They stay in these relationships not because of love or devotion but because it seems safer.[3]

Depression keeps many people tied into unhappy relationships, and the stress and degradation of living with jealous people often accentuates extreme depression. Social scientists have noted a significant degree of depression in spouses who are dominated or less powerful. Power imbalances are typical in jealousy-based relationships, so a high occurrence of depression is to be expected. Depression results in loss of energy, drive, assertiveness, and decisiveness—the very qualities that are necessary to implement such a major life decision as ending a marriage, breaking up a home, and creating a new environment.[4]

This is how it happens that staying in a jealous marriage may well seem better for some people, even when the jealousy is severe and dangerous. There is no guarantee that life will be better after a divorce for the person who makes this choice. In fact, there is some evidence to the contrary.

Some social scientists who conduct follow-up studies about the eventual outcome of divorce believe that many people do not do so well as they anticipated. One recently concluded ten-year study of divorce found that in two-thirds of all divorcing couples only one of the spouses actually experienced an improved quality of life. Among only 10 percent of divorced couples did the quality of life improve for both ex-partners.[5]

An all-too-prevalent reason for remaining with a jealous person is fear. People are understandably afraid of financial destitution, social ostracism, and even of the unknown. However, the most troublesome and realistic of these factors is fear of the jealous person.

Being afraid of the jealous person is frequently quite justified. The very jealous person is likely to be strongly opposed to the idea of separating. The opposition will probably not take the form of reasonable discussion or of positive efforts to correct the problem. Rather, it is more likely to take the form of violence, destructive behavior, and revenge-seeking activities. The person will have a desire to get even and make the other go through the same humiliation and loss.[6]

Wives of very jealous men are the ones most vulnerable in such situations. Unfortunately, too many of them have probably experienced difficulty in getting prompt help and continued protection from the law enforcement authorities. The legal system typically applies a double standard when it comes to marital relationships. Married victims of abuse are not always protected by law enforcement agencies with the same diligence as are nonmarrieds. Until recently, for example, the California penal code stated that a wife must be injured more seriously than commonly allowed for battery in order to press charges against her husband.[7]

A wife may recognize that calling the authorities for help will cause her more problems in the long run. The action is likely to make her husband angry. When the law enforcers leave, as they inevitably will, the wife faces greater possibility of retaliation. Even when the law does take action against the jealous partner who is abusive, much of the punishment is ultimately inflicted on the family. Any punishment would take the form of fines or incarceration, both of which could lead to serious financial consequences for the family as well as the perpetrator.

Thus, though it might at first seem ironic and even unbelievable that people who have control of their mental faculties would not try to get away from the sources of their fears, mental health professionals and social science researchers have found that this is precisely what happens with many abused women. Their response is not necessarily masochistic; rather, it is the response most commonly found among disaster victims. Those involved in such crises as airplane crashes, wars, and epidemics behave consistently. They feel personally vulnerable and are overwhelmed by feelings of fear, isolation, guilt, apathy, and "frozen fright." During these times they want to be with their closest associates, even if those people are not very positive influences.[8]

Similarly, the abused wives of jealous husbands cling to what is familiar to them, including their homes and all their family members, even the abuser. Though they are at risk, they stay because they fear the loneliness, nonsupport, and physical discomfort they will encounter if they leave. As bad as the relationship may be, at least it is familiar.[9]

This type of fear is also related to the pattern of learned helplessness noted earlier. Many studies of the victims of spouse abuse have shown how certain people gradually become immobilized and feel ineffectual in coping with their problem. They have been subjected to so much degradation that they lose the self-confidence needed to take action. Many of these people wait passively for years, looking for signs of improvement and seeing hope where no one else can see any reason for optimism. This condition has been described by psychiatrists as "pathological tolerance"—a trait found in some individuals who endure treatment that would be unacceptable to normal, healthy people.[10]

Staying together "for the sake of the children" also causes many unhappy jealousy-based relationships to endure. Some couples fear that the divorce would be damaging to the children's well-being and so elect to stay married, at least until the children become independent. Peter found that this was a reasonable choice for himself and his children even though his marriage to a very jealous woman was painful.

Peter was thirty-five, the father of two young children, and had for twelve years been the husband of an intensely jealous woman. Her possessiveness made the relationship barely tolerable for him. He didn't consider himself to be a masochist and did not appreciate the discomfort of his situation. He could easily have sought a divorce, except that he knew he would be giving up the daily care of his children. Despite recent judicial movement toward placing children in the care of their fathers or into joint custody, the odds still greatly favor the awarding of young children to the mother.[11]

This is especially true when the mother is not explicitly seen as "unfit."

Peter knew it would have been impossible to prove his wife an unfit parent or pathologically jealous. It would even have been hard to prove that it was unfounded, though he knew there were no rational reasons for her suspicions about him.

Peter also had reason to believe that his wife would impose her jealousy problem on the children if he were gone. She already did that to a great extent when he was away on business. Peter was unhappy for himself and for his family, yet he felt he had to consider the children's needs paramount. He took the position that he should preserve the marriage in order to continue having a strong and healthy influence with his children. Thus he made a fairly rational judgement to stay in the marriage, solely for the sake of the children.

Keeping a marriage intact only for the children's well-being has had few advocates in recent years. Most professional therapists still conclude that children are probably not better served if their parents remain together unhappily. This view has been reiterated so often that it sounds like a proved fact, but actually no scientific study has proved or disproved this hypothesis.[12] In fact, it is well known that the children of divorced parents as a group have many more problems than do the children of parents who have remained together. The rates of delinquency, truancy, school dropouts, substance abuse, mental illness, and subsequent divorces are very much higher among the children of divorced parents. However, this does not mean that divorce is the cause of such outcomes. Other factors play a part in these problems. For example, divorcing couples themselves have far more economic, emotional, and physical problems than do nondivorcing couples. The resulting stress and difficulty can lead to more problems for the children. Divorced parents have more emotional and health problems and fewer social supports. These factors, not divorce itself, can help explain why some children of divorcing parents have more of these problems.[13]

Given the current limitations in research technology and resources, it is still not possible to determine in advance whether children are better off staying in homes with unhappy parents or being part of a separation. Testing this question accurately would require comparing at least three large groups of children throughout their lives—children whose parents were unhappy but stayed together, those whose parents were unhappy and eventually divorced, and those whose parents were happy and stayed together. Then some way would have to be found to make sure the groups compared were equal in every other relevant aspect, including economic well-being, stresses in daily life, parental stability, and ability to provide for the emotional needs of the children. It would surely be difficult to tell whether children from supposedly "happy" homes really had such homes or not. Every home has some moments of unhappiness—and every home, no matter how wretched otherwise, has some positive moments. To test such a hypothesis, it would also be necessary to define and objectively measure overall well-being. Any consensus would be very difficult to achieve, because the question essentially remains a value judgment to be decided by each individual.[14]

Even if these formidable obstacles could be overcome, how could anyone conclude that the parents' action years earlier was the cause of a subsequent better outcome? Too many other factors, intervening variables, in each person also play a part in whatever outcome is achieved. In other words, taking the children into account in making the decision to stay or leave a jealous home is important but complex. Because it is so complicated, a parent cannot clearly or accurately base the decision on that single issue.

Another reason many people remain in unhappy marriages is that they don't believe in divorce or have an aversion to it. No one can be very enthusiastic about divorce or separation as a way to resolve problems. It is not for everyone, even for everyone who lives in a pathologically jealous household. But for some, it may be the only viable option. Anyone who continues to be physically or mentally abused even after trying unsuccessfully for a long time to improve the situation has to consider separation. In the words of psychotherapist Howard Halpern, "The pain of ending it won't last forever. In fact it won't last nearly as long as the pain of not ending it." He adds that ending a possessive relationship can open the door to new possibilities.[15]

Divorce or permanent separation must be considered before one gives up all hope of happiness, all reasonable chance to be fulfilled and productive, because of some dubious notion that people must remain together no matter what. It makes little sense for people to sacrifice themselves, their children, even their jealous partners, to lives of continued pain because they have once made a commitment. Being married and sharing lives are supposed to contribute to one's happiness and well-being. Relationships exist to give people some fulfillment. They permit people to have more security, companionship, and love. But if relationships don't do this or if they provide only the opposite of this, needless and pointless sacrifices are being made.

Nevertheless, most people don't look on divorce very favorably. It is often associated with the breakdown of society and an indication that a nation's morals are in decay. Divorce, say its critics, is symptomatic of a society's declining standards, lack of family values, individual selfishness, and impulsiveness. Despite these warnings, the American divorce rate is among the highest in the world. Rarely do people point out that this high frequency also indicates something positive—that divorce is more likely to happen when people are permitted freedom of choice and have relative sexual equality and economic opportunity to be independent.

Even if divorce is considered to have some redeeming social merit, however, most individuals don't consider it a desirable thing to do. People rarely marry thinking of divorce or eventually planning to end the relationship. Many feel too ashamed to divorce. They feel it represents failure and is a tangible sign, for all the world to see, of their incompetence. They fear that others will reject and isolate them.

Because of these apprehensions, many people endure considerable pain and displeasure to avoid divorce. Donald Cantor, a divorce lawyer who reviewed courtroom testimony for a serious study about the motivations of divorce, concluded that most people do not divorce frivolously or without regret and personal conflict. In fact, he said, they seem loath to terminate their marriages. "What most people endure during marriage before finally resorting to divorce," he said, "is practically unbelievable."[16]

Perceptions about divorce have been changing dramatically in recent years. While the high divorce rate is still universally regrettable, there is greater acceptance of individuals who divorce. This is true in large part because few Americans remain personally untouched by it. Every year over 1,200,000 families break up through divorce.[17]

Almost anyone who hasn't been divorced is probably married to, related to, or friendly with someone who has been divorced. Divorced people are no longer looked upon as pariahs. Political leaders, entertainment and sports personalities, and businesspeople seem accepted or rejected for reasons that have nothing to do with their divorce status. The American public twice voted for Ronald Reagan's presidency, and his divorce wasn't a campaign issue. The social disgrace once inevitably attached to divorce now seems like an archaic remnant of a simpler time.

In other words, divorce is a painful but not fatal ordeal. It is more like a toothache—it may hurt at the dentist's office getting the extraction and it may hurt for a while after, but in the long run it hurts a lot less than it would if the problem were ignored.

No matter what reasons a person has, the decision to stay or leave a very jealous person can be made objectively and rationally. No matter how formidable the obstacles to be encountered in staying or going, one can implement the decision through careful planning and preparation. Before discussing how to plan, however, it will be useful to consider the example of Pamela Flynn, who went through the process with effective results.

Pamela Flynn was forty-five, the mother of three teenagers, and had been unhappily married for twenty-two years. The doctor who referred her for therapy was concerned that her long-standing marital problems accounted for her growing depression. She had just returned to her husband after a two-month separation when she saw the therapist for the first time. This is a slightly edited version of the way she described her situation:

> I couldn't make it on my own. So I swallowed my pride and came back. Now it's worse than ever. Kevin knows I'm stuck with him now, no matter what he does. I wish I could have stayed away. Well, I guess I shouldn't have left in the first place. The truth is I shouldn't have married the bastard!
>
> My life with him has been a nightmare. He's got a terrible temper. I got clobbered plenty of times. He's the most jealous guy you ever saw. He hates it when I want to have friends. He figured I'd fall in love with someone if I did. For years I kept threatening to leave him. That didn't make him improve, it just made him crazier. He knew I wouldn't go, he figured I couldn't afford it. It costs a lot to feed three teenagers. I told him the law would force him to support us, and he said we could starve for all he cared, no matter what the law said. He'd burn the house down and never be seen again. I believed him too.
>
> My lawyer didn't get the picture at first. He said I could get a divorce, easy, and I could get a good financial settlement too. Ha! He didn't know my husband. Kevin's so stubborn he'd rather go to jail than do what anyone told him to do.
>
> One day I went to the lawyer just after Kevin beat me up. I had a black eye and my arms were all bruised. The lawyer asked if there were any witnesses, but no one else saw the fight. The lawyer told me to move out now, no matter what. So I did. I had to get away even without a settlement.
>
> I went right out from the lawyer's office and found a cheap apartment. I had a little money stashed, just enough for the rent and deposit and a few things to keep us going. Then I picked up the kids at school. They were great. They didn't want to leave their school or home, but they didn't want me getting killed either. And they sure didn't want to stay around the house with their father acting so nutty.
>
> We rented a truck and moved some beds and furniture out of the house.

It was a good thing Kevin was still at work. I figured we could stay in the apartment for a few months until things calmed down. Maybe Kevin would move out and we could all go back home. Or, if not that, then maybe the lawyer would find a way to make Kevin help with the support. Then we could move into something decent.

The apartment was in an awful area—it would give you the creeps. We only had two little bedrooms for the four of us, and a tiny kitchen. We didn't have hardly anything to cook with or eat on for a while. I got a government job. I filed papers all day. It was boring. The pay was terrible. I couldn't even get help from the welfare or food stamps or anything. They said that since I wasn't legally separated, our family income was too high to qualify. The kids were scared of the neighborhood and their new school. It was really rough for them. Other kids picked on them. They just stayed in the apartment all the time they weren't in classes.

Our apartment got broken into twice. The burglars gave up after the second time. I guess they realized there wasn't anything worth stealing. They must have told the other crooks not to bother with that place.

I let the kids call Kevin, and he got them to say where we lived. Pretty soon he started showing up all the time, day and night. We wouldn't let him in so he'd stand out in the hall saying he wanted us back. Then he'd cuss me out. Sometimes he would yell that I was having an orgy inside. He'd cry, make promises, threaten to break in. He'd say anything. We called the police a couple times. They took him in the second time, but they let him go. It really embarrassed me in front of the other tenants. I think they all got a big kick out of it.

Kevin kept it up for weeks. It was driving me crazy. I couldn't take it anymore. The kids couldn't either. They wanted to go back to their old school and friends. They started making sounds about moving back with Dad. That was the last straw for me. So I finally gave in. We packed up and moved home.

Kevin was nice at first. He helped us with the move. The kids really were happier so I guess it was worth it. I wasn't happy, though. Nothing had really changed. In fact, it got worse. Now he badgers and threatens me all the time, and he knows I can't do anything about it. Now I'm just going to wait until the kids are on their own. Then I'll probably leave again. Only I'll be prepared next time.

Pamela Flynn did as she had planned. She stayed in therapy just long enough to restore some self-confidence, make some objective plans for her future, and learn that Kevin would never participate in the sessions. Later she took courses at the local community college and learned to be a computer operator. Eventually her children all became independent. One joined the Army; one got a job and moved into a group home with several other young people; and the third married and established a new home.

Pamela used her new computer skills to find a well-paying job. She had started her job long before she finally separated, over Kevin's loud objections. She moved into a nice apartment that was secure from unwanted intruders and was able to be more forceful in keeping Kevin from interfering in her life. She established new friendships and found that life could be more pleasant than she had imagined. To this day, Pamela says, Kevin still lives in the home, alone and seemingly very bitter. He is probably waiting in vain in the expectation that Pamela will realize her folly and beg to return. She says there's not a chance.

Mrs. Flynn's example is not unusual in dealing with jealous people, but the way things turned out for her are only one of many possible outcomes. For some, separating will prove to be a blessing, for others a serious mistake. Some, like Pamela Flynn, will undertake the separation without adequate forethought and preparation, causing a valid decision to turn out badly. Others will weigh the factors systematically and make a decision that works for them, whether it is to stay or to leave. Others will do nothing but wait. They will tell themselves that they still don't have enough information to permit a rational decision.

Those who wait for more information before deciding whether to stay or go are generally avoiding the inevitable. Many of them have unconsciously made a decision already; it is to remain immobilized and to avoid deciding anything.[18] People in this situation may dwell on the issue in rather directionless ways. They keep thinking the same thoughts without much forward motion and along these lines: If I leave, everyone will get hurt. If I stay, everyone will get hurt. I don't want to hurt anyone. Maybe things will get better. Everyone changes. Anyone can grow up. But what if the problem stays the same? Then if I don't leave everyone will get hurt again.

The indecisive spouse of the jealous person will be immobilized until some unpleasant truths are faced. One truth is that no action or solution won't hurt someone, and some people can't accept this. They continue to tell themselves that such possibilities exist but they just haven't been discovered yet. They think that if they wait a little longer and get some new information, they will find the solution. The truth is that there will be pain whatever is done. It can't be eliminated. It can only be minimized.

Another truth is that there is no reason to think that the future will be any different. Many spouses of jealous partners remain immobilized be-

178

cause they keep waiting for changes. They think or hope that the jealousy will end as the spouse gets older or richer or when the children are gone, move to a different area, get different jobs, or whatever. But pathologically jealous people don't necessarily mellow with age. Flexibility and adaptability are not typical features of the jealous person's character. If the spouse has already done everything possible to bring about changes and not enough improvements have been achieved, it is unrealistic to think that change will come in the future. In other words, continuing to plan for change in these circumstances is simply a rationalization. It is far more realistic to assume that there will be no more changes and to proceed with a decision on that basis.

Still another truth is that the decision will have to be made based on incomplete information. If people in this situation wait the rest of their lives, essentially they will have no more significant information that is relevant to the decision than what presently exists. No "facts" are suddenly going to emerge during the waiting process that will tell anyone what to do. Nor can anyone base a decision on what has proved right for others. Every person's obstacles and opportunities are unique.

The decision to stay or go comes down to one difficult question: Overall, is my present life better for me and those I care about than my life would become if I separated? No one can ever be sure of discovering the right answer in advance, because this would require an accurate prediction of the future where, at best, only educated guesses are possible. There will be unanticipated risks as well as benefits in independence, just as there are known securities as well as hardships in staying.

The question also requires a look at one's present circumstances. How much is a person willing to tolerate at home before risking the unknown future of independence? There is no one answer to this either. Each person's unique circumstances greatly influence what he or she is willing to endure. A person who is emotionally secure, independently wealthy, and surrounded by friends who encourage separation will probably put up with much less of a jealous person's behavior. On the other hand, an insecure spouse without money or friends, who believes that marriages are made in heaven and that divorce will result in eternal roasting in a fiery furnace, will probably tolerate much more. Yet, no matter what each person's unique circumstances are, each has limits as to what will be tolerated. Any decisions to stay or leave should be based on an objective assessment of the pros and cons.[19]

Many people in this position want someone else to tell them what to do. They don't know what the future might be, and they don't know how much they can or will have to tolerate at home. Of course, neither does anyone else. Thus, no one can or should try to tell them what to do. This is a decision that can only be made by the person involved. However, the decision can be made with objectivity by using some simple techniques that marital therapists often recommend.

One technique is for troubled couples to write themselves personal letters in which they weigh the pros and cons. These will be private letters, not to be read by anyone else, so they can and should be completely honest. In such letters they make three lists, each on a separate page. On the first page are written all the current benefits of the relationship. On the second, all the disadvantages. On the third page is a description of what the writer thinks will happen to all concerned if there is a separation. This can be compared with the first two pages, which constitute the writer's thoughts about what will happen by staying.

Then the pages should be put away for a week. After the week is over, three new pages are written, also listing benefits, disadvantages, and separation predictions. These are placed with the first letter. This process may be repeated several more times if desired. Eventually, after no longer than a month, all the letters are reviewed and used to develop a master list. On the first page of the master list are all the benefits that were written in the previous letters. All the duplications can be eliminated. The second master list will consolidate all the disadvantages, and so on. The result of this project will be a more objective evaluation of the situation.

Having the items in writing will make them seem more objective, as though written by someone else. Because it is essentially written over a period of several weeks, it will be less influenced by one's moods of the day, atypical events, unexpected kindnesses, or crises. Having been worked on for several weeks improves the chances that it will be the result of more careful and deep thought. The effort will help the person consider, as objectively as possible, the various factors that have to be considered. The result of this exercise is no panacea, and it can't be the only factor in determining what decision should be made. But it does explicate and organize the most important thoughts that have to be considered.

If, after this exercise, the reasons for leaving clearly outweigh the reasons for staying, the person has to do some serious thinking about how to implement the separation while minimizing the difficulties that will surely be encountered. People who are married to pathologically jealous spouses should examine their own attitudes about separations and divorce. Those who are decisive and retain the option to leave do well to prepare carefully for divorce or separation.

Once the spouse has accepted that divorce or separation is a possibility, the next step is to get prepared emotionally and economically to make the break. It isn't necessary actually to leave once the preparations are made, but now the option realistically exists. Those who are prepared can still bide their time, wait, work on the relationship, and find ways of improving it. They do this secure in the knowledge that they remain of their free choice and not simply because they lack alternatives.

Preparation might include training for more financially rewarding job skills, learning about money management, locating appropriate housing opportunities, learning more about cooking and housekeeping tasks, and so on. It might also include developing new and supportive friendships, saving money, and possibly consulting with lawyers and therapists to determine legal rights and emotional stability. This education won't be wasted even if the final decision is to preserve the relationship.

No matter how well intentioned they are, activities in preparation for a possible separation are likely to upset the jealous partner. They could have the same effect on a jealous person as the sight of a convict reading a book entitled *How to Break Out of Jail* would have on a prison guard. The jealous person would probably become more vigilant, suspicious, and unpleasant. Becoming more possessive than ever, the jealous person would be likely to put up many obstructions to the preparation.

Difficulties of this kind lead many spouses to make their preparations in haste and in secret. The apparent advantage of preparing in secret is that the threat to the jealous partner may remain concealed until it is too late for any response. Because the response might be disapproving at best and violent at worst, it is tempting to avoid resistance and confrontations wherever possible. For some spouses this may be the most desirable option. For others, secrecy and hasty preparations may result in more risks and problems than they circumvent.

If the preparation phase is of very short duration, perhaps under a month, the jealous partner will have only a little time to adjust. During this time the jealous person's fears, possessiveness, and anger may become intensified, like a ray of sunlight under a magnifying glass. In these circumstances, there are considerable chances of physical and emotional violence as well as increased determination to cause problems for the spouse after the separation.

If, on the other hand, the spouse announces that preparations are being made but that the actual separation won't be for several months, the intensity of emotions is spread out. The jealous partner will feel that the time is distant and the threat isn't as great—as if there is ample time to get the nonjealous partner to end this plan. Moreover, the longer preparation time assures that any action will be taken more rationally and less impulsively. It takes at least several months to take courses, save money, and make new friends, if they are done right.

Preparing in secret may be ineffective in dealing with jealous spouses. The very jealous person is already suspicious and alert to changed patterns of behavior. If changes are detected, the usual interrogations could begin. The nonjealous partner could ignore them, evade the questions, or lie. Any response, or no response, would further reinforce the jealous person's conviction that the other had been dishonest. It might feed the jealousy and provide "evidence" that the suspicions had been valid all along. It could preclude any improved relationship in the future. Therefore, secrecy in this matter is, in effect, burning bridges.

Because the function of the preparation process is to expand options rather than reduce them, most, but not all, spouses find careful but open and obvious preparation to be most effective. Pathologically jealous people will not ignore such activities. They are more likely to suspect that the preparations are going on because the decisions to leave have already been made. They may be hostile and threatening during this time. However, their unpleasant behavior could hardly be much worse or longer lasting than if their partners had been secretive. And the behavior might even be more subdued because the nonjealous person is being so matter-of-fact.

The nonjealous partner must have a simple, clear, honest, and unequivocal explanation to offer when confronted about these preparations. For example, a wife might say to her husband, "Well, Aaron, things haven't been too good between us lately, and I really don't know what might happen to us in the future. So I want to get myself ready just in case you or I decide we can't go on living together. I'm not planning on leaving you, and I don't think you're planning on leaving me, but I think it's best that I get ready. You never know what the future holds."

If the decision to separate is made, new sets of tasks must be accomplished. There are unique problems in leaving a jealous person. It is most helpful in this case to learn as much as possible about the actual divorce process and the probable life that awaits the divorcing person. Reading about the process and talking with those who have experienced it is important. Among the excellent books that contribute to this situation are Joseph

Epstein's *Divorced in America,* Morton Hunt's *The World of the Formerly Married,* and Edward Teyber's *Helping Your Child with Divorce.*[20]

An attorney should be consulted before the spouse actually leaves the home. This is essential even though there is increased support for the idea of do-it-yourself divorces or for going through divorce mediation in order to circumvent the legal adversarial process of terminating relationships. These innovations may be valuable for some couples but are not very helpful when the central problem is pathological jealousy. This condition almost guarantees that there will be legal disputes. The stories about so-called creative divorces and friendly separations are rarely set in jealous relationships. It seems rather improbable that any jealous people who see that their lives have been disrupted; their spouses, children, and social status taken; and their homes and property lost; will still come out of it feeling only friendship for the one they believe responsible. Thus, even if the jealous spouse appears to be cooperative in the steps toward separation, the nonjealous partner is wise to seek legal counsel.[21]

Once the decision to separate is made, but before it is carried out, it is prudent to be ready for pressure and resistance from the jealous mate. When most jealous people understand that this is "for real" and not just an idle threat, they can make dramatic changes in their behavior. Because they are terrified of rejection, they may try anything to prevent it from taking place. They may promise to change, to do better, to quit making accusations, or to enter therapy. They may also try to isolate the spouse or work to get allies to try to change the spouse's mind. They could lie to friends to convince them that the nonjealous partner is actually separating to go off with one of those who were suspected all along.

These actions put the nonjealous partner in a difficult position. The promises are inviting, although they have heard them all before and been disappointed. The nonjealous person doesn't want to be heartless and may think everyone deserves another chance. There is the fear that not permitting another chance will appear cold and merciless. It may make one seem guilty of the jealous person's accusations. The pressure can be so severe that the decision to leave a jealous partner is often followed by second thoughts and changes of mind.

Spouses who change their minds about separating, however, often regret the new decision. Changing one's mind is likely to be harmful to all concerned. Momentary relief may be felt by both, but it doesn't last long. It is almost always followed by a recurrence of the same old problems. The jealous partner might have been sincere in making promises but forgets them when things get back to "normal." This is because he or she doesn't feel much that wrongdoing or need for change really existed. Once the partner has given up the plan to leave, the jealous person is generally more intent than ever on getting back in control.

Many separating couples find it appropriate to leave the relationship with the understanding that there will be a reunion someday. The premise is that the separation will motivate the jealous person to look harder at the problem and work toward its resolution and that it will permit both spouses to see what it is like to live independently.

Trial separations have been shown to have some merit for some people, especially those who have become rigidly locked into dysfunctional patterns of behavior and interaction. However, while many troubled couples might learn and grow or achieve other objectives through trial separation, it is highly unlikely among couples who have severe jealousy-based relationships. To the jealous person, it won't really be a trial of separateness. The person is likely to consider that the relationship is continuing and that the same obligations and rules that existed before still apply. The jealous person will probably scrutinize the partner more than ever during the separation, always wondering and asking when the reconciliation is to be.[22]

Under these circumstances, neither spouse will learn much about being separate. It makes more sense to be definite about the separation. If it is going to occur it should be presented as a permanent decision. If the relationship is actually severed, both people will be able to concentrate on their own well-being rather than staying oriented to the business of the other person. Obviously, people can reunite after they have been separated. If they see that actual changes rather than promises have been made, this is a possibility. But it is more clear and effective if it occurs after the separation has existed for a while without any advanced plans to be reunited.

When the separation actually takes place, it is a time to show strength and positive determination. Of course, one is going to enter this new experience with fears, doubts, and vacillations. However, it is not necessary and probably unproductive to reveal these feelings to the jealous spouse. Uncertainties or weaknesses will probably be seen by the spouse as an invitation to reassume control, an opportunity to manipulate the situation. This is needlessly confusing and prolongs the conflict and pain everyone will experience. In implementing the separation, the spouse of the jealous person is better served by acting in a cool, businesslike, and rather aloof manner. This is clear and permits all concerned to understand what is happening. It enables everyone to act more rationally.

From an emotional standpoint, if not necessarily a legal or economic one, many spouses of jealous people seem to do better if they are the ones who leave and establish new homes. Of course, legal and financial considerations often rule this out, but when it is possible it has many advantages. If the jealous person leaves, even if required to by law, it is more likely that there will be subsequent problems. Even with restraining orders and legal prohibitions requiring the jealous person to stay away, he or she could continue to make trouble. Jealous people may keep their homes under surveillance. They may abruptly enter the home and subject the family to the same problems the separation was supposed to eliminate. Jealous people will be more inclined to regard their former homes as their property and its contents, including the family members, as possessions.

If the nonjealous spouse establishes the residence away from the former home, it will seem like something new to both. The new place will not seem like the jealous person's possession. It will make the separation seem that much more final, and it will be easier for the authorities to keep the jealous person away.

After separations have been in effect for a while, many people think about returning to their jealous partners. Studies show that many people who have separated find it very difficult to stay that way. Emotional separation usually occurs long after the physical separation. They might still feel love and compassion for their partners and concern for their well being. Moreover they are facing difficulties on their own. The memories of the good times become magnified, while those of the bad begin to fade from memory. The temptation to return grows. However, doing so is exceedingly risky and should be undertaken only after much caution and soul-searching.[23]

If the couple is serious about reuniting, the chances of minimizing future problems can be improved. A worthwhile activity for both parties, prior to reconciling, would be to consult a family mediation specialist. These professionals can help couples delineate ground rules for handling future disputes and help them to "fight fair."[24]

Whether or not professional help is sought, the reunion will be more successful if it takes place in a systematic fashion. There are five steps the spouse or partner could insist upon in reconciling with a jealous person. If any of these stages has not been gone through, there is a great likelihood that the same jealousy patterns will be reestablished.

First, the reconciliation shouldn't be rushed. Enough time should have elapsed so that the return is based on a positive decision rather than an impulse or failure to cope independently. If the return occurs before independence is established, it is probable that the previous problems will recur. Ideally, a return should only be considered after the spouse has lived independently, has coped independently, and has experienced life successfully as an autonomous person. Then, when the reunion occurs, it will be harder to give up this sense of independence. When they reunite this way, both spouses will have equal power and the rejoined relationship can become stronger than it was before.[25]

Second, the jealous person must demonstrate sincere motivation to make changes. Promises are only the beginning. All jealous people in this situation should also indicate how they intend to keep those promises. They should at least be willing to learn about the problem of jealousy. They should have read something on the subject and talked to people about jealousy. They should spend time talking with their former spouses about the nature of jealousy and acknowledge their own problems with it. Psychotherapy might be required. If they promise to partake of therapy, the sessions should be well under way before any reunions are considered. If therapy is in progress, the spouses should consult with the therapist and not reunite until all concerned agree that there have been improvements.

Third, eventually some unpressured social time should be spent with the jealous person before returning home. Instead of a trial separation, there should be a "trial togetherness." The time with the jealous person should come after changes have been supposedly made but still without promises to return. The spouse should not imply that this is a test or "audition" to see if reconciliation is possible. (This may only result in a more polished performance.) Instead, the time together should be treated as a new friendship with no implications that more will come of it. After a while, having such a relationship will be beneficial in any event. And, even though it may not be acknowledged, it is certainly a good opportunity to test the possibility of a reconciliation.

Fourth, when the couple is spending time together, the spouse could talk about subjects the jealous person once found threatening—for example, equal rights for women, separate vacations, and sex role differences. Open discussion about current friendships with members of the opposite sex can also occur, with the understanding that neither spouse will seek further information about these relationships once the reconciliation takes place. Failure to agree to this condition should automatically rule out reconciliation. The purpose of this is not to threaten the partner or cause anger but rather to see if things have really changed. It is better to fight during this time than after a reunion.

The fifth step toward the reconciliation process comes when the couple writes down everything both partners understand as agreements for their future together. They develop a list of mutual expectations. The list includes such things as how each will spend his or her time and what the other partner will or will not do about it. When an agreement is reached, the couple signs two copies, one for each, to be kept for future reference. These statements will prove valuable to remind both about agreed terms and clarify misunderstandings. Almost all couples will have some violations of the agreement, no matter how determined or sincere they are. For the old patterns of behavior to be gone would require major personality changes, not good intentions. However, if both people have equally strong positions, along with their improved lines of communication, and understand their expectations of one another, the new relationship can be greatly improved.

The person who decides never to return to the jealous partner might face a rather lonely future unless a new person enters the scene. Yet, those who have lived in a jealous marriage or relationship tend to enter new relationships with caution. And well they should. Not only has the jealous reaction conditioned them to avoid other relationships but they also fear getting involved with people who have the same problem. Many people choose a new spouse whose personality characteristics are similar to those of the previous spouse. Thus a thoughtful person wants to know how to avoid repetition of a prior problem.[26]

The goal is to rule out new relationships with anyone who is excessively jealous. Unfortunately, no one wears signs that reveal this characteristic. The clues are sometimes elusive, especially in the beginnings of new relationships, when people tend to be on their best behavior. Often jealousy isn't revealed until after some commitment is made and the jealous person feels some "right" to be possessive.

It is also difficult to determine these traits simply by asking. Any response, whether it affirms or denies jealousy, will be inconclusive. If the response is "No, I'm not jealous at all," it is impossible to be sure that the person is truthful and insightful. It is also confusing when the response is an admission of jealousy. The response could be something like, "Why, yes, darling, I'm very jealous whenever I'm around anyone as wonderful as you." It would be hard to know how to take such a disarming comment.

One probably learns more by indirectly observing the behavior of the prospective companion and noting the attitudes expressed in a variety of situations. Observing the kind of people with whom someone associates can also be revealing. One could have conversations with the prospective partner about relationships, particularly those pertaining to the roles of men and women. The first warning signal is seen if someone seems very rigid about the way people should be and intolerant of deviations from one set of norms. One might also want to find out about someone's prior relationships. Why did they end? What is the current feeling about those people? The answers can be revealing.

It is also worthwhile to get to know some of the new companion's friends and family members. If they seem very rigid and role bound, another warning signal appears. Furthermore, at some point it should be made clear to the prospective partner and that person's family and friends that one's own individuality and autonomy are highly valued. Yet another warning may be seen if the prospect disapproves of this trait and, with humor or seriousness, tries to influence a change.

After the relationship has gone on a while, but before any commitment or "understandings" are reached, the evaluation becomes more direct. A woman could casually mention other dates or interesting men that she has recently seen. She could also show friendly, but not flirtatious, interest in some of her friend's friends who might also be his potential rivals. She can talk with these friends in his presence or do so privately and tell him about it. A man could describe some of the attractive women in his office or show interest in other women in front of his companion.

The response to these actions may provide further information, but it won't be entirely conclusive. Whether very jealous or not, most people who seem interested in involvement won't be enthused about these activities. And even if someone turns out to be pathologically jealous, these activities won't necessarily result in venomous tirades or even verbal disapproval. One must be alert for more subtle clues. One way would be to use the test in Chapter 2 of this book. Because of the way the test is constructed, the person who is evaluating the prospect need not reveal that a test is being used. It may take several days of casual questions from the test that the jealous person isn't directly aware of. However, it would be better if the nonjealous person was candid about the test and the reasons for using it.

If any of these activities suggest that the new companion has some problem about jealousy, it might be advisable to avoid any further serious involvement. That doesn't mean a friendship with the person shouldn't continue. It can be a very valuable experience to be friends with a very jealous person—without commitment and intense involvement.

Even with many danger signals and warnings that someone may have a serious jealousy problem, some people may still want to pursue a relationship. These people often forget the pain they experienced in their marriage or previous relationships. They become more lonely and seek the companionship of these new people. They may begin to rationalize that it will work out, that they have learned how to handle such problems better. When they are insistent about developing relationships with such people, they should at least be open and honest in communicating their concerns to the new person. They can explain to their potential spouses that they fear entering the same life-style they once had to endure. If the future mate is interested and caring, there will be further discussions and clarifications.

When a couple becomes more serious about a future together, the chances for a fulfilling experience are improved if mutual expectations are brought out into the open. Anyone who has experienced the serious problems of living with and separating from a very jealous person owes it to her- or himself to do everything possible to prevent a recurrence, no matter how unreasonable it might seem to others.

It must be reiterated here that there is no one answer about staying or separating that is correct for everyone. Even though much of the above discussion centered around the strategies of separating, staying together may be the best choice for many, regardless of the problems associated with it. It is often courageous, not cowardly, to remain in a jealous relationship and do everything possible to preserve it. Even if the effort doesn't save the relationship, it probably was worthwhile anyway. Then, if a marriage or relationship ends, the survivor will enter the singles world with the knowledge that he or she did everything they could do. They weren't quitters. To do less would subject them to endless doubts and second guesses. Always thinking, "If only I had . . . " is not a happy or healthy foundation on which to build a better life.

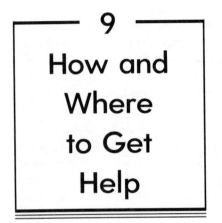

9

How and Where to Get Help

Whether one remains with or separates from a jealous person, coping with the resulting difficulties may require the services and resources of skilled, caring helpers. Outside intervention can be valuable when jealous people or their partners cannot separate but cannot seem to resolve their difficulties by themselves.

Every community has some resources to provide helpful supports and services. Nearly every community also has caring and experienced people who are trained to work with such problems. However, many people in jealous relationships don't, or feel they can't, use these services. They have many justifications:

- "I just didn't know where to go."
- "I knew about this place, but I didn't think it was for people with my kind of problem."
- "No one can help me now. Things have gotten so bad it's just hopeless."
- "It's too expensive, and we only have money for the bare necessities."
- "I'm just not the type to go to strangers for help. I like to keep my problems to myself and work them out as best I can."
- "I kept thinking things would get better."
- "My wife is the one with the problem, not me. She's the reason I'm here. I told her I'd come with her if she wanted, but not alone."
- "I didn't want everyone to think I was crazy, and that's what they'll think when they hear about me coming here."

- "My husband is so possessive and jealous that he doesn't want me to go anywhere. He gets furious if I ever talk about our problems to anyone else. So I put off coming here, I guess, just to keep the peace."

All these answers are based on incorrect assumptions, but because they are so commonly believed they keep some people from seeking help, as in the case of Esther:

Esther was attending an inpatient group therapy meeting, even though she didn't want to be there. Instead, she wanted to be dead. She had been hospitalized on the psychiatric ward of a general hospital several days before because she had attempted suicide. Having recuperated from the physical damage she had inflicted on herself, she was told she needed the help of the group and that attendance would be required in order for her to be able to return home.

Her doctor had known of her depression for years and had tried without success to get her into some type of psychotherapy program. She had told him she didn't want or need therapy. However, after she attended the hospital group therapy meetings for a few days, she began to participate, get interested in the other members' problems, and discuss her own. She began to enjoy the sessions and learn from them. By the time she was released from the hospital, she was enthusiastic about joining another group or entering a therapy program in the community.

Why had she let herself get so low before getting help? She was asked this by her new therapist and by the other members of her new group. She answered this way:

There are lots of different reasons why I tried to solve all my problems by myself, I guess. I'm kind of a loner, anyway, and fairly shy, so it's hard for me to talk about personal things to people I don't know very well. I guess I thought I could handle it. Maybe I'm too proud to ask for help. It seems like it's admitting I'm a failure if I can't take care of my own self. I already feel pretty worthless. I guess for a while I thought it would be better to be dead than admit I was so pathetic I couldn't solve my problems or even cope with them by myself.

I have a husband who has a violent temper, and he loses it often, whenever I don't do what he wants. Mostly all he wants is for me to be under his rule. He always wants me to account for my time and tell him who I see whenever I go out. He's not just jealous of other men, either. He doesn't like me with other women, kids, old people, anyone. He's been so paranoid for so long that I've always thought he needed help. But it only makes him mad when I suggest it. He says I'm the crazy one, so why should he go? I'm the one who should see a shrink, he says. But whenever I said I'd go, with him or on my own, he'd tell me I'd better not or else. I don't know what he means by 'or else,' but I don't think it means he'll give me a diamond.

We got into a stalemate about going for help. I was determined not to go unless he went too. Then I didn't want to go because I just didn't care. But he's so stubborn it's ridiculous. I guess I started thinking that suicide was my only way out. I don't think that way any more, but I know he still won't get help. So I've been thinking, Why wait for him? Who cares if anyone thinks the problems are my fault or that I'm the crazy one? Who cares if he wants me to stay away from therapy? I'm taking care of myself from now on.

Esther's reluctance to get help for herself is typical of the feelings commonly found among partners of jealous people. There is the tendency to want to avoid the partner's disapproval. There is the feeling that help for oneself is not needed or that it is only appropriate for the jealous partner. Many in this position don't seek help because their diminished self-esteem makes them feel unworthy of the attention, cost, and effort that would be expended by the potential helper. Many people avoid seeking help because they believe their jealous partners will make trouble for the helper as well as for them. These reasons are in addition to the psychological resistance that nearly all people have about baring their souls.[1]

To many people in this position, having to get help is a sign of failure. Partners of jealous people have typically been called unfaithful and no good for so long that they can't help questioning their own competence and adequacy. If they turn to others for help, it seems to confirm the idea that they are inadequate. They and their jealous partners may well agree that this proves the alleged inadequacy. So they avoid help in order not to confront this unpleasant prospect.

Of course, their premise is faulty. Getting help from others doesn't signify failure or inadequacy. It is more a sign of good sense. When doctors or dentists need surgery they don't perform it on themselves. Lawyers are considered prudent, not incompetent, when they seek legal counsel from other attorneys. Competent therapists and helpers who are married to jealous people also get outside help. The provider of help—whether a friend, support group, or professional therapist—is not necessarily more intelligent, perceptive, or capable than the person being helped. But the helper has a better, more objective vantage point from which to work on the problem.

Furthermore, the helper is not being accused, intimidated, abused, or required to be on the defensive with the jealous person. He or she can look at the situation with greater detachment and careful consideration of the long-term goals and means for achieving them.

Successful coping and problem resolution require perseverance, a positive and optimistic outlook, belief in oneself, and an objective understanding of the situation—all of which are more likely to occur in collaboration than in isolation. Conversely, the individual who works on these problems in isolation is more likely to encounter the additional problem of loneliness. This can be serious because, as studies have demonstrated, there is a significant correlation between loneliness and fewer social skills and social perceptions. In sum, working with others to find and implement solutions is effective and beneficial, no matter how healthy or personally capable an individual may be.[2]

Once the partner of a jealous person becomes convinced that obtaining help from others has merit, the next step is to deal with the jealous person's disapproval. This can also be a formidable challenge. It is not unusual for the jealous person to be extremely threatened by the idea of intervention by a third party. The jealous person may become jealous of the helper's influence on the partner and take strong actions to terminate this relationship. Many studies conducted in spouse abuse shelters have determined that abusive spouses frequently intimidate their victims to prevent them from getting help. When intimidated, the nonjealous partner is tempted to comply with the jealous person's wishes, supposedly in order to keep the peace or to avoid becoming abused.[3]

Unfortunately, keeping away from helpers usually does not avoid trouble. At best, this isolation merely postpones it and ultimately results in additional difficulties. Complying with the jealous person's unreasonable demands to keep away from outside helpers confirms the belief that the partner is weak, helpless, and a mere possession without independent rights. The inevitable conflict has only been postponed to the time when the partner finally does act independently. In fact, getting help is more likely to result in less conflict and more peace in the long run. The jealous person's objections are based on fear of losing the partner, but when help is effective it can help preserve and strengthen the relationship rather than terminate it.

Those who avoid help because they fear that their partners will become jealous of the helpers are also misguided. If the nonjealous partner avoided everyone who could be a threat, there might be no one left in the world.

Everyone is a candidate for the jealous person's suspicions. It should be remembered that most people who provide services know how to deal with jealous people, and they can help the nonjealous partner do likewise.

Another mistake is to avoid help out of the belief that all of it should go to the jealous person. Nonjealous people may feel, perhaps justifiably, that nothing will improve the situation unless their jealous partners become directly involved. But when their jealous partners reject help, they remain immobilized. They are not taking into account the helpers' skills in getting the jealous partners into treatment.[4]

Helpers and professional therapists often advise the nonjealous person to come in alone and not to try to talk the jealous partner into coming along. If pressure is placed on the jealous person to enter therapy with the nonjealous partner in the beginning, it will probably be too threatening and anxiety provoking. The jealous person will probably be very uncooperative and resistant. Furthermore, since most jealous people don't believe they need help, the suggestion will seem suspicious.

If the therapist were more direct in the beginning, and asked the nonjealous person to bring the partner along for sessions, needless problems would occur. The jealous person might well refuse, insisting that help is not needed. If refusal occurred at that stage, the nonjealous partner would feel ineffective. Or, if asked to come to the sessions too soon, the jealous person would be guarded and assume that the therapist was on the side of the nonjealous partner. To come for therapy under these conditions would probably cause the jealous person to be too defensive, hostile, and unwilling to reveal personal matters. The jealous person would probably only try to convince the therapist that the nonjealous partner was entirely to blame.[5]

For this reason, less direct approaches are often more effective in inducing jealous people to get help. In one indirect approach, the jealous person is not invited to attend the partner's helping sessions. The nonjealous spouse is seen for several weeks before there is any activity to persuade the jealous person to join in the treatment. However, the therapist encourages the partner to answer all the jealous person's questions about the meetings. After several weeks of this the jealous person becomes more curious than fearful about the sessions.

Eventually, after several therapy sessions with the nonjealous person only, the therapist finally indicates a wish to talk with the other person. If permission is granted, the therapist telephones the jealous partner. The call would sound something like this:

Therapist:	Hi, Mr. Harris. I'm the therapist who has been treating your wife for the past five weeks. I know you're concerned about her well-being, and I wanted to let you know how she's doing. Okay?
Mr. Harris:	Uh, well, okay. I didn't really like the idea of her seeing any therapists, though.
Therapist:	I understand. If you have any questions about her, I'll be glad to try to answer them.
Mr. Harris:	No, not really. I can't think of any.
Therapist:	Well, then, I was also hoping I could ask you some questions about her. If I could, it would really help me to understand her better. That way we'll finish this sooner. I think you could be a big help to her.
Mr. Harris:	What kind of questions? What did you want to know?
Therapist:	Oh, for example, I wondered if you ever noticed her having trouble with depression—you know, like does she ever get very down for long periods of time and have trouble sleeping and eating?
Mr. Harris:	Nope, I don't think I've ever seen her get like that. But maybe she does sometimes when I'm not around. I don't really know.
Therapist:	Say, Mr. Harris, I'd really like to explore this with you in more detail than we can on the phone. Do you think you could come into my office to talk about her next week?
Mr. Harris:	Uh, I don't think so. I don't really want to get involved in therapy or anything like that. Frankly, I don't actually believe in therapists too much.
Therapist:	I understand, Mr. Harris. But this is just about your wife. I promise not to put you on the hot seat. This is just so you and I can work together better to help her. You could come with her at her regular time or we could meet at another time. Okay?
Mr. Harris:	Okay, I'll come in with her. But this is just to talk about her.

In such telephone contacts, the therapist stresses that the focus of attention will not be on the jealous person but on the partner. When the meeting does occur, the therapist adheres to the promise and centers all attention on the other person. Usually, once the jealous person has come to the therapist's office, the fears and sense of being threatened are somewhat reduced.

If the call doesn't work and the jealous person refuses to come in, the therapist will just start describing the nonjealous partner's difficulties over the phone. Of course, this is also done only with the nonjealous partner's permission. The therapist will avoid suggesting that the jealous partner might have contributed to the problem. Soon the therapist starts asking the jealous person questions about the partner, indicating how the answers are proving helpful. Then the therapist promises to keep the person informed about the spouse's or partner's progress. In subsequent weeks the therapist keeps calling to give and get more information and further ideas about how to be effective in helping.

If the jealous person finally agrees to come in, the therapist continues this pattern. Nothing about the jealous person's problems, background, or contribution to the partner's troubles is initiated by the therapist. The therapist even avoids such discussions until the jealous person brings them up.

Eventually the jealous person is likely to become more comfortable with the therapist and thus become more inclined toward self-disclosure. In fact, many jealous people in such situations begin to feel left out when the therapist doesn't ask them questions about themselves, and they often start to volunteer information. They are gradually brought into the helping situation, with good potential for resolving some of their problems. However, if the jealous person never shows motivation for self-scrutiny, the therapist confines the focus to the partner.

The next step for the jealous person's partner, after overcoming the reluctance to get help and after dealing with the jealous person's uncooperativeness, is to decide which kind of help to seek. There is a remarkable variety of possibilities. They include indigenous self-help groups, social agencies, professional psychotherapists, and the individual's own personal sources of support. Indigenous self-help groups are usually run by people who share common problems and benefit from sharing their experiences, solutions, and sources of knowledge and strengths. Members of these groups help themselves through assisting others in similar circumstances. Social service agencies are staffed by well-trained and well-supervised workers, many of whom have considerable experience in helping families and couples deal with jealous relationships. Professional psychotherapists may be found in mental health clinics or in private practice, usually through referrals by family doctors or clergy. And a major source of help for many, if they know how to use it, is the "natural helping network"—including one's friends, neighbors, personal associates, members of one's church or synagogue, neighborhood associations, clubs, and similar organizations.

Each of these helping resources has its particular strengths and limitations. For example, professional therapy might be better at uncovering and resolving personality conflicts but not so useful when someone is in a crisis in the middle of the night and needs practical advice or a place to go to escape serious abuse. That's when the natural helping networks and social support groups are most crucial and capable of minimizing crises and sudden stress. In fact, natural helpers may be more accessible in most situations, but the individual's jealous partner may be too threatened by and threatening to these people. In that case, a better source of help is a formal helping organization, in which the helpers are more skilled in dealing with such situations.[6]

Because each kind of resource can best serve different needs, an individual could get help from more than one source simultaneously. Professionals and human service agencies often encourage clients to participate in self-help groups as an important supplement to their professional services, and many human service agencies are structured to work in cooperation with self-help groups and professional therapists.[7]

Friends, relatives, and personal associates are by far the most important potential source of help to those who live with seriously jealous people. Of all sources of help, only friends and relatives can be truly available at all times. They can also meet a wider variety of important needs than can any other kind of helper. Personal associates will usually know the family and its jealous member well enough to view the situation and its potential solutions more thoroughly and accurately. Friends can also directly participate in the individual's life and thus help family members change the way they relate to one another. And calling on friends is, of course, less costly than going to professionals and some social service agencies.[8]

Possibly the most important contribution made by members of the natural support system is that they tend to care personally about the individuals in need. The spouses and family members of jealous people need to know that there is someone who cares about them. Personal associates, relatives, and friends can make the individual feel worthy and loved in a way no other helping resource can duplicate. This is particularly valuable to those people who are subjected to the suspiciousness and deprecations of their jealous partners.

Many partners of jealous people are reluctant to ask their personal associates for help. They hesitate because of their own sense of pride, desire for confidentiality, and fear of involving the associate in problems with the jealous partner. These may be valid concerns, but they can be mitigated if care is taken to select the most appropriate individuals to assume this helping role.

Those who are probably most appropriate are people who want to help and who are perceptive, objective, and knowledgeable about the dynamics of this kind of problem. They should also be supportive and able to maintain confidentiality. And of course, the helpers should be readily accessible, perhaps living close enough to be prompt in giving help.

Ideally, these natural helpers should also have strong enough personalities to remain unintimidated when the jealous person tries to discourage the relationship. The jealous person can become very threatened by this type of relationship and, as a result, may try to hurt the helper as well as the nonjealous partner. Because of these potential problems, some partners of jealous people seek help only from members of their own sex. They feel that if the helper doesn't appear to be a potential sexual rival, the jealous person may not be so threatened by the involvement. (Of course, if the partners are homosexual, they might feel it safer and less troublesome to seek help from members of the opposite sex.)

There are, however, some limitations in relying on personal associates as the sole source of help. In the first place, someone with all the characteristics described above may be very hard to find. Perhaps there is no one individual in anyone's life who has all these qualities, but there are probably a few people who possess some of them. The partner can get help from more than one friend, relative, or member of the natural helping network. They can be called upon when their particular strengths are most needed at a given time.

Another limitation is that friends, relatives, and personal associates cannot always be as objective as necessary. This is true no matter how understanding and experienced they are. Objectivity requires a certain amount of detachment and an opportunity to observe the situation from some distance. Without this detachment friends might be inclined to take sides or say only what the person wants rather than needs to hear. They can sometimes give bad advice or become so involved in the situation themselves that they may contribute to the problems they were called on to help resolve. When some of these factors prove to be overwhelming obstacles, the individual can turn to professionals and organizations that are usually more experienced in knowing how to cope with such problems.

Whether or not personal supports can be called on, one might still benefit from participation in a self-help group. These groups fulfill many of the affectional, supportive, and advisory roles that are performed by personal associates, but they serve other functions as well. For isolated people who have no appropriate family members or friends, they can be crucial. Participation in them often leads to the development of personal friendships and a widening of one's natural helping network and social support group.[9]

Members of self-help groups meet regularly and somewhat formally. They share experiences and describe approaches they have found useful. They keep one another informed about other helping resources in the community. They develop communications networks so that any member who is in trouble or needs emotional support or material help can get it right away.

Self-help groups exist throughout the world and are especially popular in the United States. They are found in every community in this country to help people work together on every problem imaginable. Americans have historically been inclined to try helping themselves before relying on formal and professional institutions, which is why these groups exist in such profusion.[10]

Many communities have formal or informal self-help groups for alcoholics, drug addicts, depressed people, and people experiencing marital and relationship problems. There are effective self-help groups for neurotics, overeaters, smokers, phobics, divorced people, single parents, and victims of spouse abuse and other marital problems. There are now many self-help groups for parents who are inclined to abuse their children or people who are spouse abusers. Gay men and lesbian women have self-help groups in most larger communities to deal with the difficulties they share. Some of the best-known self-help organizations, with groups in most local communities, include Alcoholics Anonymous, Al-Anon, Batterers Anonymous, Displaced Homemakers Network, Mothers Without Custody, the National Gay Task Force, Recovery, Inc., Stepfamily Association of America, the Wives Self-Help Foundation, Women in Crisis, and Women in Transition.[11]

Unfortunately, most communities still do not have formal self-help groups exclusively for people with jealousy problems. This is because of the reticence of jealous people to open up to strangers and because they try to discourage their partners from attendance. Many people who want to attend such groups find that they must start their own. If they do, their efforts will probably be more successful if they maintain the ground rules for support groups described in Chapter 6.

Even though there are few existing self-help groups exclusively for jealous people or their relevant others, many groups include jealousy among their concerns. An individual who has a jealous partner *and* one of these other problems will almost always be welcomed and will benefit from participation. For example, nearly every city has Al-Anon chapters. These groups comprise the spouses of alcoholics who discuss ways to cope with their alcoholic partners. Al-Anon members usually maintain an active communications network that enables them to give and get support from one another. Local chapters are listed in telephone directories, and anyone is welcome to attend their open meetings. Jealousy seems to be discussed as much as any other subject, because one of the most common problems facing spouses of alcoholics is jealous possessiveness.

Self-help groups made up of the victims of spouse abuse may be the most relevant for jealous partners. While spouse abuse has been a serious problem throughout history, it has only recently received the attention and concern that it deserves. Now most cities have at least one such group. Nearly 150 of the local YWCAs around the nation have been sponsoring wife abuse programs that are largely conducted by the victims themselves. Spouse abuse, of course, consists of emotional as well as physical harm, and an abusive jealous relationship certainly qualifies.[12]

Finding the most appropriate group is not difficult. Many of them are listed in local phone books. Many groups not in the book can be located through local mental health associations, United Way offices, or the family and child welfare divisions of county human services offices. If these information sources don't suffice, many groups can be contacted through national organizations with which they are affiliated. It is estimated that about two-thirds of the nation's self-help groups have some national affiliation through which they can be contacted, while another one-third are sponsored by social agencies.[13]

Several national organizations and publishers maintain up-to-date directories of self-help groups. The *Encyclopedia of Associations*, which is available in almost every public library, lists and describes many of these organizations. Haworth Press publishes *The Resource Book*, which describes hundreds of organizations that provide help. The Women's Action Alliance publishes an annual state-by-state directory of services particularly for women in such circumstances.[14] Information about how to find, start, or improve a self-help organization can also be obtained from the National Self-Help Clearinghouse; Graduate School and University Center; City

University of New York; 33 West 42nd Street, Room 1227; New York, NY 10038.

Jealous people themselves are not usually inclined to go to self-help groups. They prefer privacy. They avoid helpers or, if they have to, are more likely to go to social agencies or private professionals. The result is that self-help groups for jealous people have been hard to get started and poorly attended.

This trend may be changing, however, An increasing number of jealous people now attend self-help groups for spouse abusers. Many groups of this type have recently been organized. Two of the older groups of this type are Denver's AMEND and Boston's EMERGE programs. The participants hold regular group discussions about different aspects of their problem, and jealousy is one of the more popular topics. They support one another and offer encouragement, advice, and potential solutions. Because they've experienced the problems, their words and ideas often have a greater impact on others in the group.

Another source of help, the social service agencies, provides information, support, tangible resources, counseling, and psychotherapy to troubled families. The agencies may be public taxpayer-funded organizations or they may be private institutions whose funds come from philanthropic contributions and from donor organizations such as United Way. The private ones include the local chapters of Family Service America, Jewish Family Services, Catholic Charities, the Child Welfare League of America, Lutheran Social Services, LDS Social Services, and many others. Most of them charge their clients nominal fees based on their ability to pay. The public agencies include the local public mental health offices, community psychiatric clinics, and family service sections of the local human services departments or social welfare offices. They, too, are usually listed in the phone book.

These organizations are staffed by a variety of helpers from experienced and highly trained professionals to closely supervised volunteers. These agencies sometimes provide practical services such as emergency transportation, shelter and material needs, referrals and contacts with other helpers, and similar types of help. They also provide clients with emotional support, advice, and psychological and vocational testing as well as psychotherapy.

Included among the social agencies, and of vital importance for some family members who live with jealous partners, are the emergency shelters that are proliferating around the nation. They exist primarily to provide temporary sanctuary for the victims of domestic violence. Often the victims can bring their children and live for a while without fear of being intimidated or hurt by the violent spouse. This creates a cooling-off period for the family, during which counseling and active professional intervention with the jealous spouse may take place. These shelters—which may be affiliated with established social agencies or autonomous and financed through private contributions, grants, or taxpayer funds—are usually staffed by reputable professionals. The residents usually find others in the same circumstances. This permits them to form self-help and support groups that they often maintain when they leave the shelter.

Professional psychotherapy may be another source of help. These people are highly trained professionals who may be psychiatrists, psychologists, social workers, family therapists, marriage counselors, and clergy counselors. As physicians, psychiatrists can prescribe any needed medications and can usually admit patients into hospitals. Psychologists use systematic tests in diagnosing specific problems to facilitate the psychotherapy they provide. Social workers provide psychotherapy and are skilled in helping their clients find additional resources in the community. Family and marital therapists are particularly effective in working with all the members of the family together. Clergy therapists and pastoral counselors provide important religious and value perspectives along with their psychotherapy skills.

Some professional therapists seem so expensive that many who might want their services feel they cannot afford them. However, this kind of help is more widely available than is generally known. Many therapists use sliding fee scales, basing their charges on the client's economic circumstances. Private health insurance now covers the majority of Americans, and mental health care is included in most of the benefits. In most states, the Medicaid program covers those who need help but have very limited financial resources. If finances still rule out private therapy, one of the 570 state- and federally funded community mental health centers all over the nation are also available at appropriate fees.

It is sometimes difficult for people with jealousy problems to know which kind of professional therapy is best for their special needs. There are many different types of therapy and conflicting views about which is most effective. For many decades the therapies that were most popular seemed to emphasize the development of self-awareness, insight, ego growth, and personality change through analytically oriented intervention. Later, more people seemed attracted to humanistic approaches that emphasized supportive relationships, self-respect, experiential growth, and self-actualization through reaching human potentials. The trend now seems to be toward therapies that are more goal directed, specific, and targeted to changing identified behaviors or situations.[15]

Many studies now seem to show that behaviorally oriented therapies may be more effective than insight-supportive ones in helping certain clients. Other researchers find that, in working with jealous relationships, a treatment approach that uses a combination of therapeutic techniques, depending on the specific needs of the client, may be most effective. Nevertheless, what probably matters more than the therapist's orientation is the degree of competence. Other factors that may be considered include the sex of the therapist, the goals of the therapy, the use of therapy teams, and the use of group versus individual therapy.[16]

Because the individual has a potential for becoming jealous of the therapist, some professionals advise seeking assistance from therapists of the same sex as the client, on the premise that the jealous partner would have less about which to be jealous. Others believe that if the therapist is skilled and knowledgeable, gender won't make a significant difference. In this regard, one must remember that jealous people are threatened by more than the possibility of sexual involvements. And they can be just as threatened by a therapist of the same sex. Furthermore, there are some advantages in working on jealousy problems with help from a member of the opposite sex. For example, a jealous husband could learn to be more trusting of his wife if she resolved some problems in therapy with a man.[17]

Nevertheless, some people know that their jealous partners will be too threatened and make too much trouble if help is sought from a member of the opposite sex. For those who find this an overwhelming obstacle, it is at least practical to choose helpers only of the same sex. This is almost always more prudent when the help of a friend or other nonprofessional is sought.

The client who seeks the help of professionals in social service agencies and clinics may find there is no choice anyway. Agencies and clinics usually assign a worker based on their own staffing criteria. Inasmuch as most social agency workers are women, this may be more of a problem for men who seek agency help. Of course, the individual can readily choose the sex of the therapist when going to a private practitioner. And if therapy is conducted by a therapeutic team, the client will be more likely to deal with members of both sexes.

Using teamwork to deliver helping services has long been recognized as an effective way to provide a wide range of services. Teams typically consist of two or more therapists or other professionals, each of whom may specialize in one aspect of the client's problem. Or they may consist only of a male and female therapist. This format is especially effective when both the jealous person and the partner are involved in therapy. The sex therapy techniques pioneered by William Masters and Virginia Johnson demonstrated that couples learn more, respond better, and overcome problems more rapidly when they can relate to therapists of both sexes. This applies equally to couples who are treated for problems that aren't exclusively sexual.[18]

A male-female treatment team can provide notable advantages for jealous relationships. The therapists can be more objective and understanding in assessing the nature of the problem. They can each provide better role models for the client of their same sex. They can show the member of the opposite sex, particularly the jealous client, that male-female relationships can be healthy. They can use cross-sex interviewing to look at the jealous situation in the clinical setting. Through the use of role playing, especially when videotaping is used, the couple can observe their own reactions to situations that formerly incited fears, conflicts, or threats.

It is no longer difficult to find therapists who work in teams, at least in larger communities. Increasingly, psychiatric clinics are finding this format quite useful. Social service agencies and centers that specialize in work with families and couples do this almost routinely. Sometimes two, three, or more therapists are used for one couple, often to break up patterns of resistance. Teams are less common among private psychotherapists, but those who specialize in work with families or couples often work in partnerships with other private practice therapists of the opposite sex if the client demonstrates that this is important. Another form of treatment, group therapy, sometimes uses teams of therapists and always uses other clients to fulfill part of the client's treatment goals.[19]

Perhaps most of the help that is given to people with jealousy problems occurs in group settings. Self-help organizations use the group method almost exclusively, and it is also the method of treating jealousy-based relationships now preferred by many agencies and professionals. The results are encouraging. Groups provide opportunities for people to understand others in similar situations, imitate the successes of others, role-play, practice communication techniques, and give mutual support that could never be duplicated in individual forms of therapy.

When groups include both the jealous person and the partner, there are additional benefits. The couple has the chance to observe how other jealous couples cope effectively or ineffectively with jealousy issues. The non-jealous partner can observe how other couples handle the same problems more effectively. Even the jealous person can benefit through observing other jealous people. Usually, jealous people who observe jealousy in others find it just as unacceptable as do the nonjealous members of the group. It is rare when jealous members endorse or support the views of other jealous group members, but it is common to see them try to change the other jealous people's views. Each jealous person in a group has more social incentives to learn about the problem and correct it than to try to defend or maintain it.

Several formats are used by self-help and professionally led groups. These include group therapy for individuals from different families, couples groups, family groups, open- and closed-ended groups, groups with frequent and long-lasting meetings, and those with short meetings and few sessions.

While most traditional group sessions are ninety minutes or two hours long, some groups may be organized to last for several hours. Marathon groups, which are rare and not usually practical for couples with jealousy problems, are typically scheduled to last twelve or twenty-four hours and sometimes longer. Naturally, those who enter marathon sessions do so of their own volition.

Most groups are open ended, but the number of closed-ended groups is growing. There are advantages to each. Closed-ended groups have a predetermined number of sessions, perhaps twelve, sixteen, or twenty-four meetings. All group members who begin together remain in the group until it ends. Often the goals are written on paper, and the focus of the group discussion is generally centered on these goals rather than on a variety of other subjects. Closed-ended groups seem most effective when all the members are concerned about the same kind of problem or have many things in common.

In open-ended groups—those with no predetermined number of sessions—there are different advantages. When a couple or an individual achieves the goals or decides to stop attending, they are replaced in the group by a new member. Eventually, this means that different people are in different stages of their therapeutic development. The more experienced group members gain by helping the newer ones get through some of their own difficult moments. This often helps them with their own problems of self-esteem, and it reminds them where they have been. It is the same effect as experienced by a member of Alcoholics Anonymous who has been sober for several years but who still benefits by helping active drinkers cope with their problems. It also shows the newer members who have problems with drinking or jealousy what kind of people they can become if they continue their efforts.

In professional group therapy, there are typically six to ten people in each group, usually of both sexes and with a variety of problems to resolve. Thus, such a group could contain some people who are themselves very jealous and other members who live with such people. In couples groups the man and woman meet with the therapist(s) along with several other couples. The number of couples is ideally three to five, so the group comprises of six to ten people. In couples groups that focus on jealousy problems it is most typical to have two therapists, one of each sex.

Many people have considerable apprehensions about groups. Their first thought is, I have enough problems of my own, so why should I want to listen to everyone else's? Some additional reluctance to participate in groups may reflect some of the stereotypes about them. Perhaps those who are reluctant to join have heard that groups are only for seriously mentally ill people or that the members scream at one another, throw things, take off their clothes, and have orgies. They often fear that their confidentiality will not be respected or that they will have problems from other group members outside of the group.

These concerns are unfounded. In professional group therapy, for example, the members are asked to refrain from any contacts with other members outside the group. They use first names only and are asked to avoid trying to identify one another in any context outside the group. There is almost never any violation of these rules. All the group members are alike in wanting to preserve confidentiality. They are not inclined to do to others what they wouldn't want done to themselves.

Members of outpatient group psychotherapy are probably just as "respectable" and no more mentally ill than any other group of people. They don't tend to be violent. They rarely do anything that is threatening or harmful or in any way likely to alienate their fellow group members. They are usually seated in a large room in a circle. They rarely leave their chairs except when they engage in role-playing. They are never forced or pressured to role-play or do anything they don't want to do. Group rules explicitly forbid any physical harm or violence. Of course, group members sometimes get loud or argue. But this is usually followed by the members' being mutually supportive.

For the most part, group psychotherapy sessions consist of various members describing their situations, their behavior, and their rationale and listening to other members offer different viewpoints, suggestions, and interpretations. The therapist-leader provides the structure, keeps the members communicating relevantly, and acts as a catalyst for new understandings or behaviors. The group method works because the members begin to care about one another and encourage the development of insights and alternative patterns of behavior.

Role playing and "doubling" are commonly used group therapy techniques that have achieved good results in working with jealousy problems. These techniques are often used to help the jealous person and the partner understand the problem from new perspectives. In role playing the jealous person and the nonjealous partner are typically asked to act as though they were other people. For example, a jealous man might be asked to pretend to be his own wife, and the wife might be asked to play the role of her jealous husband. This gives the jealous husband an experience of how it feels to be accused and interrogated, and the wife gets to see how it feels to have someone sound evasive and suspicious. They might argue, attack, and defend as though they were one another and learn to see the situation from different viewpoints.

Others in the group might play other relevant parts, too. One member might portray a potential sexual rival. Someone else could portray an innocent party who was taken for a sexual rival. Members of the group can also play people who are ancillary to the situation being discussed. For example, some members could play children who are terrorized by a jealousy based argument conducted by their parents.

This is how a role-playing episode might sound in a typical group therapy session:

> Clifton: (to the group): Last week I got home from work early, and I saw my wife talking again with that guy, Isadore, next door. I told her to stay away from him but she keeps hanging around him. Don't you, dear?
>
> Marie: No, I don't. I was just getting the mail, and he asked me if I knew where his kid was. So I walked over to tell him.
>
> Clifton: Well, you should have just said you didn't know and gone back in the house. Then there wouldn't have been any trouble.
>
> Marie: I don't have to live like a hermit. Just because you tell me

	something doesn't mean I have to do it. Does everyone else here think I have to do just what he says?
Mildred:	I don't.
Wilhelmina:	Me neither.
Clifton:	What do you mean, you don't? You people seem to be forgetting that Marie has a history of this. She gets involved with men pretty easily.
Marie:	I do not. I've never done anything like that. You're just saying that to justify being so unreasonable. It didn't happen like you said, anyway.
Therapist:	Let's see if we can recreate how this conflict started. Then we can look at how it *should* have happened so that everyone would have been more comfortable. Okay? Good. Then, Clifton, stand up and pretend you have just come home and found your wife talking to the neighbor. Marie, stand up also and act just like you did then. Wilhelmina, you play the part of Isadore. Show us how the argument went.

After the members act out what actually happened and in some ways relive the conflict in public, the other group members may comment on the situation. They discuss the parts of the argument that led to problems and suggest ways it could have been handled better. Both Clifton and Marie are told about different ways to understand and cope with such situations.

If explaining it to them is not clear or convincing, the group may show them how the argument appeared by playing the parts themselves while Clifton and Marie watch. One member might play the part of Clifton and another the part of Marie. The other members then act out the exchange and mimic Clifton and Marie as closely and faithfully as they are able. They imitate their speech and mannerisms and typical ways of thinking and even jealousy reactions. Clifton and Marie observe this performance and are able to see how they are behaving—or at least how they are seen as behaving. Then, in a second run-through, the group members play the couple as they could behave in a more healthy manner.

This accomplishes two benefits for the group. It permits Clifton and Marie to witness more effective ways of achieving the same result. It also gives the other group members, who share these problems, a forum safely to find more effective ways of handling these situations.

Finally Clifton and Marie are invited to portray themselves in the situation, first as they believe they actually lived it and then as they could have done it more effectively.

Doubling is a role-playing technique that has also been used very successfully in work with jealous couples. It is prominently featured in Robert Blood's jealousy workshops and in many other group therapy and self-help groups. As people play roles, others act as their doubles, saying aloud what their thoughts might be. It could sound something like this:

Clifton: Marie, come in here a minute, would you please? Hi, Isadore, how are you?

Clifton's double: Aha! I caught them together and they weren't expecting me. She'd better have a good explanation.

Marie: (not hearing or responding to Clifton's double): Okay. I'll be with you in a second. Yes, Isadore, I think he's at the Bergs' house. I saw him there an hour ago.

Marie's double: What's Clifton doing home so soon? Now he'll probably think I've been with Isadore all day.

Clifton: (not hearing or responding to her double): Marie, I really need to see you for a minute—right away.

Clifton's double: I know what you're doing, Marie. You're getting cozy with Isadore, so he'll want to see more of you when I'm not home.

Marie: Okay, I have to go now, Isadore. When you're at the Bergs could you tell Jimmy to come home, too? His Dad's home early.

Marie's double: I'd better move it or I'm going to have trouble. He's getting steamed. But if I come running every time he calls, I'm only giving in to him.

Clifton: I'm really hungry. Have you been working on dinner or what?

Clifton's double: What I'm really wondering about is, Have you been in the house where you belong or out here talking to that nerd all day?

Marie: (not hearing the double): No, I thought we'd go out for a pizza.

Marie's double: I should have cooked something. Now he's really going to think I've been with Isadore all day even though I was just reading my new book and watching the soaps.

After the role-playing and doubling exchanges conclude, the group members offer their comments. Usually they do this in a nonthreatening manner, often with compliments on the participants' acting abilities, and containing much laughter and affection for one another. The jealous person is not made to feel at fault but is helped to realize that there are other ways of understanding and dealing with the situation. All the members are able to look at themselves differently and not take themselves so seriously. When the other group members eventually become the subject of a discussion, it makes them feel worthy of attention, a prime requisite in the psychology of the jealous person.

Some people who have jealousy problems find that, for whatever reason, they need outside help but cannot tolerate the group experience. Because self-help and social support efforts for the most part use groups, their best alternative is individual psychotherapy.

Many people with jealousy problems prefer individual psychotherapy to all the other possibilities. They sometimes believe that this is the only type of help that can get rid of the underlying causes of their problems and thus eradicate jealousy completely and forever. Actually, there is no conclusive evidence that any type of therapy or intervention, including individual psychotherapy, can do this, or that the other forms of help are less effective than individual therapy. However, there is good reason to believe that individual therapy has helped many people with such problems. And it is obvious that this is the only type of treatment that some jealous people will permit for themselves.[20]

Many people who have jealousy problems prefer individual therapy for its essential privacy. They feel that there is less chance of having their problems disclosed to others. They fear that group members would discuss their problems and possibly ridicule them or take sides against them. They are more confident that this can't occur in individual sessions. Many partners of jealous persons also prefer individual sessions, for virtually the same reasons. They also feel they might have a more understanding and sympathetic helper than would always be the case when dealing with groups of peers.

The treatment approaches encountered in individual therapy will be influenced by the therapist's particular orientation and training. Two orientations are now the most frequently used to treat jealous people or their partners. The behavioral orientation is highly focused and directed specifically at the jealousy reaction. The insight orientation seeks greater overall self-awareness and understanding that can lead to a reduction of symptomatic behavior. Both approaches try to help clients learn how to communicate more effectively.

The primary treatment method used by behaviorally oriented therapists to deal with jealousy problems is systematic desensitization. This is the process of helping individuals feel increasingly relaxed and comfortable with any given idea, situation, or potential experience. It is similar to the treatment of allergies in which the physician gradually introduces a slight amount of the substance to which the person is allergic. The body gradually builds up a tolerance to the effects of the allergen.

In jealousy desensitization, either the jealous person or the partner may be asked to remember some pleasurable event. The jealous person may be asked to think of some mildly disruptive potential jealous threat. For example, a man remembers a picnic he once enjoyed with his wife. Then he is asked to imagine that another man happens along—a handsome man who had dated his wife before the marriage. The wife invites the man to join them. The man visits briefly and then departs. The pleasant picnic resumes. A threat occurred but, because the man handled himself well, it had a good outcome.

The husband is then asked to imagine a series of such experiences, each with some jealous threat, each having a happy resolution. However, each imagined event is progressively more threatening. For example, the man imagines another picnic in which his wife's former boyfriend stays longer and stares fondly at the wife before going away. Then he imagines that the man stays throughout the picnic and devotes all his attention to the wife while ignoring him.

Each of these scenes is interspersed with support and approval or something rewarding from the therapist. The man becomes increasingly able to tolerate such thoughts because they are associated with pleasant outcomes. The man then starts to handle actual threatening experiences better. The amount of stress that the jealous person can accommodate expands and the jealousy reaction is considerably reduced. This technique is more complicated and elaborate than is described here, but it illustrates what a client might encounter by going to such a therapist. Behaviorally oriented therapists, of course, have many other techniques that work similarly.

Insight-oriented therapists are less inclined to advise or tell the client what to do to overcome the problem. They usually find it more effective to discuss the individual's personality and approaches to various aspects of life. The client begins to understand that these ways of thinking and behaving are the result of unconscious conflicts or motivations, and as they are resolved, the personality changes. Jealousy is often seen as symptomatic of fears that are the product of these conflicts. Eliminating fears through self-understanding is seen as eliminating the jealousy.

All these helping activities are designed to minimize or eliminate the problems caused by jealousy. Even though there are many different techniques and methods, the goals are similar. Essentially, there are several basic goals that all helpers—whether personal associates, self-help organizations, social agencies, or professional therapists—try to accomplish. They try to help jealous people or their partners to

- Understand the situation more objectively and realistically
- Know more clearly what the partner wants and expects of the relationship
- Communicate more effectively with one another
- Loosen rigid, unreasonable expectations to permit more flexible roles
- Reduce sensitivity to jealousy threats
- Behave more effectively in the relationship

No one method can honestly claim that it alone can achieve all these goals. No doubt some sources of help are better for some people than others; it depends on the unique needs and circumstances of the person with the problem. No doubt all the methods have worth for some people or they wouldn't have survived and gained so many supporters. It is better for people who suffer from jealousy to know of many alternative sources of outside help. Knowledge is the most formidable weapon that can be used against jealousy.

10

Ten Steps for Surviving Jealous Relationships

Denial may be the most popular device used to survive the problems of living with very jealous people. Pretending that there is no problem, or that it is not so serious, seems to be the easiest and safest course to take. Many people who deny the problem don't know what else to do, or they fear the consequences of any known alternative. Many people who deny the existence of the problem tell themselves that jealousy is not so bad or at least that it is endurable.

These people can find support from certain scholars, writers, and laypersons who claim that jealousy is a good thing, necessary to the survival of society. They justify the existence of jealousy by saying that it helps save marriages, motivates positive actions in people, and helps maintain stability in human relationships.[1]

The way it is supposed to save marriages, say these people, is by reducing the risk of adultery. The institution of marriage is preserved because husbands and wives are afraid to get involved with others. They refrain from such conduct because they know they would be caught at it. Their jealous partners are so vigilant that no one could get away with anything. In other words, jealousy is supposedly beneficial because it makes husbands and wives more attentive to one another than they otherwise would be. Without the jealousy mechanism, according to this view, couples would feel unrestricted in their desires to explore extramarital sexual relationships.

This is a poor justification for jealousy. As a force for preserving the sanctity of marriage, preventing adultery, or reducing the number of divorces, jealousy has been a wretched failure. It has contributed to far more unhappiness, breakups, abuse, and divorces than it has prevented. Some people may remain married only because they fear some jealous retribution but they do so at the cost of their well-being in so many other ways. They maintain the marriage not because of its inherent rightness but because of controls, threats, and fear. In this sense jealousy is like a prison. It might prevent escape in some instances, but it certainly doesn't preserve the purpose of the relationship.

The idea that jealousy is good because it motivates positive behavior is another poor argument. This premise says that when jealousy becomes intolerable the victim is compelled to act. The response is to fight back, to grow, and take positive steps to find a better life. If jealousy were not so bad, the individual would be more likely to do nothing but accept conditions as they are. This is the view of Ruth, a thirty-eight-year-old divorced mother of two girls, who believed she benefited from her jealousy-based relationship problems. She revealed this notion just as she was successfully concluding her sessions in a group therapy program for jealous people.

"How come we're always bad-mouthing jealousy? I think it's the best thing that ever happened to me."

"You must be kidding, Ruth. What good did it ever do you—after what you told us about your husband? Gee, maybe you really *do* belong in here."

"No, really, I mean it. I'm better off now than I would have been if Ralph hadn't been jealous. If he hadn't been that way I'd still be with him. And I'd still be a doormat too. I feel pretty good about myself now. It was his jealousy that got me going."

"But jealousy doesn't get the credit. *You* were the one who did something."

"Yeah, didn't you tell us your husband was always accusing you of cheating on him and then hitting you when you denied it?"

"And you said he'd never let you out of his sight—like you were some kind of prisoner or something. You call that good?"

"Well, no, I'm not saying that part was good. Ralph's craziness pulled me down, that's for sure. But, you know, I wasn't that much to start with—no, come on, everyone, I really wasn't. I never even thought about having a say in my family. Even if Ralph was a creep, he was the man—so he knew best. I had to do what he said. I wanted it that way. I liked the way he guarded me and kept me away from everyone. It made me feel he loved me. I still feel that way sometimes."

"Uh, Ruth, did you forget what we talked about—that possessiveness and jealousy don't mean love?"

"Yes, I *know* it, but I still *feel* the other way. Anyway, I didn't even think about whether it was good or not. I just took it for granted. Then the ERA movement and women's lib stuff got my girls thinking. They started asking me things like why men are the bosses over women—why women stay home and men get to to out and why men always get to do the fun things in life. I didn't have any good answers. Those questions really blew Ralph's mind. Mine too, I guess. He told them to quit talking that way. It wasn't right, he said. It was unnatural. He blamed their ideas on women's libbers and said all those bra-burners ought to be given hysterectomies."

"I don't understand what you're getting at, Ruth. You sound like you're saying jealousy caused your kids to become libbers or something."

"Not really. I just started thinking like the girls were thinking, and it made Ralph uptight. We fought, only now I started fighting back. That threatened him. He got worse. He started saying I had a boyfriend again. He told the girls he knew my boyfriend and I were going to run off and desert them. Naturally that upset them and confused them. I told them I wasn't involved with anyone and would never leave them. But he just kept it up. It got so bad I couldn't stand it anymore."

"What did you do?"

"I told him I was going to make some changes. I told him I was going to get a job and go to school and get some counseling. He said no, but I didn't care. I got a job selling children's clothes at the department store. I told Ralph I wanted both of us to go to a marriage counselor. He wouldn't go so I came alone. I was in individual therapy for a while before I started this group. I also started taking psychology courses so I could understand what made Ralph and me tick."

"How did Ralph take all this?"

"Not too well, as I expected. He just got madder and tried harder to get me back like I was. The more he tried, the more determined I got. One day, in a fit of rage, he said he didn't care if I *was* running around because he was too. He was in love with his secretary. I was hurt at first, but secretly relieved. It gave me an excuse to get a divorce. He's strange—even while he kept on with his girlfriend he fought against our divorce. But he didn't have much of a case."

"What happened to him after you split up?"

"Well, he's living with that woman. I don't think they're too happy, though. A couple months ago she called to ask if he had been real jealous with me. I guess he's never going to get over that problem, no matter who he's with, if he doesn't get help. But that's his problem. He won't hurt me anymore. I'm happy on my own. The girls seem to be adjusting too, except when they visit him. They see him about once a month, and when they come back they're kind of nervous for a while. But we'll work that out."

"What do you think will happen to you in the future, Ruth?"

"Well, work is going just fine and it's helping me with my self-confidence. They made me the manager of the children's department, and they're talking about a promotion to be a buyer. I probably won't get married again. But that's okay. I've still got the girls. And I'll always have *me*. Sometimes I feel lonely, but never as much as I felt when I was with Ralph. I'll never feel that lonely again."

After Ruth ended her group therapy sessions, she continued with the department store for several years and received several more promotions. She hasn't remarried but has dated several men. Ralph married his secretary but they were soon divorced. He never did try to resolve his jealousy problem. Ruth continues to believe that his jealousy was a good thing for her, a catalyst that led her to a new and positive outlook on life. Jealousy, she believes, provides the incentive many people need to improve their circumstances.

This also is a dubious argument. Ruth and others like her accomplish important goals despite, not because of, jealousy. People who try to grow and change because they won't tolerate the abuse of the jealous relationship are giving credit where it isn't due. It isn't the jealousy but their own strength and determination that are the catalysts for action and the source of motivation. Saying jealousy is good because it motivates a positive action is like saying disease is good because it motivates people toward better hygiene.

Jealousy causes much more harm than the minor benefits that may sometimes come from it. If it stimulates a few people to improve their lives, it has the opposite effect on many more. Rather than encouraging most people to grow and improve themselves, it tends to discourage most efforts to change. It is a repressive characteristic and generally contributes to a loss of self-confidence and self-sufficiency. The victims of jealousy often become immobilized, too frightened to do anything positive, and certainly less likely to change their circumstances actively.[2]

Claiming that jealousy is good because it helps preserve the stability of relationships between men and women is also a poor argument. This idea derives from the notion that each has natural and definite roles to play. For example, men are supposed to be the leaders in the relationship, the decision makers, the breadwinners, the protecters. Women are supposed to be the followers, the nurturers, the emotional supporters, the ones who are protected. Deviations from these norms are often seen as threats to society and precursors to many other social problems.[3]

Jealousy, says this view, is a mechanism to preserve these roles. It causes the husband or wife to watch the other for deviations from the expected norms. It causes the jealous person to become angry with the partner who doesn't conform to expectations. Rather than risk being subject to such anger, the partner conforms, remains docile, and the "stability" of the relationship is preserved.[4]

This argument presumes that the existing relationship is the best possible alternative. It says any change from this tradition is to be avoided. The trouble with this idea is that one person might benefit by the status quo at the expense of the other. Supposedly the natural order of things is for one member of the relationship, usually the man, to control the other partner, usually the woman. It is a way of saying that one partner is merely a piece of "property," a possession that must be guarded and protected from those who covet it. Who says this is the natural way to be? And even if this is decided, why would jealousy be considered the best way—or even a good way—to maintain existing relationships? It is fundamentally a de-stabilizer because it is based on distrust and controls, not mutual respect and love.

Jealousy exists when people believe they "own" other people and fear having to give up their controls. Jealousy happens when people are taught that the object of their love has no rights of independence, no rights other than those allocated, and no opportunity to deviate from prescribed rules or roles. Those who believe that they must control others to keep from losing them—as they control their possessions to keep from losing *them*— are living terribly constricted lives. These people tie up themselves and their partners and then wonder why their lives are so constricted. Jealousy does not grow in relationships where there is trust, self-confidence, and respect for the other person. Such relationships foster openness, giving and sharing, and flexibility and equality—elements that make up the bane of jealousy.

Other writers and scholars believe that although there is little in jealousy that is redeeming, there is no cause for much concern. To some it is merely an amusing little foible in human loving. To others it may be a serious affliction but, because of recent social changes, one that is headed toward extinction. The respected sociologist Jesse Bernard, for one, makes this prediction. She says that jealousy will become meaningless if the current trend toward sexual equality continues.[5]

According to this view, if society accepts individual differences and re-jects sex role stereotyping and sexual possessiveness, there will be little im-petus for jealous behaviors. When women are no longer viewed as posses-sions of men, and vice versa, there will be little justification for sexually motivated jealous reactions. This prediction sees jealousy becoming an archaic affectation, something read about in outdated novels rather than seen in everyday contemporary life—something that will eventually seem as quaint as swooning or having a "fit of the vapors" now seems to be.

However, other scholars and mental health professionals are not so optimistic about the demise of jealousy problems. Although they agree that once there is greater equality of opportunity for both sexes and more flexibility in the way couples see their respective roles, there will be fewer jealousy-based conflicts, they believe jealousy will remain with us through the foreseeable future. Already there is strong social resistance to the trend toward sexual equality. There is also an effective backlash against the changes in traditional family role patterns and relationships. If these movements remain strong, the predicted changes will be less probable.[6]

Even if equality between the sexes became the norm, jealousy would continue in its many other forms. As we have stressed, jealousy is not restricted to relationships between men and women and third-party rivals but can potentially take place in all types of relationships. It is nurtured more by the cultural values of competition for the possession of material objects. Competition and materialism are not necessarily undesirable characteristics in themselves, but they are strongly associated with jealousy behaviors. In those cultures in which these traits are important, including that of the United States, it appears unlikely that jealousy will soon become extinct or unimportant.

If the social and cultural changes necessary to minimize jealousy do somehow occur, no one thinks they can happen very soon. It takes many generations before society undergoes a major shift in social values. Those who are now being victimized by the problem would be unwise to deny its existence or wait until society changes. They must act now, individually, in order to cope with and overcome the problems they face successfully. So, to summarize and conclude, here are the ten practical steps that help people survive jealous relationships.

1. *Acknowledge the problem.* Many people who live in pathologically jealous households tell themselves there is no problem. They make excuses for their partners' jealous behavior: "Aw, he's basically okay." "She doesn't act that way very often." "She'll grow out of it." "He's not too jealous, it's just that he loves me so much." They play ostrich, pretending that the problem doesn't exist if it isn't recognized.

Why do some people fail to acknowledge the existence of this problem when—if they stopped their denials—they might be able to do something about it? The question is logical, and the reasons for denial are many. Some don't see the problem because they assume it is normal. Perhaps they grew up in jealous homes and have come to expect such behavior in everyone with whom they share lives. Others don't admit there is a problem because they don't know what to do about it. If they saw a problem, they would have to act. And because they know of no specific action to take, they are immobilized.

Whatever the reasons, people who fail to acknowledge the problem are far more vulnerable to harm than they would be otherwise. Even though a solution may not be found immediately or ever, and even though admitting the problem is discomforting, acknowledging that it exists is the initial, most important step toward successfully coping with and surviving the jealous relationship.

2. *Learn about jealousy.* It takes knowledge to deal effectively with any problem. Trying to cope without knowledge is about as effective as sword fighting while blindfolded. To learn about jealousy means reading about it. The books and articles listed in the Bibliography present the existing knowledge about jealousy. From these sources one can learn how jealousy starts, what sets it off, how and why it continues, what makes it get worse, and what helps to minimize it.

Books and articles aren't the only sources of this knowledge. The process of learning about jealousy also includes talking with others who have had to cope in jealous relationships, both as victims and perpetrators. Such people can be located easily because there are so many of them. They can be found in self-help support groups or almost anyplace where people gather and discuss relationship problems. Basically, all it takes to find them is openly disclosing one's own situation and expressing interest in sharing experiences about it. Talking with these people will result in valuable emotional support as well as practical ideas about how to cope.

3. *Understand the specific kind of jealousy.* Jealousy has many forms, expressions, causes, and degrees of intensity. Every person's jealousy is unique. Therefore, it is not enough to learn only about the nature of jealousy in general. It is also important to know about the specific kind of jealousy that affects one's partner, family, relationships, or oneself. Is it normal or pathological? Does it occur because the jealous partner was taught as a child that such behavior was appropriate? Is it based on objective threats or only on feelings of insecurity and inadequacy? What are its patterns? Does the jealousy flash occur randomly or does it seem to follow certain events or situations?

Understanding the specifics of the jealousy requires a serious and objective look at the jealous partner. It means applying one's knowledge about jealousy in general to this unique person. It means talking frankly and supportively with the jealous person about the problem—not during angry confrontations but during more peaceful times. Specific knowledge is also obtained by talking with the jealous person's family. This is not to be done in a way that suggests tattling or disclosing personal confidences in a harmful way. It is done positively by showing an interest in knowing more about the person's childhood and youth and looking for patterns that seem relevant to the jealous condition. Once this particular jealousy is identified, it is possible to take more purposeful and effective action.

4. *Preserve good family health.* Whatever the nature of the jealousy problem, the most fundamental and important response is to make sure that everyone in the home stays healthy. Many members of a jealous person's family allow themselves to become run down, depressed, and dispirited. Their self-esteem is so battered they sometimes act as though they deserve to get sick. A spouse who is too depressed or physically weakened by the stresses of the jealous environment can hardly be effective in resolving the problem. Neither will this person be in a good position to act if distracted by concern for the health of the children or other dependents.

Successful coping, therefore, is built on keeping the home environment emotionally and physically healthy. This means making sure that everyone gets good nutrition, a clean environment, sufficient exercise, and proper rest. It also includes providing the family with some positive experiences. All the members of the family, including the jealous person, deserve and need respite from stress through vacations, holidays, and daily good times. It is important for all family members to maintain friendships, too. Some families find it convenient to forgo some of these activities because of the jealous person's disapproval. But even though such activities may lead to short-term conflicts, they are offset by long-term benefits.

5. *Establish goals.* Many people who live in jealous households never seem to make progress because they haven't really decided what they want. They may be ambivalent about their objectives, unsure of where they want the relationship to go. At one level of their feelings they are so angry at their partners they want to inflict pain and vengeance. At another level they want to get out of the relationship altogether and be free of the heavy burdens they have had to endure. At still another level they retain their affection and sympathy for their partners and want to do whatever they can to help. They want to improve the relationship, to make the jealousy

go away, to rekindle the love and mutual respect that led to their initial attraction.

As long as these competing objectives remain, the individual cannot get very far. An internal war will be conducted, and efforts to work on the relationship will be diminished. Thus, it is important to establish goals before any further action is taken. The specific actions to be taken can vary tremendously depending on what these goals are.

The individual who wants to survive a jealous relationship must answer several important questions about goals: Is the objective to find a way to separate amicably or to find a way to improve the relationship? Is it to help the jealous partner become a healthier individual or is it to get even for the pain that was caused? Is it to minimize the pain and discomfort in the relationship while otherwise maintaining the status quo? Is it to avoid any behavior that leads the jealous partner into jealous anger? Is it to make the best of a bad situation without making any other changes in the relationship? Is it to cure the partner of the jealous affliction? Once these questions are honestly answered and the goals are established, the individual can focus on more specific actions that can help achieve the objectives.

6. *Develop an effective plan.* It is tempting and usually easier to rely on one's immediate feelings in coping with the jealous partner. It is also compelling to use trial-and-error methods in trying to determine what works. But once goals are established, it is more effective to rely on a logical plan and stick to it.

For example, when the goal is to help minimize the partner's jealousy problem, the plan will include supportiveness, encouragement, positive reinforcement of acceptable behaviors, and improved communications. These would not be desirable actions if the goal is to bring about a separation. In that case the plan might include such specific preparations as getting oneself ready emotionally, economically, and socially. If vengeance is the goal, there are many effective strategies that could effectively inconvenience or hurt the jealous partner. But these actions should not be mixed up with attempts to improve the relationship.

The point is to develop a plan and stay with it and to avoid getting it mixed up with feelings or passing moods that might be contrary to the overall objective.

7. *Avoid isolational behavior.* There is a tendency among those who live with very jealous people to cope by avoidance or isolational behavior. Because of the jealous partner's disapproval of relationships and because of

his or her unpredictable moods, it seems an effective defense to avoid people and thus the possibility of confrontations.

Isolational behavior takes many forms. Some people pout, remain sullen and noncommunicative, stay away from others, and say as little as possible to the jealous person. These self-protective devices may offer some immediate protections but are ultimately counterproductive. More than almost anyone, the person who lives in a jealous relationship needs to be with people and needs to communicate and interact. To do otherwise will ultimately accentuate the problem.

To cope in a jealous relationship, it is more effective to keep talking and expressing feelings, wherever these exchanges may lead. It is effective to maintain one's friendships, no matter how doing so is interpreted by the jealous person. These actions provide needed supports, better understanding, and opportunities to clarify issues with the jealous person. Granted, when communication occurs there will be greater likelihood of confrontations and the expression of antagonisms. Yet even this, unpleasant as it may be, is more effective in reaching whatever goals one may have. And when communication is effective it results in improved understanding.

Effective communication includes proper selection of subjects for discussion and good timing. Among the subjects that should be discussed with the jealous partner is jealousy itself. Both partners in a relationship can learn more by discussing things together rationally. Talking should not be confined to problems, however. This would soon lead both members of the relationship to dread talking with one another. They would associate it with unpleasantness and more pain. If both members of the couple can think of talking as including opportunities for fun, pleasant exchanges, and understanding, they won't be so reluctant to do it.

8. *Don't provoke jealous behaviors.* Jealousy itself comes from within the individual and not from the actions of the other person. Nevertheless, people sometimes intentionally or unconsciously provoke the jealous person. Provocation might take the form of flirting with potential rivals, ridicule, or unpleasant teasing of the jealous person; always defeating the jealous person in competitive encounters; or even leaving clues to infidelity when none has actually taken place.

The partners of jealous people may feel they have valid reasons for their provocative behaviors. They may hold the widespread but mistaken belief that jealousy is a sign of love. They may feel a sense of power or distorted self-esteem when their partners are worried about losing out in the relationship. They may feel anger at their partners for past hurts and may want to reciprocate. Or they may be caught up in a "jealousy game" with their partners, in which both get certain neurotic gratifications through relating with one another in a jealous way.

Whatever the reason, provoking jealous behaviors is not a positive or effective way to survive the relationship. At best it can only provide some temporary satisfaction or release of anger. But eventually it harms all concerned, leading to more confrontations, less love, and a diminished possibility of a working relationship. Avoiding provocative behavior doesn't mean, however, that the partner should be passive, docile, or submissive in the relationship. This is also counterproductive. It projects a weak and helpless stance and demonstrates to the jealous person that any behavior is acceptable no matter how bad it is. A strong but nonprovocative stance occurs when the partner states a position clearly and unequivocally and then avoids repeated explanations.

For example, a jealous person may insist on knowing more details about the partner's recent whereabouts. When this is explained once, the jealous person demands additional details, proof, corroboration, and clarification of possible discrepancies. Getting caught up in such explanations is fruitless. The only reasonable response, after the initial explanation, is to stop discussing it. Changing the subject or complete silence about that issue becomes necessary until the jealous person realizes that continuing the interrogation is fruitless.

9. *Improve flexibility and negotiation skills.* Whether the goal is to improve the relationship, dissolve it, or do anything in between, the relationship will benefit when the partners show some flexibility and interest in negotiating their differences. Jealous people tend to be rigid and feel they are right and that there is no room for negotiation. Thus, the nonjealous partner may have to develop these skills unilaterally. They include getting the jealous partner to feel more comfortable about change and less threatened about compromise, offering praise and rewards whenever the jealous person shows some flexibility or tolerance for differences, making concessions on smaller issues in order to convince the jealous partner of the need to yield on others, and expressing views in a nonconfrontative way so that the jealous person doesn't feel threatened or guarded.

Once the jealous partner is more comfortable with compromise and negotiation, the couple is more ready to discuss their mutual expectations and clarify their respective roles. When these discussions take place before any arguments, the resulting agreements may be used later to reconcile conflicts. Of course, this is a long and tedious process in dealing with the seriously jealous person, and it requires great patience before any positive results can be expected.

10. *Grow and expand horizons.* Couples can help minimize their problems with jealousy as their sights are directed outward. If they look beyond themselves and their personal concerns and concentrate more on the world in which they live, they will be taking an immensely productive step. Taking an interest in people, in social causes, in the well-being of others, will always be of value to both partners.

The desire to grow and learn makes for an atmosphere in which jealousy cannot thrive. It is an attitude that can offer hope for the jealous person and the nonjealous partner. Through it the couple can work together to express love and mutual respect and show that their future lives together can be worthwhile. Thus, when each person has an incentive to learn, to look at other people's points of view, and to understand other ways of living, there will be less room for jealousy-based conflict. There will be more self-confidence, feelings of personal worth, and inner security. What was once a cause of deprivation, a source of fear and loneliness, can be changed and become the foundation for a rich and fulfilling relationship.

Notes

CHAPTER ONE What Is Jealousy?

1. Murray A. Straus, Richard Gelles, and Suzanne K. Steinmetz (1980), *Behind Closed Doors: Violence in the American Family* (Garden City, N.Y.: Anchor Books, Doubleday and Co.), p. 32.
2. Murray M. Schwartz (1973), "Leontes' Jealousy in *The Winter's Tale*" *American Imago* 30, Fall, pp. 250–51.
3. George M. Foster (1972), "The Anatomy of Envy: A Study in Symbolic Behavior," *Current Anthropology* 13, April, p. 165.
4. John P. Docherty and Jean Ellis (1976), "A New Concept and Finding in Morbid Jealousy," *American Journal of Psychiatry* 133, June, pp. 679–80; Hubert Tellenbach (1974), "On The Nature of Jealousy," *Journal of Phenomenological Psychology* 4, Spring, p. 462.
5. S. Schneider (1985), "Jealousy is Hell," *Mademoiselle*, July, p. 56.
6. Ronald Mazur (1973), "Beyond Jealousy and Possessiveness," in *The New Intimacy! Open-Ended Marriage and Alternative Lifestyles* (Boston: Beacon Press), p. 95.
7. The students were attending a graduate course in social work conceptual frameworks taught by the author at The Catholic University of America, Washington, D.C., in 1986.
8. David Lester, et al. (1985), "Jealousy and Irrationality in Love," *Psychological Reports* 56, February, p. 216.
9. Eugene Mathes, Heather E. Adams, and Ruth M. Davies (1985), "Jealousy: Loss of Relationship Rewards, Loss of Self-Esteem, Depression, Anxiety and Anger," *Journal of Personality and Social Psychology* 48, June, p. 1552.
10. R. Joseph (1985), "Competition Between Women," *Psychology* 22, March, pp. 1–12.
11. Ralph B. Hupka, et al. (1985), "Romantic Jealousy and Romantic Envy: A Seven-Nation Study," *Journal of Cross-Cultural Psychology* 16, December, pp. 423–446; also Hupka (1981), "Cultural Determinants of Jealousy," *Alternative Lifestyles* 4, Fall, pp. 310–14.
12. Kingsley Davis (1936), "Jealousy and Sexual Property," *Social Forces* 14, Spring, pp. 395–405; also Mazur, "Beyond Jealousy," p. 95.
13. Robert A. Stewart and Gerald T. Hotaling, eds. (1980), *The Social Causes of Husband-Wife Violence* (Minneapolis: University of Minnesota Press), pp. 36–43; Anthony Pietropinto (1982), "Current Thinking on Jealousy in Marriage," 16, *Medical Aspects of Human Sexuality*, July, pp. 37–42.
14. Theodore I. Rubin (1978), "Myths of Jealousy," *Ladies Home Journal*, May, p. 44.

15. Anthony Pietropinto and Jacqueline Simenauer (1979), *Husbands and Wives: A Nationwide Survey of Marriage* (New York: Times Books), pp. 88–91.
16. Tellenbach, "On the Nature of Jealousy," p. 463.
17. Margaret Mead (1958), "Jealousy: Primitive and Civilized," in *Women's Coming of Age*, eds. Samuel D. Schmalhausen and V. F. Calverton (New York: Liveright Publishing Co. p. 36); Otto Fenichel (1945), *The Psychoanalytic Theory of Neurosis* (New York: W. W. Norton), p. 186; Howard M. Halpern (1982), *How to Break Your Addiction to a Person* (New York: McGraw-Hill), p. 73.
18. Lester et al., "Jealousy and Irrationality," p. 214.
19. Abraham Maslow (1968), *Toward a Psychology of Being*, 2nd ed. (Princeton, N.J.: Van Nostrand), pp. 49–67.
20. Robert J. Sternberg (1986), "A Triangular Theory of Love," *Psychological Review* 93, February, pp. 119–35.
21. Gregory White (1981), "A Model of Romantic Jealousy," *Motivation and Emotion* 5, December, p. 309; Eugene Mathes and Donna J. Deuger (1982), "Jealousy, A Creation of Human Culture?" *Psychological Reports* 51, October, pp. 351–54.
22. Judy Dunn (1983), "Sibling Relationships in Early Childhood," *Child Development* 54, April, p. 787–811; Vicki Morris (1982), "Helping Lesbian Couples Cope with Jealousy," *Women and Therapy* 1, Winter, pp. 27–34; G. Schwartz (1985), "Your Guy and Your Sis: Too Close for Comfort?" *Seventeen*, October, p. 118; E. Sweet (1984), "The Electra Complex: How Can I Be Jealous of My Four-Year-Old Daughter?" *Ms.*, May, p. 148; J. O. Wisdom (1976), "Jealousy in a Twelve-Month-Old Boy," *International Review of Psychoanalysis* 3, March, pp. 365–68; Lucy Waletzky (1979), "Husband's Problems With Breast Feeding," *American Journal of Orthopsychiatry* 49, April, pp. 349–52; E. A. Ziman (1949), *Jealousy in Children: A Guide to Parents* (New York: A. A. Wyn).
23. Peter B. Neubauer (1983), "The Importance of the Sibling Experience," *Psychoanalytic Study of the Child* 38, pp. 325–36.
24. Sigmund Freud (1955), "Some Neurotic Mechanisms in Jealousy, Paranoia, and Homosexuality," in *The Complete Psychological Works of Sigmund Freud*, ed. and trans. James Strachey (London: Hogarth Press), pp. 221–32.
25. Mathes and Deuger, "Jealousy, A Creation" p. 352.
26. Paul A. Hauck (1981), *Overcoming Jealousy and Possessiveness* (New York: Westminster Press), pp. 36–40.
27. Frank Pittman (1985), "Gender Myths," *Family Therapy Networker* 9, pp. 24–33.
28. Martin Daly, Margo Wilson, and Suzanne J. Weghorst (1982), "Male Sexual Jealousy," *Ethology and Sociobiology* 3, January, pp. 11–27; G. Mitchell (1981), *Human Sexual Differences: A Primatologist's Perspective* (New York: Van Nostrand Reinhold), pp. 119–37.
29. Daly, Wilson, and Weghorst, "Male Sexual Jealousy," p. 12.
30. E. Maccoby and C. Jacklin (1974), *The Psychology of Sex Differences* (Palo Alto, Calif.: Stanford University Press), p. 18.
31. Joseph, "Competition Between Women," p. 12.
32. Jane Barr Stump (1985), *What's the Difference? How Men and Women Compare* (New York: William Morrow & Co.) p. 56.
33. James Wagenvoord and Peyton Bailey (1978), *Men: A Book for Women* (New York: Avon); James Wagenvoord and Peyton Bailey (1979), *Women: A Book for Men* (New York: Avon).
34. Stump, *What's the Difference?*, p. 66.

35. Ibid.
36. Tim Hackler (1983), "Biology Influences Sex Roles," in *Male/Female Roles*, eds. Bruno Leone and M. Teresa O'Neil (St. Paul, Minn.: Greenhaven Press), pp. 16–26.
37. Pietropinto and Simenauer, *Husbands and Wives*, p. 233.
38. Jesse Bernard (1971), "Jealousy in Marriage," *Medical Aspects of Human Sexuality* 5, April, p. 209.
39. Pietropinto, "Current Thinking," p. 39.
40. Herbert S. Strean (1983), *The Sexual Dimension* (New York: Free Press), p. 181.
41. Alfred C. Kinsey, Wardell Pomeroy, and Clyde Martin (1948): *Sexual Behavior in the Human Male* (New York: W. B. Saunders), pp. 583–91; Alfred C. Kinsey, Wardell Pomeroy, and Clyde Martin (1953), *Sexual Behavior in the Human Female* (New York: W. B. Saunders), pp. 276–84.
42. Robert Atchley and Mildred Seltzer (1976), *The Sociology of Aging* (Belmont, Calif.: Wadsworth Publishing Company), pp. 18–24.
43. Steven Frankel and Ivan Sherick (1977), "Observations on the Development of Normal Envy," *Psychoanalytic Study of the Child* 32, pp. 257–81; Peter A. Titelman (1981), "A Phenomenological Comparison Between Envy and Jealousy," *Journal of Phenomenological Psychology* 12, Fall, pp. 189–204; I. A. van Krogten et al. (1983), "Afgunst en Jaloezie gescheiden" (Envy and jealousy differentiated), *Tijdschrift voor Psychotherapie* 9, September, pp. 238–45.
44. Maury Silver and John Sabini (1978), "The Social Construction of Envy," *Journal for the Theory of Social Behavior* 8, October, pp. 313–32.
45. Titelman, "A Phenomenological Comparison," p. 190.
46. Gary L. Hansen (1982), "Reactions to Hypothetical Jealousy-Producing Events," *Family Relations: Journal of Applied Family and Child Studies* 31, October, pp. 516–18.
47. Robert W. Hibbard (1975), "A Rational Approach to Treating Jealousy," *Rational Living* 10, Fall, pp. 25–27.
48. Neubauer, "The Importance of the Sibling Experience," pp. 130–31.

CHAPTER TWO   Is It Harmless or Destructive?

1. Federal Bureau of Investigation (1986), *Uniform Crime Reports for the United States* (Washington, D.C.: U.S. Department of Justice).
2. Murray A. Straus and Gerald T. Hotaling, eds. (1980), *The Social Causes of Husband-Wife Violence* (Minneapolis: University of Minnesota Press), pp. 23–24.
3. Suzanne K. Steinmetz (1977), "Wife Beating, Husband Beating—A Comparison of the Use of Violence Between Spouses to Resolve Marital Conflicts," in *Battered Women: A Psychosocial Study of Domestic Violence*, ed. Maria Ray (New York: Van Nostrand); Richard K. Goodstein and Ann W. Page (1981), "Battered Wife Syndrome: Overview of Dynamics and Treatment," *American Journal of Psychiatry* 138, August, pp. 1036–37; Elaine Hilberman (1980), "Overview: The Wife Beater's Wife Reconsidered," *American Journal of Psychiatry* 137, November, p. 1336.
5. B. Sokoloff (1947), *Jealousy: A Psychiatric Study* (New York: Howell, Soskin), p. 13.
6. P. C. Hoaken (1976), "Jealousy as a Symptom of Psychiatric Disorder," *Australian and New Zealand Journal of Psychiatry* 10, March, pp. 47–51.
7. J. Richard Udry and Bruce K. Eckland (1984), "Benefits of Being Attractive: Differential Payoffs for Men and Women," *Psychological Reports* 54, February, pp. 47–56.
8. Ernest Jones (1953), *The Life and Work of Sigmund Freud* (New York: Basic Books), pp. 114–15.

9. Ayala Pines and Elliot Aronson (1983), "Antecedents, Correlates and Consequences of Sexual Jealousy," *Journal of Personality* 51, March, pp. 108–136.

10. Carol H. Hoskins (1982), "Biorhythms and Marital Conflict," *Medical Aspects of Human Sexuality* 16, March, p. 43.

11. Gary L. Hansen (1983), "Marital Satisfaction and Jealousy Among Men," *Psychological Reports* 52, April, p. 366.

12. Janice Wood Wetzel (1984), *Clinical Handbook of Depression* (New York: Gardner Press), pp. 31–34.

13. Braun Buunk (1984), "Jealousy as Related to Attributions for Partner's Behavior," *Social Psychology Quarterly* 47, March, p. 107; Hupka, "Cultural Determinants," Fall, p. 310.

14. American Psychiatric Association (1980), *DSM-III: Diagnostic and Statistical Manual of Mental Disorders*, 3rd ed. (Washington, D.C.: American Psychiatric Association), p. 171.

15. Eugene Schoenfeld (1980), *Jealousy: Taming the Green-Eyed Monster* (New York: Holt, Rinehart & Winston), pp. 5–7.

16. Mathes, Adams, and Davies (1985), "Jealousy: Loss of Relationship Rewards," p. 1553.

17. Hilberman, "Overview: The Wife Beater's Wife," p. 1336.

18. The Jealousy Rating Scale was developed and used in a briefer form by the author beginning in 1976. Several versions, each more complex, have been produced and used since then. The version that appears in this book was completed in 1982. Most of the 300 subjects have been college students, volunteers, and marital therapy clients.

19. Emil R. Pinto (1978), "Pathological Tolerance," *American Journal of Psychiatry* 136, June, pp. 698–701.

20. B. M. Campbell (1981), "Jealousy: The Ugly Side of Love," *Ebony* 36, August, pp. 125–27; Joseph L. White (1984), *The Psychology of Blacks: An Afro-American Perspective* (Englewood Cliffs, N.J.: Prentice-Hall).

CHAPTER THREE   The Causes of Jealousy

1. Carolyn Ellis and Eugene Weinstein (1985), "Jealousy and the Social Psychology of Emotional Experience," *American Journal of Sociology* 107, April, p. 633; Steven D. Solomon (1982), "An Integrated Theory of Jealousy," doctoral dissertation, Los Angeles: California School of Professional Psychology.

2. Bernard Berlson and Gary Steiner (1964), *Human Behavior: An Inventory of Scientific Findings* (New York: Harcourt, Brace & World).

3. Charles Darwin (1871/1970), *The Descent of Man, and Selection in Relation to Sex* (New York: Penguin), ed., Philip Appleman, reprinted in *Darwin* (New York: Norton, pp. 199–276).

4. Melanie Klein (1977): *Envy and Gratitude and Other Works, 1946–1963* (New York: Delacorte).

5. George M. Foster (1972), "The Anatomy of Envy: A Study in Symbolic Behavior," *Current Anthropology* 13, April, pp. 165–202; Frankel and Sherick (1977), "Observations," pp. 257–281.

6. Ashley Montagu (1978), *Touching: The Human Significance of the Skin*, 2nd ed. (New York: Harper & Row); Paula Alderette and Donald F. deGraffenreid (1986), "Nonorganic Failure to Thrive Syndrome and the Family System," *Social Work* 31, May–June, pp. 207–13.

7. Wisdom, "Jealousy in a Twelve-Month-Old Boy," p. 368.
8. William C. Nichols (1978), "When Jealousy Threatens," *Parents Magazine*, August, p. 20.
9. Ziman, "Jealousy in Childhood," pp. 22–35.
10. Erik Erikson (1963), *Childhood and Society*, 2nd ed. (New York: W. W. Norton).
11. Neubauer, "The Importance of the Sibling Experience," p. 325.
12. D. C. McClelland and D. A. Pilon (1983), "Sources of Adult Motives in Patterns of Parent Behavior in Early Childhood," *Journal of Personality and Social Psychology* 44, June, pp. 564–74.
13. R. D. Enright et al. (1980), "Parental Influences on the Development of Adolescent Autonomy and Identity," *Journal of Youth and Adolescence* 9, August, pp. 529–45.
14. Leslie Farber (1976), *Lying, Despair, Jealousy, Envy, Sex, Suicide, Drugs and the Good Life* (New York: Basic Books).
15. Gary L. Hansen (1985), "Dating Jealousy Among College Students," *Sex Roles* 12, Summer, pp. 57–61.
16. Wetzel, *Clinical Handbook*, p. 16.
17. M. Zentner (1984), "Paranoia," in *Adult Psychopathology*, ed. Francis J. Turner (New York: Free Press), pp. 368–70.
18. American Psychiatric Association, *DSM-III*, p. 68; Kenneth S. Kendler (1980), "Are There Delusions Specific for Paranoid Disorders and Schizophrenia?" *Schizophrenic Bulletin* 6, January, pp. 1–3.
19. Norman Cameron (1967), "Psychotic Disorders: Paranoid Reactions," in *Comprehensive Textbook of Psychiatry*, eds. Alfred Freeman and Harold Kaplan (Baltimore, Md.: Williams and Wilkins, pp. 665–75).
20. Albert Bandura (1977), *Social Learning Theory* (Englewood Cliffs, N.J.: Prentice-Hall).
21. Martin Sundel and Sandra Stone Sundel (1985), *Behavioral Modification in the Human Services*, 2nd ed. (Englewood Cliffs, N.J.: Prentice-Hall).
22. Sigmund Freud, "Some Neurotic Mechanisms," p. 221.
23. J. P. Cobb and I. M. Marks (1979), "Morbid Jealousy Featuring an Obsessive-Compulsive Neurosis," *British Journal of Psychiatry* 125, March, pp. 301–5.
24. Anna Freud (1946), *The Ego and the Mechanisms of Defense*, trans. Cecil Baines (New York: International Universities Press).
25. Herbert S. Strean (1985), *Resolving Resistances in Psychotherapy* (New York: John Wiley & Sons).
26. Stump, *What's the Difference?*, pp. 61–62.
27. Amelie O. Rorty (1974), "Some Social Uses of the Forbidden," *Psychoanalytic Review* 58, Winter, pp. 497–510.
28. John Turbott (1981), "Morbid Jealousy: Reciprocal Appearance of Psychopathology in Either Spouse," *Australian and New Zealand Journal of Psychiatry* 15, June, pp. 164–67.

CHAPTER FOUR   Unhealthy Jealous Relationships

1. Steven A. Roth (1986), "The Symbiotic Marriage," *Medical Aspects of Human Sexuality* 16, July, p. 39.
2. Julian R. Hafner (1979), "Agoraphobic Woman Married to Abnormally Jealous Man," *British Journal of Medical Psychology* 52, June, pp. 99–104.
3. Michael F. Hoyt (1986), "Neuroticism and Mate Selection," *Medical Aspects of Human Sexuality* 16, July, p. 11.

4. William I. Grossman (1986), "Notes on Masochism: A Discussion of the History and Development of a Psychoanalytic Concept," *Psychoanalytic Quarterly 55*, Fall, pp. 379–413.

5. C. Socarides (1977), "On Vengeance: The Desire to 'Get Even'," in *The World of Emotions* ed. C. Socarides (New York: International Universities Press).

6. Hupka et al., "Romantic Jealousy and Romantic Envy," p. 424.

7. J. Cameron (1985), "He's a Little Too Jealous—You Like It a Little Too Much," *Mademoiselle*, July, p. 56.

8. Docherty and Ellis, "A New Concept and Finding," p. 680.

9. Robert L. Barker (1986a), "Slaying the Green-Eyed Monster," *USA Today Magazine*, April, p. 12.

10. Eric Berne (1964), *Games People Play* (New York: Grove Press).

11. Eric Berne (1972), *What Do You Say After You Say Hello?* (New York: Grove Press).

12. Grossman, "Notes on Masochism," p. 340.

13. David Brandt (1986), *Don't Stop Now, You're Killing Me: The Sadomasochistic Game in Everyday Life and How Not to Play It* (New York: Poseidon).

CHAPTER FIVE   Helping One's Jealous Partner

1. Robert W. Hibbard (1975), "A Rational Approach to Treating Jealousy," *Rational Living* 10, Fall, pp. 25–27.

2. S. Schneider (1985), "Jealousy Is Hell," *Mademoiselle*, July, p. 56.

3. Larry Constantine (1976), "Jealousy: Techniques for Intervention," in *Treating Relationships*, ed. David H. Olson (Lake Mills, Iowa: Graphic Publishers), pp. 141–58.

4. Schoenfeld, *Jealousy: Taming the Green-Eyed Monster*, pp. 124–34.

5. B. Wein (1983), "Dealing With Jealousy," *Harper's Bazaar*, October, pp. 204–7.

6. Peter Salovey and Judith Rodin (1985), "The Heart of Jealousy," *Psychology Today* 19, September, pp. 22–25.

7. Murray Bowen (1978), *Family Therapy in Clinical Practice* (New York: Jason Aronson).

8. Robert N. Whitehurst (1971), "American Sexophobia," in *The New Sexual Revolution*, eds. L. A. Kirkendall and R. N. Whitehurst (New York: Donald Brown, Inc.)

9. Elahé Mir-Djalali (1980), "The Failure of Language to Communicate," *International Journal of Intercultural Relations* 4, Spring, pp. 307–28.

10. Hibbard, "A Rational Approach," p. 27.

11. The instructions on how to settle conflicts fairly with one's spouse was developed by the author for work with his marital therapy clients and not intended to be limited to couples with jealousy problems.

12. Constantine, "Jealousy: Techniques for Intervention."

13. Sundel and Sundel, *Behavioral Modification.*

CHAPTER SIX   Self-Defense Strategies

1. Daniel O'Leary and Alison D. Curley (1986), "Assertion and Family Violence: Correlates of Spouse Abuse," *Journal of Marital and Family Therapy* 12, July, pp. 281–89; Pinto, "Pathological Tolerance," p. 700.

2. Ellis and Weinstein (1985), "Jealousy and the Social Psychology of Emotional Experience" *American Journal of Sociology* 107, April, p. 633.

3. Herbert S. Strean (1980), *The Extramarital Affair* (New York: Free Press); Laurel Richardson (1985), *The New Other Woman* (New York: Free Press).

4. Buunk, "Jealousy as Related," p. 109.

5. Gregory White (1980), "Inducing Jealousy," *Personality and Social Psychology Bulletin* 6, June, pp. 222–27.

6. Susan F. Turner and Constance Hoenk Shapiro (1986), "Battered Women: Mourning the Death of a Relationship," *Social Work* 31, Sept.–Oct., pp. 372–384.

7. Phillip D. Tomporowski and Norman R. Ellis (1986), "Effects of Exercise on Cognitive Processes: A Review," *American Psychologist* 99, May, pp. 338–46.

8. Joseph Flaherty et al. (1983), "The Role of Social Support in the Function of Patients With Unipolar Depression," *American Journal of Psychiatry* 140, April, pp. 473–76.

9. George R. Bach and R. M. Deutsch (1976), *Pairing* (New York: Avon Books); Carl Rogers (1972), *Becoming Partners: Marriage and Its Alternatives* (New York: Dell Publishers); Virginia Satir (1972), *Peoplemaking* (Palo Alto, Calif.: Science and Behavior Books).

10. Susan Folkman and Richard S. Lazarus (1986), "Stress Processes and Depressive Symptomatology," *Journal of Abnormal Psychology* 95, May, pp. 107–113.

11. Mary Kay O'Neil (1984), "Affective Disorders," in *Adult Psychopathology*, ed. Francis J. Turner (New York: Free Press), pp. 148–80.

12. Marcia Lasswell and Norman Lobsenz (1977), "How to Handle Sexual Jealousy," *McCall's*, July, p. 86.

13. Morton Friedman (1979), "Obsessions with Mate's Sexual Experiences," *Medical Aspects of Human Sexuality* 13, February, pp. 54–57.

14. Sidney Cobb (1976), "Social Supports as a Moderator of Life Stress," *Psychosomatic Medicine* 38, December, pp. 407–17.

15. Women's Action Alliance (1987), *Women Helping Women: A State-by-State Directory of Services* (New York: Neal-Schuman Publishers).

CHAPTER SEVEN Protecting Children from Jealous Parents

1. Dunn, "Sibling Relationships," p. 790; A. C. Bernstein (1979), "Jealousy in the Family," *Parents Magazine*, February, pp. 47–49.

2. Robert Bringle and Larry J. Williams (1979), "Parental Offspring Similarities on Jealousy and Related Personality Dimensions," *Motivation and Emotion* 3, September, pp. 265–86.

3. E. Sweet (1984), "The Electra Complex," p. 148.

4. G. V. Laury (1979), "Child in Bed as Chastity Belt," *Medical Aspects of Human Sexuality* 13, October, p. 68.

5. Waletzky, "Husband's Problems," p. 352.

6. D. C. McClelland and D. A. Pilon, "Sources of Adult Motives," pp. 565–67.

7. Bringle and Williams, "Parental Offspring Similarities," p. 265.

8. Straus, Gelles, and Steinmetz, *Behind Closed Doors*, pp. 17–26.

9. Friedlander, "Learned Helplessness," p. 100.

10. McClelland and Pilon, "Sources of Adult Motives," pp. 566–67.

11. Ibid., p. 555.

12. Grossman, "Notes on Masochism," p. 410.

13. Peter B. Neubauer (1982), "Rivalry, Envy, and Jealousy," *Psychoanalytic Study of the Child.* Vol. 37. pp. 121–42.

14. Karen Gail Lewis (1986), "Sibling Therapy With Multiproblem Families," *Journal of Marital and Family Therapy* 12, July, pp. 291–300.

15. Lucille Forer and Henry Still (1976), *The Birth Order Factor* (New York: David McKay).

16. Ibid., p. 9.

17. Frankel and Sherick, "Observations on the Development," pp. 263–69.
18. A. C. Bernstein (1979), "Jealousy in the Family," *Parents Magazine*, February, p. 47.
19. McClelland and Pilon, "Sources of Adult Motives," pp. 567–68.
20. Enright et al. "Parental Influences," pp. 535–37.
21. Foster, "The Anatomy of Envy," pp. 200–202.

CHAPTER EIGHT Ending Jealous Relationships

1. James L. Framo (1985), "Breaking the Ties That Bind," *Family Therapy Networker* 9, September–October, pp. 51–56.
2. Laura B. Hansen and Joan F. Shireman (1986), "The Process of Emotional Divorce: Explanations of Theory," *Social Casework* 67, June, pp. 323–31.
3. P. L. Moffitt, N. D. Spence, and R. D. Golding (1986), "Mental Health in Marriage: The Roles of Need for Affiliation, Sensitivity to Rejection and Other Factors," *Journal of Clinical Psychology* 42, January, pp. 68–76.
4. O'Neil, "Affective Disorders," pp. 150–55; Wetzel, "Clinical Handbook of Depression."
5. Judith S. Wallerstein (1986), "Women After Divorce: Preliminary Report from a Ten-Year Follow Up," *American Journal of Orthopsychiatry* 56, January, pp. 65–77.
6. Socarides, "On Vengeance."
7. Richard K. Goodstein and Ann Page (1981), "Battered Wife Syndrome: Overview of the Dynamics and Treatment," *American Journal of Psychiatry* 138, August, pp. 1036–43.
8. M. Symonds (1975), "Victims of Violence: Psychological Effects and After Effects," *American Journal of Psychoanalysis* 36, January, pp. 39–46.
9. Turner and Shapiro, "Battered Women," pp. 383–84.
10. Christopher Peterson (1985), "Learned Helplessness: Fundamental Issues in Theory and Research," *Journal of Social and Clinical Psychology* 3, February, pp. 248–54.
11. A. P. Derdeyn (1976), "Child Custody Contests in Historical Perspective," *American Journal of Psychiatry* 133, December, pp. 1369–76.
12. Karen E. Rosenblum (1986), "Leaving as a Wife, Leaving as a Mother," *Journal of Family Issues* 7, June, pp. 197–213.
13. Judith S. Wallerstein and J. B. Kelly (1976), "The Effects of Parental Divorce: Experiences of the Child in Later Latency," *American Journal of Orthopsychiatry* 46, Fall, pp. 256–69; B. L. Bloom, S. J. Asher, and S. W. White (1978), "Marital Disruption as a Stressor: A Review and Analysis," *Psychological Bulletin* 85, September, pp. 867–94.
14. John W. Jacobs (1986), "Divorce and Child Custody Resolution: Conflicting Legal and Psychological Paradigms," *American Journal of Psychiatry* 143, February, pp. 192–97.
15. Howard M. Halpern (1982), *How to Break Your Addiction to a Person* (New York: McGraw-Hill), p. 240.
16. Donald Cantor, quoted in Joseph Epstein (1974), *Divorced in America* (New York: Dutton), p. 36.
17. Jacobs, "Divorce and Child Custody Resolution," pp. 192–97.
18. Theodore I. Rubin (1985), *Overcoming Indecisiveness: The Eight Stages of Effective Decision Making* (New York: Harper & Row).
19. Stuart Berger (1983), *Divorce Without Victims* (Boston: Houghton Mifflin).
20. Epstein, *Divorced in America*; Edward Teyber, *Helping Your Child with Divorce* (New York: McGraw-Hill); Morton M. Hunt (1963), *The World of the Formerly Married* (New York: McGraw-Hill).

21. A. J. Cornblatt (1985), "Matrimonial Mediation," *Journal of Family Law* 23, pp. 99–109; Robert Coulton (1983), *Fighting Fair: Family Mediation Will Work For You* (New York: Free Press); Helen R. Weingarten (1986), "Strategic Planning for Divorce Mediation," *Social Work* 31, May–June, pp. 194–200; James L. Framo (1976), "The Friendly Divorce," *Psychology Today,* September, pp. 76–81.
22. Donald K. Granvold and Roxanne Tarrant (1983), "Structured Marital Separation as a Marital Treatment Method," *Journal of Marital and Family Therapy* 9, April, pp. 189–98.
23. Eric E. McCollum (1985), "Recontacting Former Spouses: A Further Step in the Divorce Process," *Journal of Marital and Family Therapy* 11, October, pp. 417–20.
24. Coulton, *Fighting Fair.*
25. John Mirowsky (1985), "Depression and Marital Power," *American Journal of Sociology* 91, November, pp. 557–92.
26. Michael F. Hoyt (1986), "Neuroticism and Mate Selection," *Medical Aspects of Human Sexuality* 20, July, p. 11.

CHAPTER NINE   How and Where to Get Help

1. Herbert S. Strean (1985), *Resolving Resistances in Psychotherapy* (New York: John Wiley & Sons).
2. Mitchell T. Wittenberg and Harry T. Reis (1986), "Loneliness, Social Skills, and Social Perception," *Personality and Social Psychology Bulletin* 12, March, pp. 121–30.
3. Goodstein and Page, "Battered Wife Syndrome," pp. 1041–43.
4. Martin H. Ritchie (1986), "Counseling the Involuntary Client," *Journal of Counseling and Development* 64, April, pp. 316–18.
5. Robert L. Barker (1984), *Treating Couples in Crisis* (New York: Free Press), p. 73.
6. Cobb, "Social Supports as a Moderator," pp. 414–17.
7. James K. Whittaker and James Garbarino (1983), *Social Support Networks: Informal Helping in the Human Services* (Hawthorne, N.Y.: Aldine Publishing Co.).
8. Benjamin H. Gottlieb (1985), "Assessing and Strengthening the Impact of Social Support on Mental Health," *Social Work* 30, July–Aug., pp. 293–300.
9. Gertrude Goldberg et al. (1986), "Spouseless, Childless, Elderly Women and Their Social Supports," *Social Work* 32, March–April, pp. 104–13.
10. Michael Belyea (1985), "Self-Care and the Politics of the Body in the Welfare State," paper presented at the annual meeting of the Mid-South Sociological Association, 14 October 1985, Chapel Hill, N.C.
11. Carol D. Hunka, Anita W. O'Toole, and Richard O'Toole (1985), "Self-Help Therapy in Parents Anonymous," *Journal of Psychosocial Nursing and Mental Health Services* 23, July, pp. 24–32.
12. Jane H. Pfouts and Connie Renz (1981), "The Future of Wife Abuse Programs," *Social Work* 26, November, pp. 451–53.
13. Daniel Remine, Robert M. Rice, and J. Ross (1984), *Self-Help Groups and Human Service Agencies: How They Work Together* (New York: Family Service America).
14. *Encyclopedia of Associations* (1986), (Detroit, Mich.: Gale); Robert L. Barker (1986c), *The Resource Book* (New York: Haworth Press); Women's Action Alliance, *Women Helping Women.*
15. Toksoz Karasu (1986), "The Psychotherapies: Benefits and Limitations," *American Journal of Psychotherapy* 50, July, pp. 324–42.
16. Won-gi Im, Stefanie Wilner, and Miranda Breit (1983), "Jealousy: Interventions in Couples Therapy," *Family Process* 22, June, pp. 211–19.

17. J. O. Cavenor and D. S. Werner (1983), "The Sex of the Psychotherapist," *American Journal of Psychiatry* 140, January, pp. 85–91.
18. Robert L. Barker and Thomas L. Briggs (1969), *Using Teams to Deliver Social Services* (Syracuse, N.Y.: Syracuse University Press); William Masters and Virginia Johnson (1970), *Human Sexual Inadequacy* (Boston: Little, Brown & Co.).
19. Ronald W. Toseland et al. (1986), "Teamwork in Psychiatric Settings," *Social Work* 31, Jan.–Feb., pp. 46–52; Shirley Braverman (1985), "One Couple, Three Therapists: Therapeutic Overdose or Collusion-Breaker?" *Journal of Marital and Family Therapy* 11, April, pp. 179–86.
20. United States Congress, Office of Technology Assessment (1980), "The Efficacy and Cost Effectiveness of Psychotherapy," background paper no. 3. (Washington, D.C.: U.S. Government Printing Office).

CHAPTER TEN Ten Steps for Surviving Jealous Relationships

1. Amelie O. Rorty (1974), "Some Social Uses of the Forbidden," *Psychoanalytic Review* 58, Winter, pp. 497–510; Mathes and Deuger, "Jealousy, A Creation," pp. 352–54.
2. Hilberman, "Overview," pp. 1336–47.
3. Kenneth L. Woodward (1983), "Children Need to Learn Traditional Sex Roles," in *Male/Female Roles*, eds. Bruno Leones and M. Teresa O'Neill (St. Paul, Minn.: Greenhaven Press), pp. 27–30.
4. Edward Westermarck (1922): *The History of Human Marriage* (New York: Allerton).
5. Jesse Bernard (1977), "Infidelity: Some Moral and Social Issues," in *Marriage and Alternatives*, eds. Roger Libby and Robert Whitehurst (New York: Scott, Foresman and Co.), pp. 131–46; also Bernard (1982) *The Future of Marriage*, 2nd ed. (New Haven, Conn: Yale University Press).
6. Dorothy Wheeler (1985), "The Fear of Feminism in Family Therapy," *Family Therapy Networker* 9, Nov.–Dec., pp. 53–55.

Bibliography

Adams, Virginia (1980). "Getting at the Heart of Jealous Love." *Psychology Today*, October, pp. 37–44.

Alderette, Paula, and Donald F. deGraffenreid (1986). "Nonorganic Failure-to-Thrive Syndrome and the Family System." *Social Work*, May–June, 31, pp. 207–13.

American Psychiatric Association (1980). *Diagnostic and Statistic Manual of Mental Disorders*, 3rd ed., *DSM-III*. Washington, D.C.: American Psychiatric Association.

Ammon, Gunter (1984). "Eifersucht" (Jealousy). *Dynamische Psychiatrie* 17, May, pp. 456–67.

Ascher, B. L. (1983). "The New Jealousies." *Vogue*, September, p. 216.

Atchley, Robert, and Mildred Seltzer (1976). *The Sociology of Aging*. Belmont, Calif.: Wadsworth Publishing Co.

Bach, George R., and R. M. Deutsch (1970). *Pairing*. New York: Avon Books.

Bandura, Albert (1977). *Social Learning Theory*. Englewood Cliffs, N.J.: Prentice-Hall.

Barker, Robert L. (1984). *Treating Couples in Crisis*. New York: Free Press.

—— (1986a). "Slaying the Green-Eyed Monster," *USA Today Magazine* 114, April, p. 12.

—— (1986b). "The Marriage-Problem Conference." Paper presented at the National Association of Social Workers Symposium, 21 April 1986, Washington, D.C.

—— (1986c). *The Resource Book*. New York: Haworth Press.

—— (1987). *The Social Work Dictionary*. Silver Spring, Md.: National Association of Social Workers.

——, and Thomas L. Briggs (1969). *Using Teams to Deliver Social Services*. Syracuse, N.Y.: Syracuse University Press.

Barnes, Julian (1984). "Retro-Jealousy." *Vanity Fair*, April, p. 18.

Barrell, James J., and Anne C. Richards (1982). "Overcoming Jealousy: An Experimental Analysis of Common Factors." *Personnel and Guidance Journal* 61, September, pp. 40–47.

Beecher, Marguerite, and Willard Beecher (1971). *The Mark of Cain: An Anatomy of Jealousy*. New York: Harper & Row.

Belyea, Michael (1985). "Self-Care and the Politics of the Body in the Welfare State."

235

Paper presented at the annual meeting of the Mid-South Sociological Association, 14 October, 1985, Chapel Hill, N.C.

Berger, Stuart (1983). *Divorce Without Victims.* Boston: Houghton-Mifflin.

Berlson, Bernard, and Gary Steiner (1964). *Human Behavior: An Inventory of Scientific Findings.* New York: Harcourt, Brace & World.

Bernard, Jesse (1971). "Jealousy in Marriage." *Medical Aspects of Human Sexuality* 5, April. p. 209.

——, (1977). "Infidelity: Some Moral and Social Issues." In *Marriage and Alternatives,* eds. Roger Libby and Robert Whitehurst. Glenview, Ill.: Scott, Foresman and Co., pp. 131–46.

—— (1982). *The Future of Marriage,* 2nd ed. New Haven, Conn.: Yale University Press.

Berne, Eric (1964). *Games People Play.* New York: Grove Press.

—— (1972). *What Do You Say After You Say Hello?* New York: Grove Press.

Bernstein, A. C. (1979). "Jealousy in the Family." *Parents Magazine,* February, p. 47.

Bers, Susan A., and Judith Rodin (1984). "Social Comparison Jealousy: A Developmental and Motivational Study." *Journal of Personality and Social Psychology* 47, October, pp. 766–79.

Blood, Robert, and Margaret Blood (1972). *Marriage.* New York: Free Press.

Bloom, B. L., S. J. Asher, and S. W. White (1978). "Marital Disruption as a Stressor: A Review and Analysis." *Psychological Bulletin* 85, May, pp. 867–94.

Boris, Harold N. (1986). "The 'Other' Breast: Greed, Envy, Spite and Revenge." *Contemporary Psychoanalysis* 22, January, pp. 45–59.

Bowen, Murray (1978). *Family Therapy in Clinical Practice.* New York: Jason Aronson.

Bowker, L. (1984). "Coping With Wife Abuse: Personal and Social Networks." In *Battered Women and Their Families,* ed. A. R. Roberts. New York: Springer Publishing Co., pp. 96–121.

Bowlby, J. (1969). *Attachment.* New York: Basic Books.

Brandt, David (1986). *Don't Stop Now, You're Killing Me: The Sadomasochistic Game in Everyday Life and How Not to Play It.* New York: Poseidon.

Braverman, Shirley (1985). "One Couple, Three Therapists: Therapeutic Overdose or Collusion-Breaker." *Journal of Marital and Family Therapy* 11, April, pp. 179–86.

Bringle, Robert, et al. (1979). "Measuring the Intensity of Jealous Reactions." *Catalogue of Selected Documents in Psychology* 9, May.

——, and Larry J. Williams (1979). "Parental Offspring Similarities on Jealousy and Related Personality Dimensions." *Motivation and Emotion* 3, September, pp. 265–86.

Buunk, Braun (1982). "Anticipated Sexual Jealousy: Its Relationship to Self-Esteem, Dependency and Reciprocity." *Personality and Social Psychology Bulletin* 8, February, pp. 310–16.

—— (1984). "Jealousy as Related to Attributions for Partner's Behavior." *Social Psychology Quarterly* 47, March, pp. 107–12.

Cameron, J. (1985). "He's a Little Too Jealous—You Like It a Little Too Much." *Mademoiselle,* July, p. 56.

Cameron, Norman (1967). "Psychotic Disorders: Paranoid Reactions." In *Comprehensive*

Textbook of Psychiatry, eds. Alfred Freeman and Harold Kaplan. Baltimore, Md.: Williams and Wilkins, pp. 665–75.

Campbell, B. M. (1981). "Jealousy: The Ugly Side of Love." *Ebony*, August, p. 125.

Cash, Thomas F. and Claire A. Trimmer (1984). "Sexism and Beautyism in Women's Evaluation of Peer Performance." *Sex Roles* 10, January, pp. 87–98.

Cavenor, J. O., and D. S. Werner (1983). "The Sex of the Psychotherapist." *American Journal of Psychiatry* 140, January, pp. 85–91.

Clanton, Gordon, and L. G. Smith, eds. (1977). *Jealousy*. Englewood Cliffs, N.J.: Prentice-Hall.

Cobb, J. P. and I. M. Marks (1979). "Morbid Jealousy Featuring an Obsessive-Compulsive Neurosis." *British Journal of Psychiatry* 125, March, pp. 301–5.

Cobb, Sidney (1976). "Social Supports as a Moderator of Life Stress." *Psychosomatic Medicine* 38, December, pp. 407–17.

Constantine, Larry (1976). "Jealousy: Techniques for Intervention." In *Treating Relationships*, ed. David H. Olson. Lake Mills, Iowa: Graphic Publishers, pp. 141–58.

——, and Joan Constantine (1973). *Group Marriage*. New York: Macmillan.

Cornblatt, A. J. (1985). "Matrimonial Mediation." *Journal of Family Law* 23, January, pp. 99–109.

Coulton, Robert (1983). *Fighting Fair: Family Mediation Will Work for You*. New York: Free Press.

Daly, Martin, Margo Wilson, and Suzanne J. Weghorst (1982). "Male Sexual Jealousy." *Ethology and Sociobiology* 3, January, pp. 11–27.

Darwin, Charles (1871/1970). *The Descent of Man, and Selection In Relation to Sex*. Ed. Philip Appleman. Reprinted in *Darwin*; New York: Norton, pp. 199–276.

Davis, Kingsley (1936). "Jealousy and Sexual Property." *Social Forces* 14, Spring, pp. 395–405.

—— (1949). *Human Society*. New York: Macmillan.

Derdeyn, A. P. (1976). "Child Custody Contests In Historical Perspective." *American Journal of Psychiatry* 133, December, pp. 1369–76.

Docherty, John P., and Jean Ellis (1976). "A New Concept and Finding in Morbid Jealousy." *American Journal of Psychiatry* 133, June, pp. 679–83.

Dunn, Judy (1983). "Sibling Relationships in Early Childhood." *Child Development* 54, April, pp. 787–811.

Eitzen, D. Stanley (1983). "Sexual and Family-Based Social Problems: Illegitimacy, Abortion and Family Violence." In *Social Problems*, ed. D. S. Eitzen, 2nd ed. New York: Allyn and Bacon.

Ellis, Albert (1962). *The American Sexual Tragedy*. New York: Grove Press.

Ellis, Carolyn, and Eugene Weinstein (1985). "Jealousy and the Social Psychology of Emotional Experience." *American Journal of Sociology* 107, April, pp. 624–35.

Encyclopedia of Associations (1986), Detroit Mich. Gade.

Enoch, M.D. (1980). "Sexual Jealousy." *British Journal of Sexual Medicine* 30, July, pp. 32–41.

Enright, R. D., et al. (1980). "Parental Influences on the Development of Adolescent Autonomy and Identity." *Journal of Youth and Adolescence* 9, August, pp. 529–45.

Epstein, Joseph (1974). *Divorced in America.* New York: E. P. Dutton.

Erikson, Erik (1963). *Childhood and Society,* 2nd ed. New York: W. W. Norton.

Evans, William N. (1975). "The Eye of Jealousy and Envy." *Psychoanalytic Review* 62, Fall, pp. 481–92.

Faber, Stuart, and Teddi Levison (1975). *The Upside Downs of Jealousy, Possessiveness and Insecurity.* New York: Good Life Press.

Farber, Leslie (1976). *Lying, Despair, Jealousy, Envy, Sex, Suicide, Drugs and the Good Life.* New York: Basic Books.

Federal Bureau of Investigation (1986). *Uniform Crime Reports for the United States.* Washington, D.C.: U.S. Department of Justice.

Fenichel, Otto (1945). *The Psychoanalytic Theory of Neurosis.* New York: W. W. Norton.

Fishman, Stephen M. (1985). "Self as Forming the Formless." *Journal of Humanistic Psychology* 25, Summer, pp. 57–61.

Flaherty, Joseph, et al. (1983). "The Role of Social Support in the Function of Patients with Unipolar Depression." *American Journal of Psychiatry* 140, April, pp. 473–76.

Folkman, Susan, and Richard S. Lazarus (1986). "Stress Processes and Depressive Symptomatology." *Journal of Abnormal Psychology* 95, May, pp. 107–13.

Forer, Lucille, and Henry Still (1976). *The Birth Order Factor.* New York: David McKay.

Foster, George M. (1972). "The Anatomy of Envy: A Study in Symbolic Behavior." *Current Anthropology* 13, April, pp. 165–202.

Framo, James L. (1985). "Breaking the Ties That Bind." *Family Therapy Networker* 9, Sept.–Oct., pp. 51–56.

——— (1976). "The Friendly Divorce." *Psychology Today,* September, pp. 76–81.

Frankel, Steven, and Ivan Sherick (1977). "Observations on the Development of Normal Envy." *Psychoanalytic Study of the Child,* vol. 32. pp. 257–81.

Freud, Anna (1946). *The Ego and the Mechanisms of Defense,* trans. Cecil Baines. New York: International Universities Press.

Freud, Sigmund (1955). "Some Neurotic Mechanisms in Jealousy, Paranoia, and Homosexuality." In *Complete Psychological Works of Sigmund Freud,* ed. and trans. James Strachey. London, England: Hogarth Press, pp. 221–32.

Friday, Nancy (1985). *Jealousy.* New York: William Morrow.

Friedlander, Steven (1985). "Learned Helplessness in Children's Perception of Control and Causal Attributions." *Imagination, Cognition and Personality* 4, January, pp. 99–116.

Friedman, Morton (1979). "Obsessions with Mate's Sexual Experiences." *Medical Aspects of Human Sexuality* 13, February, pp. 54–57.

Gage, D. and M. Hibsch (1986). "When You're Jealous of Your Best Friend." *Seventeen,* April, pp. 170–71.

Galbreath, Judy (1986). *The Gifted Kids' Survival Guide.* Minneapolis, Minn.: Free Spirit Publishing Co.

Gaylin, Willard (1984). *The Rage Within: Anger in Modern Life.* New York: Simon and Schuster.

Gellert, Shepard (1976). "Mixed Emotions." *Transactional Analysis Journal* 6, April, pp. 129–30.

Gelles, Richard (1976). "Abused Wives: Why Do They Stay?" *Journal of Marriage and the Family* 38, November, pp. 659–67.

—— (1974). *The Violent Home: A Study of Physical Aggression Between Husbands and Wives* Beverly Hills, Cal.: Sage Publications.

Goldberg, Gertrude, et al. (1986). "Spouseless, Childless, Elderly Women and their Social Supports." *Social Work* 32, March–April, pp. 104–13.

Goldscheider, Frances, and Linda J. Waite (1986). "Sex Differences in the Entry into Marriage." *American Journal of Sociology* 92, July, pp. 91–109.

Goodstein, Richard K., and Ann W. Page (1981). "Battered Wife Syndrome: Overview of Dynamics and Treatment." *American Journal of Psychiatry* 138, August, pp. 1036–43.

Gottlieb, Benjamin H. (1985). "Assessing and Strengthening the Impact of Social Support on Mental Health." *Social Work* 30, July–Aug., pp. 293–300.

Graff, Robert W., and George I. Whitehead (1986). "Group Treatment with Divorced Women Using Cognitive-Behavioral and Supportive-Insight Methods." *Journal of Counseling Psychology* 33, July, pp. 276–81.

Granvold, Donald K., and Roxanne Tarrant (1983). "Structured Marital Separation as a Marital Treatment Method." *Journal of Marital and Family Therapy* 9, April, pp. 189–98.

Grossman, William I. (1986). "Notes on Masochism: A Discussion of the History and Development of a Psychoanalytic Concept." *Psychoanalytic Quarterly* 50, Autumn, pp. 379–413.

Hackler, Tim (1983). "Biology Influences Sex Roles." *Male/Female Roles*, eds. Bruno Leone and M. Teresa O'Neil, St. Paul, Minn.: Greenhaven Press, pp. 16–26.

Hafner, Julian R. (1979). "Agoraphobic Woman Married to Abnormally Jealous Man." *British Journal of Medical Psychology* 52, June, pp. 99–104.

Halpern, Howard M. (1982). *How to Break Your Addiction to a Person.* New York: McGraw-Hill.

Hansen, Gary L. (1982). "Reactions to Hypothetical Jealousy Producing Events." *Family Relations: Journal of Applied Family and Child Studies* 31, October, pp. 513–18.

—— (1983). "Marital Satisfaction and Jealousy Among Men." *Psychological Reports* 52, April, pp. 363–66.

—— (1985a). "Dating Jealousy Among College Students." *Sex Roles* 12, Summer, pp. 57–61.

—— (1985b). "Perceived Threats and Marital Jealousy." *Social Psychology Quarterly* 48, September, pp. 262–68.

Hansen, Laura B., and Joan F. Shireman (1986). "The Process of Emotional Divorce: Explanations of Theory." *Social Casework* 67, June, pp. 323–31.

Hauck, Paul A. (1981). *Overcoming Jealousy and Possessiveness.* New York: Westminster Press.

Hibbard, Robert W. (1975). "A Rational Approach to Treating Jealousy." *Rational Living* 10, Fall, pp. 25–27.

Hilberman, Elaine (1980). "Overview: The Wife Beater's Wife' Reconsidered." *American Journal of Psychiatry* 137, November, pp. 1336–47.

Hoaken, P. C. (1976). "Jealousy As a Symptom of Psychiatric Disorder." *Australian and New Zealand Journal of Psychiatry* 10, March, pp. 47–51.

Horney, Karen (1967). *Feminine Psychology.* New York: W. W. Norton.

Hoskins, Carol H. (1982). "Biorhythms and Marital Conflict." *Medical Aspects of Human Sexuality* 16, March, p. 43.

Hoyt, Michael F. (1986). "Neuroticism and Mate Selection." *Medical Aspects of Human Sexuality* 20, July, p. 11.

Hunka, Carol D., Anita W. O'Toole, and Richard O'Toole (1985). "Self-Help Therapy in Parent's Anonymous." *Journal of Psychosocial Nursing and Mental Health Services* 23, July, pp. 24–32.

Hunt, Morton M. (1983). "How Jealous Are You?" *Reader's Digest,* October, p. 27.

—— (1963). *The World of the Formerly Married.* New York: McGraw-Hill.

—— (1974). *Sexual Behavior in the 1970s.* Chicago: Playboy Press.

Hupka, Ralph B. (1981). "Cultural Determinants of Jealousy." *Alternative Lifestyles* 4, Fall, pp. 310–14.

——, et al. (1985). "Romantic Jealousy and Romantic Envy: A Seven-Nation Study." *Journal of Cross-Cultural Psychology* 16, December, pp. 423–46.

Im, Won-gi, Stefanie Wilner, and Miranda Breit (1983). "Jealousy: Interventions in Couples Therapy." *Family Process* 22, June, pp. 211–19.

Jacobs, John W. (1986). "Divorce and Child Custody Resolution: Conflicting Legal and Psychological Paradigms." *American Journal of Psychiatry* 143, February, pp. 192–97.

Johnson, Harriette C. (1984). "The Biological Bases of Psychopathology." In *Adult Psychopathology,* ed. Francis J. Turner. New York: Free Press, pp. 6–72.

Jones, Ernest (1953). *The Life and Work of Sigmund Freud.* New York: Basic Books.

Joseph, R. (1985). "Competition Between Women." *Psychology* 22, March, pp. 1–12.

Karasu, Toksoz (1986). "The Psychotherapies: Benefits and Limitations." *American Journal of Psychotherapy* 50, July, pp. 324–42.

Kendler, Kenneth S. (1980). "Are There Delusions Specific for Paranoid Disorders and Schizophrenia?" *Schizophrenic Bulletin* 6, January, pp. 1–3.

Kinsey, Alfred C., Wardell Pomeroy, and Clyde Martin (1948). *Sexual Behavior in the Human Male.* New York: W. B. Saunders.

Klein, Melanie (1977). *Envy and Gratitude and Other Works, 1946–1963.* New York: Delacorte.

Land, Helen (1986). "Social Support Networks." *Social Work* 31, Jan.–Feb., p. 72.

Lasswell, Marcia, and Norman Lobsenz (1977). "How to Handle Sexual Jealousy." *McCall's,* July, p. 86.

Laury, G. V. (1979). "Child in Bed as Chastity Belt." *Medical Aspects of Human Sexuality* 13, October, p. 68.

Lee, J. A. (1977). "A Typology of Styles of Loving." *Personality and Social Psychology Bulletin* 3, March, pp. 197–82.

Lester, David, et al. (1985). "Jealousy and Irrationality in Love." *Psychological Reports* 56, February, pp. 210–16.

Levay, Alexander N., and Josef H. Weissberg (1980). "Habits that Infuriate Mates." *Medical Aspects of Human Sexuality* 14, September, pp. 8–10.

Lewis, Karen Gail (1986). "Sibling Therapy With Multiproblem Families." *Journal of Marital and Family Therapy* 12, July, pp. 291–300.

Livsey, Clara G. (1981). "Marital Fights Over Relatives." *Medical Aspects of Human Sexuality* 15, February, pp. 81–85.

Lobel, B., and Robert M. A. Hirschfeld (1984). "Depression: What We Know" (DHHS Publication ADM 84–1318). Rockville, Md.: National Institute of Mental Health.

Lobsenz, Norman (1975). "Taming the Green-Eyed Monster." *Redbook*, March, p. 74.

Lunde, D. T. (1975). "Our Murder Boom: Murder and Madness." *Psychology Today*, July, pp. 35–40.

Maccoby, E., and C. Jacklin (1974). *The Psychology of Sex Differences*. Palo Alto, Calif.: Stanford University Press.

Maslow, Abraham (1968). *Toward a Psychology of Being*, 2nd ed. Princeton, N.J.: Van Nostrand.

Masters, William, and Virginia Johnson (1970). *Human Sexual Inadequacy*. Boston: Little, Brown & Co.

Masterson, J. (1984). "Pretty Eyes and Green, My Love." *Psychology Today*, February, p. 71.

Mathes, Eugene, and Deuger, Donna J. (1982). "Jealousy, A Creation of Human Culture?" *Psychological Reports* 51, October, pp. 351–54.

——, Heather E. Adams, and Ruth M. Davies (1985). "Jealousy: Loss of Relationship Rewards, Loss of Self-Esteem, Depression, Anxiety, and Anger." *Journal of Personality and Social Psychology* 48, June, pp. 1552–61.

Maynard, R. (1978). "The Green-Eyed Monster." *Woman's Day* 14, June, p. 74.

Mazur, Ronald (1973). "Beyond Jealousy and Possessiveness." In *The New Intimacy: Open-Ended Marriage and Alternative Lifestyles*. Boston: Beacon Press, pp. 94–108.

McCary, James L., and Stephen P. McCary (1982). *McCary's Human Sexuality*, 4th ed. Belmont, Calif.: Wadsworth Publishing Co.

McClelland, D. C., and D. A. Pilon (1983). "Sources of Adult Motives in Patterns of Parent Behavior in Early Childhood." *Journal of Personality and Social Psychology* 44, June, pp. 564–74.

McCollum, Eric E. (1985). "Recontacting Former Spouses: A Further Step in the Divorce Process." *Journal of Marital and Family Therapy* 11, October, pp. 417–20.

Mead, Margaret (1958). "Jealousy: Primitive and Civilized." In *Women's Coming of Age*, eds. Samuel D. Schmalhausen and V. F. Calverton. New York: Liveright Publishing Co.

Mir-Djalali, Elahe (1980). "The Failure of Language to Communicate." *International Journal of Intercultural Relations* 4, Spring, pp. 307–28.

Mirowsky, John (1985). "Depression and Marital Power." *American Journal of Sociology* 91, November, pp. 557–92.

Mitchell, G. (1981). *Human Sexual Differences: A Primatologist's Perspective*. New York: Van Nostrand Reinhold.

Mithers, C. L. (1985). "How Envious Are You?" *Ladies Home Journal* October, p. 88.

Moffitt, P. L., N. D. Spence, and R. D. Golding (1986). "Mental Health in Marriage: The Roles of Need for Affiliation, Sensitivity to Rejection and other Factors." *Journal of Clinical Psychology* 42, January, pp. 68–76.

Montagu, Ashley (1978). *Touching: The Human Significance of the Skin*, 2nd ed. New York: Harper & Row.

Morris, Vicki (1982). "Helping Lesbian Couples Cope With Jealousy." *Women and Therapy* 1, Winter, pp. 27–34.

National Center for Health Statistics (1981). *Differentials in Health Characteristics*, Vital and Health Statistics, Series 10, No. 108. Bethesda, Md.: U.S. Department of Health and Human Services.

Neubauer, Peter B. (1982). "Rivalry, Envy, and Jealousy." *Psychoanalytic Study of the Child* 37, pp. 121–42.

—— (1983). "The Importance of the Sibling Experience." *Psychoanalytic Study of the Child* 38, pp. 325–36.

Nichols, William C. (1978). "When Jealousy Threatens." *Parents Magazine*, August, p. 20.

O'Brien, J. E. (1971). "Violence in Divorce-Prone Families." *Journal of Marriage and the Family* 33, Winter, pp. 692–98.

Okun, Lewis (1986). *Woman Abuse: Facts Replacing Myths*. Albany, N.Y.: State University of New York Press.

O'Leary, Daniel, and Alison D. Curley (1986). "Assertion and Family Violence: Correlates of Spouse Abuse." *Journal of Marital and Family Therapy* 12, July, pp. 281–89.

Olson, Sandra K., and Sarah L. Brown (1986). "A Relocation Support Group For Women In Transition." *Journal of Counseling and Development* 64, March, pp. 454–55.

O'Neil, Mary Kay (1984). "Affective Disorders." In *Adult Psychopathology*, ed. Francis J. Turner. New York: Free Press, pp. 148–80.

O'Neill, Nena, and George O'Neill (1972). *Open Marriage: A New Life Style for Couples*. New York: Evans and Co.

O'Reilly, Jane (1983). "Wife Beating: The Silent Crime." *Time*, 5 September, p. 86.

Peterson, Christopher (1985). "Learned Helplessness: Fundamental Issues in Theory and Research." *Journal of Social and Clinical Psychology* 3, February, pp. 248–54.

Pfouts, Jane H. and Connie Renz (1981). "The Future of Wife Abuse Programs." *Social Work* 26, November, pp. 451–53.

Pietropinto, Anthony (1982). "Current Thinking on Jealousy in Marriage." *Medical Aspects of Human Sexuality* 16, July, pp. 37–42.

——, and Simenauer, Jacqueline (1979). *Husbands and Wives: A Nationwide Survey of Marriage*. New York: Times Books.

Pines, Ayala, and Elliot Aronson (1983). "Antecedents, Correlates and Consequences of Sexual Jealousy." *Journal of Personality* 51, March, pp. 108–36.

Pinto, Emil R. (1978). "Pathological Tolerance." *American Journal of Psychiatry* 136, June, pp. 698–701.

Pittman, Frank (1985). "Gender Myths." *Family Therapy Networker* 9, Nov.–Dec., pp. 24–33.

Policoff, Stephen P. (1986). "Obsessed Men and How to Spot Them." *Cosmopolitan*, July, p. 162.

Remine, Daniel, Robert M. Rice, and J. Ross (1984). *Self-Help Groups and Human Service Agencies: How They Work Together*. New York: Family Service America.

Richardson, Laurel (1985). *The New Other Woman*. New York: Free Press.

Ritchie, Martin H. (1986). "Counseling the Involuntary Client." *Journal of Counseling and Development* 64, April, pp. 316–18.

Rogers, Carl (1972). *Becoming Partners: Marriage and Its Alternatives*. New York: Dell Publishing Co.

Rorty, Amelie O. (1974). "Some Social Uses of the Forbidden." *Psychoanalytic Review* 58, Winter, pp. 497–510.

Rosenblum, Karen E. (1986). "Leaving as a Wife, Leaving As a Mother." *Journal of Family Issues* 7, June, pp. 197–213.

Roth, Steven A. (1986). "The Symbiotic Marriage." *Medical Aspects of Human Sexuality* 16, July, p. 39.

Rubenstein, Carlin (1981). "Money and Self-Esteem, Relationships, Secrecy, Envy, and Satisfaction." *Psychology Today*, January, p. 36.

Rubin, Theodore I. (1978). "Myths of Jealousy." *Ladies Home Journal*, May, p. 44.

—— (1985). *Overcoming Indecisiveness: The Eight Stages of Effective Decision Making*. New York: Harper & Row.

Ryan, William (1976). *Blaming the Victim*. New York: Pantheon Books.

Salovey, Peter, and Judith Rodin (1984). "Some Antecedents and Consequences of Social Comparison Jealousy." *Journal of Personality and Social Psychology* 47, October, pp. 780–92.

—— (1985). "The Heart of Jealousy." *Psychology Today*, September, pp. 22–25.

Saltzman, Leon (1980). "Why Some Women Fall In Love With Men Who Are 'Heels.'" *Medical Aspects of Human Sexuality*, September, pp. 106–9.

Satir, Virginia (1972). *Peoplemaking*. Palo Alto, Calif.: Science and Behavior Books.

Schneider, S. (1985). "Jealousy Is Hell." *Mademoiselle*, July, p. 56.

Schoenfeld, Eugene (1980). *Jealousy: Taming the Green-Eyed Monster*. New York: Holt, Rinehart & Winston.

Schwartz, G. (1985). "Your Guy and Your Sis: Too Close for Comfort?" *Seventeen*, October, p. 118.

Schwartz, Murray M. (1973). "Leontes' Jealousy in *The Winter's Tale*." *American Imago* 30, Fall, pp. 250–73.

Silver, Maury, and John Sabini (1978). "The Social Construction of Envy." *Journal for the Theory of Social Behavior* 8, October, pp. 313–32.

Socarides, C. (1977). "On Vengeance: The Desire to Get Even." In *The World of Emotions*. New York: International Universities Press.

Sokoloff, B. (1947). *Jealousy: A Psychiatric Study*. New York: Howell, Soskin.

Solomon, Robert C. (1976). *The Passions*. Garden City, N.Y.: Anchor Press.

Solomon, Steven D. (1982). "An Integrated Theory of Jealousy." Doctoral dissertation, Los Angeles: California School of Professional Psychology.

Span, Paula (1981). "New Theories, New Research on Sexual Jealousy." *Glamour,* September, p. 298.

Spendlove, David, James Gavelek, and Val MacMurray (1981). "Learned Helplessness and the Depressed Housewife." *Social Work* 26, November, pp. 474–79.

Steinmetz, Suzanne K. (1977). "Wife Beating, Husband Beating—A Comparison of the Use of Violence Between Spouses to Resolve Marital Conflicts." In *Battered Women: A Psychosocial Study of Domestic Violence,* ed. Maria Ray. New York: Van Nostrand.

Sternberg, Robert J. (1986). "A Triangular Theory of Love." *Psychological Review* 93, February, pp. 119–35.

Stewart, Robert A., and Michael J. Beatty (1958). "Jealousy and Self-Esteem." *Perceptual and Motor Skills* 60, February, pp. 153–94.

Straus, Murray A., and Gerald T. Hotaling, eds. (1980). *The Social Causes of Husband-Wife Violence.* Minneapolis: University of Minnesota Press.

———, Richard J. Gelles, and Suzanne K. Steinmetz (1980). *Behind Closed Doors: Violence in the American Family.* Garden City, N.Y.: Anchor Books, Doubleday and Co.

Strean, Herbert S. (1980). *The Extramarital Affair.* New York: Free Press.

——— (1983). *The Sexual Dimension.* New York: Free Press.

——— (1985). *Resolving Resistances in Psychotherapy.* New York: John Wiley & Sons.

Stump, Jane Barr (1985). *What's the Difference?: How Men and Women Compare.* New York: William Morrow and Co.

Sundel, Martin, and Sandra Stone Sundel (1985). *Behavioral Modification in the Human Services,* 2nd ed. Englewood Cliffs, N.J.: Prentice-Hall.

Sweet, E. (1984). "The Electra Complex: How Can I Be Jealous of My Four-Year-Old Daughter?" *Ms.,* May, p. 148.

Symonds, M. (1975). "Victims of Violence: Psychological Effects and Aftereffects." *American Journal of Psychoanalysis* 36, January, p. 27.

Teismann, Mark W. (1979a). "Jealous Conflict: A Study of Verbal Interaction and Labeling of Jealousy Among Dating Couples Involved in Jealousy Improvizations." Doctoral dissertation, New London: University of Connecticut.

——— (1979b). "Jealousy: Systematic Problem-Solving Therapy With Couples." *Family Process* 18, June, pp. 151–60.

Tellenbach, Hubert (1974). "On The Nature of Jealousy." *Journal of Phenomenological Psychology* 4, Spring, pp. 461–68.

Tennov, Dorothy (1979). *Love and Limerence.* New York: Stein and Day.

Tester, Sylvia R. (1980). *Jealous: What Does It Mean?* Chicago: Children's Press.

Theodoracopulos, T. (1984). "Love Only Me." *Esquire,* March, p. 25.

Titelman, Peter A. (1981). "A Phenomenological Comparison Between Envy and Jealousy," *Journal of Phenomenological Psychology* 12, Fall, pp. 189–204.

Tomporowski, Phillip D., and Norman R. Ellis (1986). "Effects of Exercise on Cognitive Processes: A Review." *American Psychologist* 99, May, pp. 338–46.

Toseland, Ronald W., et al. (1986). "Teamwork in Psychiatric Settings" *Social Work* 31, Jan.-Feb., pp. 46–52.

Truesdell, Donna L., John McNeil, and Jeanne P. Deschner (1980). "Incidence of Wife Abuse in Incestuous Families." *Social Work* 31, March–April, pp. 138–39.

Turbott, John (1981). "Morbid Jealousy: Reciprocal Appearance of Psychopathology in Either Spouse." *Australian and New Zealand Journal of Psychiatry* 15, June, pp. 164–67.

Turner, Susan F., and Constance Hoenk Shapiro (1986). "Battered Women: Mourning the Death of a Relationship." *Social Work* 31, Sept.–Oct., pp. 372–84.

Udry, J. Richard, and Bruce K. Eckland (1984). "Benefits of Being Attractive: Differential Payoffs for Men and Women." *Psychological Reports* 54, February, pp. 47–56.

United States Congress, Office of Technology Assessment (1980). "The Efficacy and Cost Effectiveness of Psychotherapy," background paper no. 3. Washington, D.C.: U.S. Government Printing Office.

Van Krogten, I. A., et al. (1983). "Afgunst en Jaloezie gescheiden" (Envy and jealousy differentiated). *Tijdschrift voor Psychotherapie* 9, September, pp. 238–45.

Veereshwar, Anand (1983). "Jealousy and the Abyss." *Journal of Humanistic Psychology* 23, Spring, pp. 70–84.

Wagenvoord, James, and Peyton Bailey (1978). *Men: A Book For Women.* New York: Avon.

—— (1979). *Women: A Book For Men.* New York: Avon.

Waletzky, Lucy (1979). "Husband's Problems With Breast Feeding." *American Journal of Orthopsychiatry* 49, April, pp. 349–52.

Wallerstein, Judith S. (1986). "Women After Divorce: Preliminary Report from a Ten-Year Follow Up." *American Journal of Orthopsychiatry* 56, January, pp. 65–77.

——, and Kelly, J. B. (1976). "The Effects of Parental Divorce: Experiences of the Child in Later Latency." *American Journal of Orthopsychiatry* 46, Fall, pp. 256–69.

Wein, B. (1983). "Dealing With Jealousy." *Harper's Bazaar*, October, p. 207.

Weingarten, Helen R. (1986). "Strategic Planning for Divorce Mediation." *Social Work* 31, May–June, pp. 194–200.

Westermarck, Edward (1922). *The History of Human Marriage.* New York: Allerton.

Wetzel, Janice Wood (1984). *Clinical Handbook of Depression.* New York: Gardner Press.

Wheeler, Dorothy (1985). "The Fear of Feminism in Family Therapy." *The Family Therapy Networker* 9, Nov.–Dec., pp. 53–55.

White, Gregory L. (1976). "The Social Psychology of Romantic Jealousy." Doctoral dissertation, Los Angeles: University of California.

—— (1980). "Inducing Jealousy." *Personality and Social Psychology Bulletin* 6, June, pp. 222–27.

—— (1981a). "A Model of Romantic Jealousy." *Motivation and Emotion* 5, December, pp. 295–310.

—— (1981b). "Some Correlates of Romantic Jealousy." *Journal of Personality* 49, June, pp. 129–47.

White, Joseph L. (1984). *The Psychology of Blacks: An Afro-American Perspective.* Englewood Cliffs, N.J.: Prentice-Hall.

Whitehurst, Robert N. (1971). "American Sexophobia." In *The New Sexual Revolution,* eds. L. A. Kirkendall and R. N. Whitehurst. New York: Donald Brown, Inc.

Whittaker, James K., and James Garbarino (1983). *Social Support Networks: Informal Helping in the Human Services.* Hawthorne, N.Y.: Aldine Publishing Co.

Windmiller, M., et al. (1980). *Moral Development and Socialization.* Boston: Allyn and Bacon.

Wisdom, J. O. (1976). "Jealousy in a Twelve-Month-Old Boy." *International Review of Psychoanalysis* 3, Fall, pp. 365–68.

Wittenberg, Mitchell T., and Harry T. Reis (1986). "Loneliness, Social Skills, and Social Perception." *Personality and Social Psychology Bulletin* 12, March, pp. 121–30.

Woodward, Kenneth L. (1983). "Children Need to Learn Traditional Sex Roles." In *Male/Female Roles,* eds. Bruno Leones and M. Teresa O'Neill. St. Paul, Minn.: Greenhaven Press, pp. 27–30.

Women's Action Alliance (1987). *Women Helping Women: A State-By-State Directory of Services.* New York: Neal-Schuman Publishers.

Zenter, M. (1984). "Paranoia." In *Adult Psychopathology,* ed. Francis Turner. New York: Free Press.

Ziman, E. A. (1949). *Jealousy in Children: A Guide to Parents.* New York: A. A. Wyn.

Index